TRIUMPH TWIN
RESTORATION

The start of it all – front view of the Speed Twin as shown on the cover of the 1938 brochure. Note girders, large headlamp and slim lines as for a twin port single

TRIUMPH TWIN

RESTORATION

The essential guide to the renovation, restoration
and development history of all pre-1972 production
Triumph Twins. Plus how to recognize parts, improve
specifications and maintain this classic motorcycle

ROY BACON

OSPREY

First published in 1985 by Osprey Publishing,
Reed Consumer Books, Michelin House,
81 Fulham Road, London SW3 6RB
First reprint early 1987
Second reprint spring 1988
Third reprint spring 1989
Fourth reprint summer 1990
Fifth reprint spring 1993
Sixth reprint spring 1995
Seventh reprint autumn 1996

British Library Cataloguing in Publication Data

Bacon, Roy H.
    Triumph twin restoration: the essential guide to the
    renovation, restoration and development history of all
    pre-1972 production Triumph twins.—(Osprey
    motorcycle restoration guides)
    1. Triumph motorcycle
    I. Title
    629.28'775   TL448.T7
ISBN 0–85045–635–5

Editor Tim Parker

Filmset by Tameside Filmsetting Limited,
Ashton-under-Lyne, Lancashire
Printed in Great Britain by
The Bath Press, Bath

For a catalogue of all books published by Osprey Automotive
please write to:

The Marketing Manager,
Consumer Catalogue Department,
Osprey Publishing Limited,
Michelin House, 81 Fulham Road,
London SW3 6RB

CONTENTS

Acknowledgements

The idea for this book came from the type of question I was receiving through the *Classic Bike* reader service or agony column. Over the years this changed as the simple dating data was published in the Osprey Collector's Library series and I found myself drawn more into the detailed changes from one year to the next.

The basic queries of date, colour, spares and data continued but as the 1980s rolled along so the classic movement became keener to know about the fine detail. Hence this book to deal with that problem laced with restoration information and guidance as appropriate.

The original idea was Tim Parker's and from this I compiled a report to set it out in some detail. Osprey approved and away I went on a detailed data hunt. In this my good friend Don Mitchell was very helpful indeed and was able to supply me with much that I needed from his stocks of secondhand motorcycle literature.

Specific pieces of information came from Alan Blake of Avon Tyres, Derek Dyson of Champion Plugs and Martyn Ashwood of NGK and my thanks go to all. I must especially thank John Gregory, a local friend and fellow member of the Isle of Wight British Motorcycle Society, who read through the entire text and gave me the benefit of his experience of restoring and rebuilding many machines.

Most of the pictures and line drawings came from the EMAP archives which hold the old *Motor Cycle Weekly* files for which my grateful thanks. Others were from the *Classic Bike* files courtesy of Mike Nicks and a number were from Triumph brochures, parts lists and manuals of the era. A number of the electrical line drawings were from Lucas originally. One picture was from Mike Jackson of Andover Norton and a few I took myself at the 1000 bike rally at Brands Hatch in 1984.

Some of the pictures carried the imprint of a professional and work used came from Richard Bailey, Donald Page, P. W. and L. Thompson and P. J. Worden. As usual all the pictures were returned to their files after publication and I have tried to make contact to clear copyright. If my letter failed to reach you or I have used an unmarked print without realising this, please accept my apologies.

Finally my thanks to my editor, Tim Parker, who supported me throughout the longer than expected time it took to research and write this book. His help and guidance enabled me to keep going when the going got sticky.

Roy Bacon
Niton, Isle of Wight
July 1985

Our policy

This book is written on the basis of a restoration back to original factory specification for the model and year. It is fully appreciated that not every reader will want to aim for this but it is the only practical way to write the words.

Restorations can range from a mild check-over to concours standard and further to add features and a finish never seen on a production machine. Alterations may be carried out and these again can range from discreet rider improvements to accepted changes to update the specification, or even total rework into a hardtail chopper.

In all cases and regardless of the final aim it is hoped that this book will assist and guide the reader to produce the machine of his or her dreams. It is also hoped that the result will be sound in wind and limb and every endeavour has been made to offer advice which is helpful and safe. However, the onus is always with the reader to ensure that any machine he or she works on or rides is in a safe and legal condition. If you decide to carry out a modification you must make certain that it will work properly.

Neither the author or publisher can accept any liability for anything contained in this book which may result in any loss, damage or injury and the book is only available for purchase or loan on that basis.

Note It is worth noting that each chapter of this book contains both general principles and specific information. The first can really apply to any make or model, while the second is very much only applicable to particular cases, such as a part made for a model that was only available for one year.

The most sporting road twin, the T120 in its 1968 guise. Points to note are the twin leading shoe front brake and cable, tank badges and Concentric Amals. Characteristic of the 650 cc unit construction models and a great favourite of many Triumph enthusiasts

Machine year

Chapter 1 contains details of the way in which models are dated which causes for example 1955 model to run from late 1954 to late 1955. It also covers the habit of using up 1954 stocks in early 1955 models to clear the bins at the factory. Because of these points the text will use the model year without constant repetition that the feature or model was introduced late in the previous calendar year. Thus a late 1954 model is referred to as 1955 because that is the specification to which it was made.

The use of old parts is ignored by the Triumph factory parts lists and by this book. By definition they had to inter-change by form and function so any notes on parts has to bypass this area. It does mean, however, that it is possible for an all-original machine with known history to have an incorrect part. It is the owner's decision as to whether to keep it or change to the correct parts list specification.

Engine and frame numbers take precedence over model year in determining when a change took place and have been noted where necessary. Parts lists, coupled with these numbers, are always the correct way back to original specification.

Scope

This book sets out to deal with production road models from 1938 to 1972 specification and so to just before the Meriden sit-in began. It does not cover the later machines as these are felt to fall currently outside the realms of a restoration project although these notes will be of considerable use when rebuilding or refurbishing such a model.

The data quoted applies to standard UK specification machines as these are the basis from which any factory variations were derived. Thus while the data will assist when dealing with a machine to USA or any other overseas specification, it cannot be assumed to be exact. The same applies to all machines built for the police as these had their own specification and could vary in detail from one force to the next. The most famous of these was known as the Saint and while it was based on the Thunderbird it had a fair number of internal and external changes which can confuse.

The military side-valve models and racing GP machines are not covered as they are both specialist versions of the production line and neither prototypes or one-off specials are mentioned. If you are lucky enough to have such a machine I am sure you appreciate its rarity and will look after it without my help.

Remember that some models were only made in small numbers, so their spares could be hard to locate.

Export specification models may pose similar problems even in the country they were destined for, and worse problems outside it. A further pitfall arises where an attempt has been made to create a rare model from a prosaic one or to convert from one market specification to another. Very rarely will the change be totally complete, thus another hybrid appears and can cause headaches to sort out.

Your skills

This book is not a workshop manual and neither is it a primer on being a motorcycle mechanic. It has to assume that you know how your machine works and have a good idea as to how to maintain it. Also that you have a degree of mechanical aptitude and have worked on motorcycles to some extent.

In many cases a good restoration is a combination of skill, available tools and knowledge of techniques and tricks that get the job done. Together they equate to experience and no book can give you that. It can only advise that you don't attempt more than you can cope with and add the suggestion that with the right information, care and attention to detail this could be more than you think. Proceed slowly with confidence.

Address list

Always a problem in a book as they tend to be out of date by publication.

If in difficulties the 'agony' columns of the specialist magazines are there to help so you can send them your query as long as you include some method of return postage.

Specifications

Many books of this type carry extensive tables of data to the fourth place of decimals which have been compiled from endless hours of research. This does not as much of it is in *Triumph Twins & Triples* (Osprey Publishing) and the rest in workshop manuals.

It is recommended that before any restoration is attempted that data and information is collected to cover your model and its year. In many areas the four figure dimensions are of little moment as parts are reamed to fit and made to size. Part of the art is knowing which ones matter and no book can teach that any more than it can show you how to paint a masterpiece or write an opera. Well not one that is any good.

So there are no endless lists of bushes and bearings, gaps and settings or tolerances and gauges. The figures and data that are provided are there to back up the manual you should have and to help you sort out what you may have bought.

1 In the beginning

The Edward Turner Triumph twin of 1937 set up a machine type that remained little changed for many years and had many imitators. In itself it was modified over the years but remained in both concept and reality a simple machine of unaltered basic form.

The classic Triumph twin ranged in engine size from 350 to 750 cc. It was built in pre-unit and unit forms, with dynamo or alternator electrics and with a variety of cycle parts. From first to last it had overhead valves, two high mounted camshafts, pushrod tubes and an unmistakable line.

History

The Speed Twin was first shown to the public in the autumn of 1937 as was the practice of the English industry of that time. It was thus as a 1938 model that initial production began and as a 1939 model that the first Tiger 100 joined it. There was to have been a Tiger 85 for 1940 but it was cancelled when war broke out. Its design led to the military 3TW but this was bombed and Triumph spent the war making singles.

Postwar the machines changed from girders to telescopic forks, the T85 failed to appear but the 350 cc model 3T did join the range for a while. The sprung hub was introduced in lieu of either a plunger or swinging fork frame and in 1949 the Trophy was added to the list.

In 1950 the engine size was increased to 650 cc with the arrival of the Thunderbird and the tank styling underwent a major revision. The sports 500 cc engines were fitted with a die-cast top half the next year when the 3T was dropped, 1952 brought the SU carburettor for the Thunderbird and 1953 an alternator for the Speed Twin. The same year also brought the T100c, a short lived model which replaced the factory race kit sold for the T100.

1954 saw the alternator on the 6T and a sports

The 1938 Speed Twin with girder forks, instrument panel in tank top, mag-dyno and pressure oil feed to valve gear. This one has a painted headlamp shell although the brochure shows and quotes chrome plating

ABOVE *Drive side of a restored 5T with correct six stud barrel and crankcase used for the first 1938 season*

BELOW *1938 5T engine showing the oil feed to the rockers but not the pipe to the oil gauge which came from the same point*

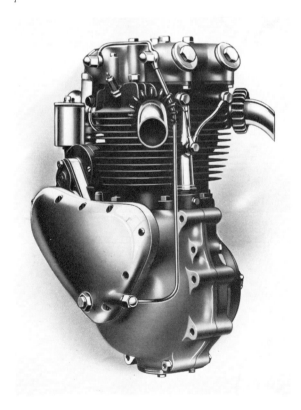

650 cc model, the Tiger 110. It and the 500 version went into swinging fork frames and were fitted with an 8 in. front brake to stop them. The next year saw all the models in the new frame and the year after, 1956, a 650 cc version of the Trophy with the label TR6.

In 1957 the first unit construction twin, the 350 cc 3TA, appeared complete with its bathtub rear enclosure. It introduced a new tank style and was joined by a 500 cc version in 1959, the year the T120 Bonneville was first seen. 1960 brought the T100A unit construction Tiger in place of the old one that dated from prewar days and this completed the changeover to the modern design in the smaller engine capacities.

The 650 model continued with its separate gearbox until 1963 when the bigger unit construction engine was introduced. As before this was built in touring form as the 6T Thunderbird and in super sports form as the T120 Bonneville. Between the two came the TR6, no longer a dual purpose or off-road model, but simply a single carburettor Bonnie much as the old Tiger 110.

The basic touring 350 and 500 cc models were joined by the sporting Tiger 90 as well as the Tiger 100A and the latter became the T100SS and in time the Daytona, a very quick machine. The full bathtubs changed to partial skirts during this period and then were discarded as fashions in the late sixties swung to the café racer style and away from an enclosed touring image.

For 1971 there was a major revision to the range and the effects of this and other factors was to run the company into deep water along with BSA. There were major design problems, financial cramp and too many new models. A great deal of pruning had to take place but despite the problems 1972 brought a five-speed gearbox and a bigger twin of 750 cc capacity.

1973 saw the last of the 500 cc models produced with a few in a trail bike format as the Adventurer. The big twins carried on but that year the Triumph company and the Meriden works became a political football. The outcome of all the meetings, discussions, amalgamations and cash injections culminated with a sit-in by the workforce late in the year.

The men and women at Meriden were disillusioned by the setting up of the NVT group under Dennis Poore, by the BSA influences that had bedevilled them for years and the abrupt announcement that their factory was to close. So they set up their pickets and sat round the brazier for two long, hard winters.

While they sat, there were two general elections, a change of government and as a result the Meriden

Brochure picture of 1938 5T with chrome-plated headlamp as per parts list. The marque lines were to run through all models and years

workers' co-operative came into existence. In 1975 work began again on the later twins.

Model choice

Anyone who wishes to own a Triumph twin has a wide range of model types, engine capacities and years to select from. The one chosen is down to the individual and that person's choice is their decision alone, but for most people the machine they choose is determined by what is available and the depth of their purse.

Not everyone undertaking a restoration project actually starts with a complete machine. Some begin with a box of parts and often such jobs are the hardest to finish as parts are invariably missing. The box has appeared because the last owner allowed enthusiasm to run ahead of resources, stripped the machine and then gave up or was forced to give up. He is sure it is all there but has forgotten various parts already missing, lent, lost or strayed for all sorts of reasons and all problems for the new owner to solve.

The restorer also has to decide what is wanted and what is possible as the two are not always the same thing. Not everyone wants a concours machine but all should aim for a model in good running order if only because it is less likely to let one down on the road.

The aim may be to take a machine in poor condition and correct its faults so it becomes a pleasure to use on the road, even if it appears quite nondescript. It could be to repair damage as required for general use. Maybe this would include changes to enhance

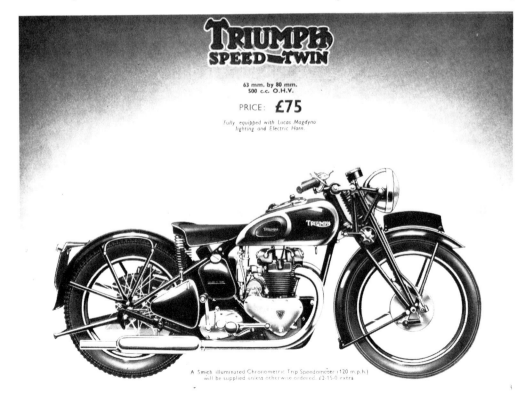

SPECIFICATION
"SPEED TWIN" MODEL

ENGINE : Entirely new design. Bore 63 m.m. Stroke 80 m.m. 497 c.c. O.H.V. double high camshaft, vertical Twin. Crankshaft mounted on massive ball bearings with central flywheel. Forced feed lubrication to big ends and valve gear. Oil gauge in instrument panel. All-gear drive to camshafts and magdyno. Totally enclosed valves with accessible tappet adjustment. This engine is designed to give sustained high power output, with even slow speed torque and mechanical silence.

CRANKCASE : High tensile aluminium alloy, heavily webbed and of great rigidity.

CRANKSHAFT : Built up construction with centrally disposed flywheel.

CONNECTING RODS : 'H' section in R.R.56 Hiduminium alloy. Split big end bearings with steel caps lined with white metal

VALVE SPRINGS : Duplex Aero quality.

CARBURETTER : Large bore Amal. Latest Triumph Special quick action twist grip control (patent applied for).

PETROL TANK : All-steel welded, combining shapely streamline contour with large capacity. All-metal permanant Triumph Badge. Flush rubber mounted illuminated instrument panel carrying oil gauge, ammeter, switch and dash lamp. Quick-opening filler cap. Capacity: 3¼ galls.

OIL TANK : All-steel welded with accessible filters, drain plug and separate vent : capacity ¾ gall.

FRAME : Brazed full cradle type, from tubes of finest alloy steel combining immense strength with lightness and correct weight distribution. Large diameter tapered front down tube. A comfortable riding position with the highest possible standard of road holding at speed is secured.

FRONT FORKS : Taper tube girder incorporating dampers with finger adjustment on the lower bridge.

GEARBOX : Four-speed all-Triumph design and manufacture. Gears and shafts of nickel-chrome steel of Triumph accuracy and precision. Large multi-plate clutch, patented positive stop foot change.

TRANSMISSION : Primary chain running in polished cast aluminium oil bath of streamline design. Rear chain adequately protected.

BRAKES : Triumph 7" diameter brakes with special alloy detachable ribbed drums and extra wide shoes. Powerful and smooth braking with long life. Finger adjustment. Front brake adjustment accessible from saddle.

SADDLE : De luxe soft top type, adjustable for height.

HANDLEBAR : Triumph, resiliently mounted, eliminating fatigue and shocks, full range of adjustment provided. Control levers grouped and adjustable to suit individual requirements. T.T. type brake and clutch levers.

MUDGUARDS : Of adequate width with streamline section stays. Detachable tail piece to facilitate rear wheel removal.

WHEELS & TYRES : Latest Triumph wheels with spokes of approximately equal length taking braking and transmission stresses. Dunlop tyres, front 26" x 3" ribbed, rear 26" x 3.50 Universal.

TOOLBOX : Large capacity and water-tight. All steel construction; rubber sealed. Complete set of good quality tools, grease gun and instruction booklets.

FINISH & EQUIPMENT : Entirely finished in Amaranth (dark) Red. Petrol tank finished in chromium plate with Amaranth panels lined out in gold. Spokes and rims chromium plated, rim centres Amaranth, lined out in gold. Specially shaped knee grips for comfort and security at high speeds. Lucas 6-volt Magdyno lighting with voltage control, 8" diameter chromium plated, anti-glare head lamp. Altette horn. Chromium plated down-swept exhaust pipes. All aluminium parts smooth and highly polished and both chromium plate and enamel of the highest quality. All nuts Cadmium plated.

2

THE TRIUMPH SPEED TWIN

DESIGNED to combine a very high performance with the reliability which has always been associated with the name of Triumph the new 500 c.c. Speed Twin is a notable contribution to motor cycle development.

The cylinders are mounted vertically side by side, the crank assembly being such that even firing intervals are obtained. This form of construction results in an engine of extremely compact overall dimensions, and the whole layout with its massive crankcase and monobloc cylinder and head castings is particularly rigid and free from distortion. Ample air spaces are provided and the cooling arrangements are superior in every way to those obtainable with a single cylinder type of power unit.

Other advantages resulting from this compact layout are that excellent weight distribution is obtained and as a result of the modest overall height, both ground clearance and accessibility are highly satisfactory.

The use of hemispherical combustion chambers with short direct inlet ports is a feature of note, as is the special patented built-up construction of the crankshaft and the H-section connecting rods of R.R. 56 alloy with split type big-ends.

A high pressure dry-sump lubrication system making use of a pair of large capacity plunger pumps forces oil not only to all main bearings but also to the overhead valve gear, which attains a high standard of mechanical silence in operation. The bearing surfaces and general proportions throughout are such that the performance is maintained for long periods and the maintenance costs are therefore small.

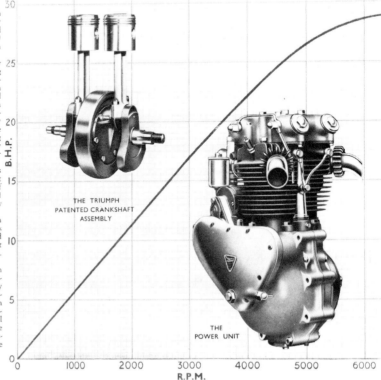

THE TRIUMPH PATENTED CRANKSHAFT ASSEMBLY

THE POWER UNIT

B.H.P.

R.P.M.

16

performance, reliability or appearance. Or the aim can be a complete restoration to original condition, or even beyond with more chrome, polish and sparkle than even a Meriden show model.

The decision belongs to the owner just as the machine does. If you want it all chromed, all original or all bituminous black that is your choice. The choice itself depends on many factors, aside from the owner's wishes for time, money and facilities will all affect what can and will be done.

Spares for all may be a problem. The situation varies from model to model, part to part and day to day. Items that were impossible to obtain at the time of writing could be easy to find when you read this book, or the reverse could apply. Because of this, the text is written on the basis that spares can be had, although this will always apply more to the engine parts than the cycle ones.

Assets

Motorcycle restoration or repair requires time, money and equipment. It is necessary to have all three to some degree and possession of a large quantity of any one will ensure the desired result can be obtained. Given plenty of time it is possible to achieve the highest of restoration standards using very limited facilities and for a minimal cost. A deep purse will enable the project to be farmed out and completed in a short time without the need for much equipment. The ultimate stage along this line is to hand the project over to a professional restorer with a wad of money and a delivery date. Even then it may require some organizational skills and a degree of determination to meet the due date but most people with that depth of purse have those attributes. Finally, anyone with the fullest of workshop facilities can accomplish a restoration at minimal cost and surprisingly quickly.

It must be noted that all three assets have to be present to some degree as no matter how well endowed the owner is in one aspect, the others are also needed, even if only in small amounts.

Abilities

The Triumph restorer must also try to make a realistic assessment of his or her abilities. Some of us are just less well blessed with manual skills than others and it is very important to realize one's limitations early on and make plans to get round them. This may mean making sure you have the correct tools for particular jobs or maybe deciding to farm some of the work out.

An example of the need for the correct tools is the camshaft gear on the Triumph. Up to 1971 a special

ABOVE LEFT *Specification page from the 1938 brochure giving the details including that of chrome plated wheel spokes*

LEFT *Also from the brochure and showing power, crankshaft and rocker oil pipe air brushed out*

puller must be used to remove it and normal practice is to buy one. But, given the equipment, one could be machined from stock quite quickly and easily. Or you take the engine assembly to someone with the equipment.

One's skill levels may vary and this must also be allowed for. Your expertise in some areas may be to a very high standard so accept that fact and that in others it is lower. You must judge which areas you have the required competence in and those where assistance will be needed.

Another answer to this problem is to lower the standard of your restoration. If you cannot do particular jobs and don't want outside help then the only answer may be to settle for less than a concours finish. It may be far more satisfying to rebuild a basket case into a complete reliable motorcycle than to attempt a perfect job and not achieve it for personal rather than financial reasons.

A further factor to be considered is the overall timescale of the job. If the machine is wanted for a particular date, then the planning must allow for some points to go wrong as they always do. It is much better not to have a deadline of any sort for your first restoration and even with the experience of several it can be hard to estimate when the project will be finished.

Better to allow for delays and more so if your aim is concours standard. If a straight rebuild is intended then it is easier to keep to a schedule as more of the work will be under your own control. Any schedule should allow for some delay although this can often be reduced by careful planning. Any series of tasks that depend on one another and run in a sequence should be started early so the work is not held up at a later date.

Wheels are a classic example as you have to de-spoke, dismantle, clean, paint hub, renovate rim, assemble spindle and rebuild the wheel in that order.

Thus the first stage of the restoration is to decide on a machine and determine the degree of restoration to be carried out. It always pays to think this through before committing oneself and proper planning not only saves time and money but makes the work more enjoyable and turns a job into a hobby.

Receipts

It also pays to keep the paperwork in order from the start. This is dealt with in more detail later but it cannot be over-emphasized that you must be able to prove that you actually own your machine which sits in the garage, shed or front hall depending on your workshop habits. Thus it is essential to obtain a receipt for the machine or, if it is built up from boxes, then get receipts for them and for all the major purchases you make. It won't do any harm to keep the till slips of even minor items and to log all these in your records.

ABOVE *Transmission side of 1947 5T fitted with sprung hub. Old style rear mudguard and lift handles*

TOP *The 1946 3T with through bolts for one piece head and rocker box*

ABOVE *The 5T timing side and cycle part details as for 1947 and common with the T100*

This will help prove ownership, be a useful record should you wish to sell, show a prospective customer exactly what has gone into the machine and maybe frighten you at the size of the cost of a restoration.

Workshop

This has been the subject of many articles which seek to describe an ideal arrangement but for most restorers it is either their garage or garden shed. Some lucky people have better premises and some much worse and the work that comes from the shop may bear little relation to its size and facilities.

It is possible to produce a concours Triumph in a small, draughty shed and many people have done just this. However the job of restoring a machine is not an easy one and the exercise is supposed to be an enjoyable hobby so it makes sense to at least be able to work in comfort.

There is seldom much you can do about the size of your workshop but basically one can say that the smaller it is the more you need to have it well organized. Whatever the size it must be clean, dry, warm and well lit. The first job is to stop the roof from leaking and the next to check the floor and consider sealing its surface. Aside from the dust problem, which sealing greatly reduces, it also makes it much easier to find anything dropped on the floor. Normal concrete is gritty and finding small screws can be difficult.

With the roof and floor fit the walls can be seen to and a coat of white emulsion brightens the atmosphere no end and helps the efficiency of the lighting. This must be good and fluorescent tubes are essential. They should be the daylight white type and may need to be supplemented by a bench light and a hand torch or wander light. It pays to wipe the tubes over occasionally as they tend to get dirty in a workshop and any reduction in illumination is a handicap. If likely to be knocked at any time they should be protected by a guard.

Some people share a workshop and this can be a great help but only if you get on well and can work side-by-side. For some jobs a pair of spare hands can save a lot of time and trouble while discussion of a problem will often solve it.

Just as important as sharing with another person is sharing the restoration site with another machine. If the same shed has to garage a machine in daily use then sooner rather than later it will come in wet and dirty. Not impossible to live with but a factor to remember when deciding what can and cannot be attempted at home.

Equipment

The workshop has to be fitted out and the first need is a bench to work on. This must be solidly built and firmly fixed in place. Next on the list is a machine bench with a means of running the motorcycle up onto it and finally come shelves of various sizes for the storage of parts, tools, equipment, spares and consumables such as oil and grease. Don't forget a place for a large box of small depth in which to store your gaskets.

The bench needs a vice and you may also wish to make up an engine stand. This can be constructed in wood or metal and its purpose is to stop the unit from falling over on the bench and maybe damaging itself. To be really useful the stand needs to be clamped down to the bench and the same effect can be achieved by holding the engine, or gearbox, in the vice. This then leaves both hands free to do the work but does emphasize the need to fix vice and bench securely. Needless to say the vice must be fitted with smooth jaws to avoid marking the castings.

Hand tools are best stored on a board so they are easy to reach but keep files beneath the bench to avoid any chance of metal particles getting into the works. Your hand tools are likely to have been accumulated over the years and may be of a variable quality. Now is a good time to get ruthless with them and separate the good from the rest.

1948 Tiger 100 engine fitted with BTH magneto. Note HT leads clipped to right of carburettor, they went on the left from 1954

1951 line drawing of the 6T Thunderbird. Points to note are tank badges, horn grill in nacelle, Amal, barrel saddle springs and Mark II sprung hub

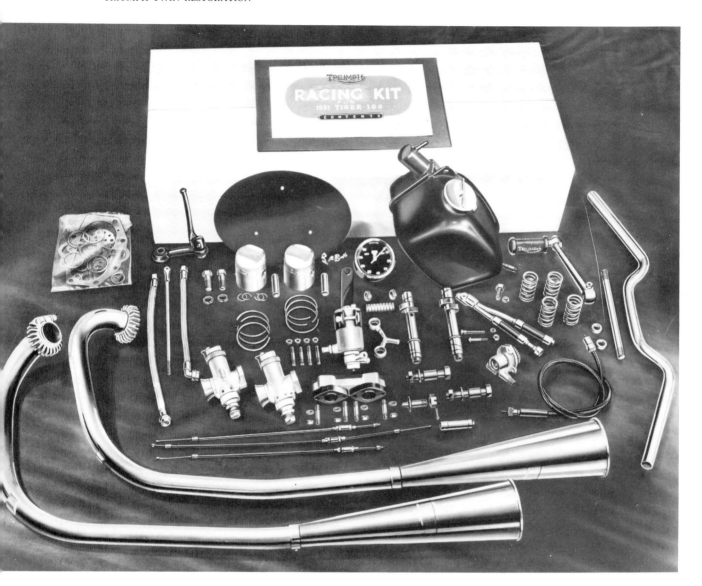

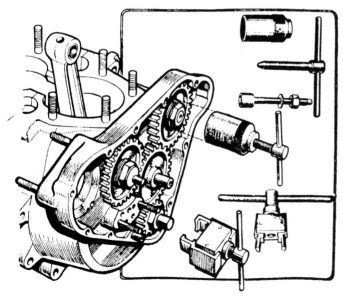

ABOVE *The complete racing kit offered for the Tiger 100 from 1951 to 1953 which included a folding kickstart. Rev-counter drive replaced dynamo*

ABOVE RIGHT *1955 style TR5 as used by an army team the previous year in the ISDT*

LEFT *Essential pullers for the Triumph timing gears and crankshaft pinion*

RIGHT *The first unit construction model, a 1957 3TA or 21 with screen and shields*

Spanner types are legion but the rules are basically to only use ones that fit and that are made from a good steel. My preference is for combination spanners with a ring and open end of the same size at the two ends, a set of $\frac{1}{4}$ in. drive sockets which give me feel on most motorcycle fixings, and a selection of $\frac{1}{2}$ in. drive sockets. Mine have been bought as needed to suit specific jobs so that thanks to the changes from Whitworth to Unified to metric threads a fairly full set is to hand. But it took many years to acquire and each of the big sockets were bought for a job.

The $\frac{1}{4}$ in. drive is thought light by many but its slimness is an asset in many situations. Often a nut may be slackened by a heavier tool and then run off with the smaller one which can tuck in better.

In addition to the hand tools for taking things apart you will need some for making things. It is at this point that you have to decide how much work you will attempt and what to farm out as the equipment becomes more specialized and expensive. Possession of a good electric drill is taken as granted and it is not too hard to adapt this to a pillar drill and as a bench grinder to sharpen drills. A flexible shaft will help with port work but the next items come into another league.

There are two pieces of equipment to consider and their relative importance depends to an extent on the work you intend to do. If you will be making spacers, machining parts and working to a greater degree on the mechanics then a lathe becomes essential. With a good set of tools and attachments a whole new world of possibilities opens up and parts can be made at a speed undreamed of. Should you intend to concentrate rather more on the cycle parts then welding

equipment is the essential for you. Standard oxy-acetylene gear enables parts to be brazed, welded, filled, loosened, bent and reformed. An alternative which helps with engine and a good deal of the cycle part work is a butane torch. In all cases when using a mobile heat source be careful where you point it and remember what items you have warmed up. A fire extinguisher of the correct type is a good investment.

For serious restoration work both are really essential although a great deal is possible without either. One area where both can help is in making special tools for working on the machine in general and the engine in particular.

A further piece of specialized equipment well worth considering is a hydraulic press which can be constructed using a car or lorry jack. Remember to disconnect the overstroke release if it has one as otherwise you can lock the press up solid and it will stay that way until a seal goes.

Also worth putting on your shopping list is an air compressor. It does not have to be new, and often it, and the motor to drive it, may be bought separately, but it can be very useful even if you have no intention of doing any paint spraying. What it will do is enable you to check oilways, pipe lines, carburettor jets and the like for obstructions. Also, an air-line will blast

RIGHT *Jack Surtees, famous John's father and a successful racer in his own right, on a T120 Bonneville. The nacelle indicates a 1959 model as this was only fitted that season*

BELOW *The sporting or off-road TR6 from the same year, a model derived from the TR5 and using the T110 engine*

your cleaning agent off the parts and can save lots of time drying with a cloth.

The equipment you decide to acquire will depend on many factors and relates to your earlier assessment of your abilities. There is no point in having more tools than you can handle but don't confuse lack of confidence with this. If welding or machining is unfamiliar to you read about them, consider attending an evening course at the local college and above all practise before working on anything expensive or hard to replace.

Data

Just as important as tools for the workshop is data for the mind. Before laying a tool on your Triumph there is a good deal of information to be collected if you want the best results. Even if you are only after a good working machine you still need certain basic engine settings while for a concours job the data needed is far more detailed.

In all cases the first step is to establish what you

have by checking engine and frame numbers for year and model type. The latter can be further checked against the machine specification and often this can reveal discrepancies. It is all too easy to fit a T110 timing cover onto a 6T engine and trust that the buyer will not notice the Thunderbird features. There are many other changes that can be made and some may date from early in the machine's life, long before the classic machine revival.

Hybrids are a common problem with any make that remained in production for many years with minimal changes to basic dimensions. Some were built years ago because the parts were to hand. Maybe an old Triumph was bought to make a Triton and years later fitted with another engine unit. Others came from autojumbles as a number of parts bought from many sources. With a rising interest in machines in original specification it is inevitable that some will be built up from spares while the numbers are added to by those that had an engine change simply because of a major blow-up.

The magazine agony columns indicate that this is a common happening with most makes and so something to be aware of and to check. For the machine to be a hybrid may be a good thing rather than bad for it may have a worthwhile improvement. The important matter is knowing exactly what you do have.

Dating is complicated by the English industry tradition of starting its model year in August or September. Like most confusion it arose from good intentions and came about because the works switched to making the new models when they returned from the annual holiday. Production thus was well underway with stocks in the warehouse or at the dealers when the new models were announced in the press in the run up to the Earls Court Show. This was held in November and thus you could view in London and the next day collect your machine from

your local dealer. In theory.

Thus the maker's year was out of step with the calendar so that it is quite possible to find a machine first registered in October of the year before its style. Further complication for the restorer lies in the changeover of parts which may not coincide with the start of a new model year. Often stocks of old parts would be used, where feasible, until run down before the new ones were phased in. In many cases the change is internal and out of sight but some are on the outside and can cause real confusion.

The only answer is to work from the engine and frame numbers using the relevant parts book. This list is a most useful publication and really an essential for the restorer along with a workshop manual. In some ways the parts list is the more important for anyone striving for originality as it lists every part used on the machine with its part number and quantity.

The T120 in 1961 still with separate gearbox but in duplex frame and now fitted with an alternator although the magneto was retained

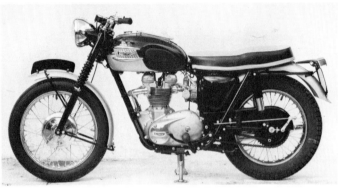

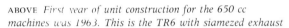

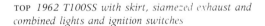

ABOVE *First year of unit construction for the 650 cc machines was 1963. This is the TR6 with siamezed exhaust*

TOP *1962 T100SS with skirt, siamezed exhaust and combined lights and ignition switches*

ABOVE *1963 Thunderbird with nacelle and skirt for its unit engine*

TOP *1963 T120, twin carburettor version of TR6*

Other literature that will help and which can be obtained from specialist book dealers is the rider's handbook in case it can add to the data in the manual and a sales brochure, often the only indication of the colours of the machine and its component parts.

A marque history is well worth having as it will fill out the background and I am biased to recommend *Triumph Twins and Triples* as I wrote it. You should also be reading the specialist magazines, *Classic Bike* and *The Classic Motor Cycle* on older machines and *Performance Bike* which covers modern techniques, to note addresses and articles that could be useful to you. The addresses to take note of are any that look to be good and helpful, those close to you and the ones offering a special service likely to be needed. Plating, painting, wheel rebuilds and crankshaft regrinds are common needs but you may also need someone to help with seat renovation, electrics or instruments so a knowledge of helpful addresses can be vital.

This type of firm is not here for two reasons. The first is the general need for them to be local. It is one thing to send a dynamo away for repair but quite another if you have 40 items for stove enamelling. The second is that firms are built up of people and their expertise. A good reputation may be due to the owner ensuring it is so or the workforce being skilled or a combination of the two. It can easily change if one or more men leave so recent recommendation is the best guide.

It will also be useful to join the Triumph Owners Club as they offer a unique combined experience. No other body has quite the same outlook and members are in the best position to carry out very real evaluation tests on machines, modifications and their effects. There is also the Vintage Motor Cycle Club in Britain (with others elsewhere) which offers a further source of data, a marque specialist and from their work has come a transfer scheme now available to all.

Yet another source of information is the show in its various forms. This may be a straight exhibition which includes the older machine, a classic machine show, a rally or a race meeting with events for older machines. All provide an opportunity to study other machines, talk to owners, gather information and find out where to get parts. Autojumbles, which are often combined with other events, can become an important part of the restorer's life for they offer the opportunity to seek out elusive spares, data and services. Local and not so local ones should be attended with dates and venues found in the specialist press pages.

Work plan

This is the grand title for you tearing the engine out and apart in the first flush of enthusiasm. Unfortunately, come winter, this fades and the mix up of parts you now have in many boxes, bags and tins becomes very unattractive. Before long another basket job hits the ad columns which is both sad and unnecessary.

Before you pick up the first tool have a long look at yourself, your facilities and the machine. *Think*, painful though it is. Make sure that you have decided what *you* want to do and that this is within the capabilities of you and your gear. Now you have to think again and decide how that happy dream of a concours win, sweet running machine or whatever, is to be reached.

In essence you have to decide whether to deal with the machine as a whole or by major parts. The first is usually quicker but requires more fortitude. Once apart you will seem to have a vast number of parts all needing attention and long before you get to the assembly stage you can run out of interest. The alternative is to take a major unit and renovate that alone. It will take longer to complete the whole machine but this method does reduce the storage space needed and you do feel that you are getting somewhere as each major lump is completed. Whichever way you go you need notes, photographs and sketches in large numbers. If you are going to rely on photos you will need to take plenty and they must be good close-ups. It is possible to do this with a very basic camera but for the best results you really need a decent SLR which can focus down to three feet or less. Unless you can get that close you just won't record the detail you need. Good lighting will help to get good photos, and a wide angle lens could be a useful asset.

TOP RIGHT *The sports 350 cc Tiger 90 of 1963, the only year it had a skirt*

SECOND RIGHT *The TR6C for the Western USA in 1966. Strictly off-road with those pipes*

THIRD RIGHT *Eastern USA guise for the TR6C in 1966 with lights and waist level exhaust systems*

BOTTOM RIGHT *Bonneville T120R for the USA in 1966, much as the UK version*

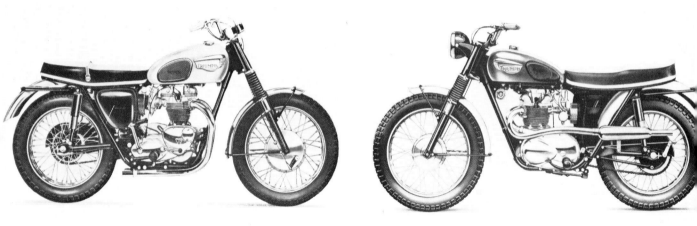

ABOVE *A T100T on test late in 1966, thus a 1967 model. Quick*

TOP LEFT *USA racer, the T120TT Bonneville in 1966*

TOP RIGHT *The T100C for the Western USA in 1966 with siamezed waist level exhaust*

RIGHT *1972 brochure worth comparing with the 1938 one to confirm the presence of the Turner line*

The ultimate in power and performance!

Trident 750

From the Isle of Man 750 Formula and Production races to the Bol d'Or and the British Championships the Trident has proved its worth time after time.

Needless to say a Trident is a masterpiece of Triumph engineering. The big three cylinder, three carb engine provides real power, the three-throw crank gives smoothness.

Trident available in large capacity (4 gall.) tank (as main illustration) or in small tank (3 gall.) specification – (right).

Bonneville . . . the most famous Triumph of them all.

Bonneville 650

The legend. The world's most consistent production race winner of its class, race bred, race proven. The high performance twin-cylinder, twin-carb engine is tough and rugged, ready for hard fast riding anywhere.

Competition-type forks, enormously strong frame are two features of a bike that has proved its worth time after time. Now in new colours for '72 with polished forks.

Bonneville is available in large tank (4 gall.) as main illustration or small tank (3 gall.) specification – shown (right).

The one that has everything!

Tiger 650

The Tiger 650 offers the best of both worlds – all the performance you need plus economy. The single carburetter unit gives instantaneous response, constant tractability and real economy. It's no surprise that hundreds of the world's police authorities rely on Tiger 650's.

The Tiger is available in large tank (4 gall.) specification, as in main illustration or small tank (3 gall.) option, (right).

. . . for the man who likes a real bike.

Daytona 500

A thoroughbred, a traditionalist's machine. A twin-cylinder, twin-carburetter engine which has been proved and proved. Slung low, with lean and hungry looks. A race-proved bike designed for purists. Now in new colours for '72.

Daytona available with 3 gall. capacity tank (as main illustration) or with small tank (2.2 gall.) specification – (right).

Common hybrid, the Triton, with Triumph engine and gearbox in Norton featherbed frame. Note awful clutch cable arrangement

Notes and sketches are a good alternative and mean that you can safely proceed without wondering if your film is going to develop satisfactorily. A pad of paper should be kept handy for rough notes in the workshop and these tidied and written up cleanly the same day. It is all too easy, especially with cycle parts, to forget the order in which parts fit onto a stud, which way round a bolt goes or even where the horn is fitted when you come to put things together months later. Plenty of labels and plastic storage bags will make life easier.

Even if the assembly you start with is wrong it is useful to record it as a basis to work from. Do not think that you can remember it all as you cannot and neither is it always obvious as to how the parts should be. Mudguard stays in particular can cause problems as often the apparently same part is used on both sides of

the machine and can be fixed in four alternative ways in each position. Four? Yes, as it can be turned over or end to end but only one way and one position will get it back where it came from. In theory this may not matter, if the stays are all the same, but in practice they always seem happier if replaced as they were. This no doubt arises because of small distortions that the parts have accommodated and if switched round they will have to begin again.

If you start with someone else's disaster as a basket case then the problem becomes more difficult as you will have to determine what each part is, where it goes and if it needs attention or was made in its present shape at the factory. A common difficulty with basket cases is rogue parts from another machine that have crept in and can give you hours of fun and frustration. These can include parts from another machine which is no trouble for you if they are stamped AJS or Norton but could be a small headache if marked BSA. If you have a late Triumph they may belong; or they may not! A larger headache is the appearance of real Triumph parts which happen to come from a single – or another model twin but not compatible with yours.

You must also beware of parts that changed in detail over the years but remained very similar in appearance, changes of thread form from Whitworth to Unified, changes brought about by metrication and some pattern parts. Of the last, some are very, very good but others can be awful. On the factory changes the threads altered over several years which can confuse but fortunately not much was changed to metric sizes.

Another headache can be proprietary parts which were common to many English machines and some of which happened to fall in with your basket. A handful of petrol taps might be useful but not if they all came from some other machine.

Lists

Some people live by lists, others abhor them, but in restoration they really are an essential and should form part of your note taking. Starting from a complete machine parts can be listed as they are dismantled with notes as to whether they need to be repaired, treated or both. By working with a parts list missing items can be highlighted and a shopping list compiled. On this will go consumables as well.

When starting with a basket case a parts list really is an essential and one or more photocopies well worth obtaining at the start. Using one as a master the parts can then be checked off one by one down to the last nut, bolt and washer. What is left on the list at the end becomes the shopping list and any parts not identified are, or ought to be, rogue.

While checking the list you can begin to establish the work needed on the parts you have depending rather on how much you are short and how essential the missing items are. How you fulfil the shopping list depends on your aims, money and the items themselves. You may have a good selection of nuts and bolts that would be fine for the job even if not correct to concours standard. If your aim is a good working machine then use them and the same philosophy can apply to many other items.

At the end of this operation you will have dismantled the complete machine and listed all the parts that require your attention or their purchase. This may have happened in stages if that is your way of working but happen it has. With this knowledge the restoration work will be easier to organize and the assembly straightforward to carry out.

Security

Classic motorcycles and their component parts are valuable and in some cases nearly irreplaceable. One professional restorer is quoted as saying 'What man has made, man can make again' which is perfectly true, but only at a price. So if you are lucky enough to own the optional bronze head which was available for the 1939 Tiger 100 it is worth a good deal both for the metal and its rarity. To remake the tooling, recast the head and to machine it might be possible but the cost would be astronomical.

Therefore security has become a point to bear in mind. This is especially true if you are forced to use a lock-up garage as your workshop and the necessary steps should be taken before the machine is on the premises. Avoid publicity as the word can quickly get about so don't leave the doors open if the premises face onto the street.

Working at home reduces the problem but may not remove it so again discretion is a good iea. It could also avoid an argument with the local council through a neighbour thinking you are using your home as a repair business.

A method used by some restorers to at least cut down their risk once a machine is partly dismantled is to store the parts in different areas of their home. This is a particularly useful way of protecting the smaller, more delicate, rather expensive and fairly universal items. These minor assemblies such as magneto, dynamo, speedometer and carburettor all lend themselves well to this arrangement and benefit from the household heating.

2 First steps

Clean machine

With your 'before' pictures safely taken work can begin on your project but not in the workshop. The very first thing is to take the machine outside and give it a good clean to remove dirt, grime, grease and oil. There are a number of cleaning agents to help with this task and the aim is to get the bulk of the dirt washed away and the machine dried before it enters the working area.

Transfers

While this chore is in hand care must be taken not to damage the finish or any transfers as reference to them may be necessary. In fact once the machine is clean and back in the workshop it is a good time to go round it and make notes as to the exact position of all the transfers with dimensions from fixed features.

If you are just overhauling the model then the transfers are unlikely to be of any major concern but for a full restoration they are. The position of the oil tank level and the 'Triumph' on the rear mudguard for instance are a fixed dimension from some other point and for a concours job should be correct.

First removals

The initial steps are to remove the parts that are fragile and easily damaged or which impede access to the major items. The first step is the fuel tank but before touching it have a look at the control cables and note how they run. Whether they are to left or right of the steering head and above or below the fixing lugs.

On some models you cannot remove the tank without taking the seat off first so if this is the case tackle it that way without forcing anything. If any of the bolts involved hold something else as well then you must note the order the parts are in as well as which way round the bolts go.

Note also the run of the petrol pipes while the tank and taps are in their correct location and watch the handlebars as you shift the tank. It is all too easy to catch the front of it on something and have the bars swing round and clout it to produce a dent or a nasty scratch.

Now get the machine up on the bike bench and make quite sure it is secure. If it is on a stand check that the feet cannot slide off the edge of the bench even when you lean on it with a tool. Check what will happen as you dismantle the machine. Most with a centre stand will keep their front wheel on the ground but if there is any doubt force a piece of wood under the back tyre to ensure stability. To have the whole machine rock back just as you try to lift the engine out can really put you off your stroke. Or worse still to dive to save the model and knock it over.

So aim for stability until you have the major weighty items out and then jack up the front and take the wheel out. Do it the other way round and you have too much mass balanced on too short a wheelbase for safety. Remember this for when you come to assemble.

With the bike up in the air and secure continue with the dismantling by removing the exhaust systems which may fall away or could stick. If the latter occurs don't tip the bike over while hauling on the pipes, just try to work them off a little at a time.

Tackle tight systems from the rear, a section at a time. Keep the pipe fixings tight and just remove the silencer bolts and clips. Work at the silencer to ease it back and off and then move on to the pipe which should respond to the same treatment. If it remains stuck to the screwed in adaptor and this is itself loose you have a problem. Don't strain at it in this instance or the port threads will be destroyed. You will have to get the cylinder head off with pipe still attached so you can then unwind the adaptor and make your repairs.

Now attend to the fragile items which start with the headlamp rim with its glass, reflector and bulb. Place something soft over the front mudguard so the assembly can rest while you disconnect the wires or pull out the bulb holders. Store with care and add the rear light lens and bulb.

Next is the speedometer, and rev-counter if fitted, noting which is to left or right. Watch the bulb holder fitted in the back of the instrument and remove the bulb itself. Tie the parts so they stay together at the end of the wire and don't slide off into the main harness. The same trick is often worth doing with the instrument drive cable to restrain the knurled end fitting. A clothes peg can be used temporarily and the run of the cables must be noted.

Remove the carburettor(s) and float chamber and store but drain the petrol out first. If a complete strip is intended the slides could best be removed from the cables and kept with the carburettor until attention is turned to that item.

The wiring is next on the list along with the control cables for they may well be inexorably linked by clips and tape holding them to the frame. More notes are needed before they are released. Then disconnect the battery and remove it. Don't hide it as it will need immediate attention if to act as a case or regular attention if it is to be used further.

The cables, suitably labelled, may come off first and the label should indicate which end is which if not obvious. The wiring is usually best detached working from the rear of the machine forward to the headlamp switch. Depending on the year of the machine it may be best to detach it from the switches and other electrical parts or it could be simpler to leave it joined and to take the parts off. Some, a dip-switch is an example, don't leave you any choice. More notes of course but also check along the harness as you remove it for any points where it has been rubbed or shows signs of damage. They are areas to do something about on assembly to prevent problems occurring.

It is likely that the rectifier will have been removed

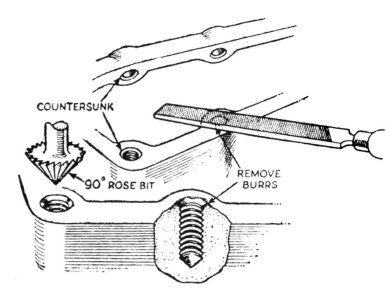

Cleaning up plain and tapped holes in a casting, essential if oil leaks are to be avoided

How to store tools even if some are Lambretta and the engine is a racing Bantam. Tube stock is stored above

during this operation but not necessarily the regulator if one is fitted. It is fragile so take it off for storage.

With the delicate details and the tangled mass or mess of cables and wiring out of the way the machine will look a lot cleaner and easier to work on. You can now really see what you are doing and can get at it without fear that you may damage something both fragile and costly. No reason not to take care of course.

Basket case

Where your Triumph has come in boxes you start your restoration with the assembly of shabby components. It is well worth cleaning the contents of each box as this will make them nicer to work on but nothing special is needed at this stage as they are going to need a lot more work and another, and better, clean before the final assembly.

What you have to do is to build up your collection of parts, each checked off against the parts list, into a complete machine. There are three problems in doing this. First is that it may not all be there. If the missing items are mainly bolts and fixings then anything from stock can be pressed into temporary service but if you lack structural items it becomes more tricky.

The next problem arises if the parts you have are damaged so they don't fit or try to distort other parts. Allowance must be made where this occurs. Finally there is the problem of rogue parts which may throw you off course.

At this stage keep everything and in fact this is a sound move with any part from any older machine. No matter how tired or worn it may be, at some time you or someone else will want to use it because it is the best one available. If you don't use it yourself you may

be able to swap it for something you do need and many a rebuild has been completed on this basis. Sometimes the swaps involve three or four people but usually all will finish up with the parts they need – often at little or no cost.

With a basket case you have to build the complete machine up as you get the parts. It is valid to leave, say, the gearbox internals out as their space is defined but beware of any assumptions with the cycle parts. It is only too easy to think all is well, begin final finishing and then have to destroy that with further fitting work.

This is why a basket case always takes so much longer to complete and tries the worker's patience as it is ages before any progress at all seems to be made.

From this first assembly exercise should come a list of missing parts and those needing attention. Once you are satisfied that it is all there and will all go together then you can continue along the same lines as someone fortunate enough to start with a complete machine.

You can now take it all apart again.

Restoration

This is another word for repair and is closely linked to service and maintenance. The philosophy is the same whether you have a 1938 Speed Twin or a 1972 Bonneville and the work involved and techniques used are similar or the same for both machines. The problems will vary enormously with no regard to the age of the machine and only spares availability will relate to the years to any degree.

The essence of the job is that the machine is reduced totally to its component parts. That means studs out of

Impact driver in use. It must fit the screw head and be held square. The hammer shown is unlikely to move it if stubborn

castings, spokes from wheels, seat cover from frame and so on so you are down to a single piece of metal, rubber or plastic for just about any item. Ball races and rectifiers you do not dismantle if you want them to continue living but most assemblies will come down to individual pieces.

Once in pieces each of these has to be checked and then mended or replaced. The first operation may be as simple as running a die down a thread to as complex as metal spraying followed by grinding to a very close tolerance. Or it could be a specialist welding process plus a careful freehand cutting using a flexible drive followed by a milling operation.

Replacement can be by a new spare or by an uprated part from a later machine which improves the performance. Or it can be by a modern component that does the job in a better way; tyres, shock absorbers and electronic ignition are just three examples.

After mending or replacement comes finishing when the outer coat goes onto the piece part and may be paint, plating or polish. In all cases they mirror the base material and reflect its preparation. You can then put it all together again.

Dismantle

There is a whole special technique to taking things apart and if you want to restore successfully you need to learn it. The first aspect is to soak things in penetrating fluid. If anything is stuck this is the opening move – and time. Let the fluid soak well in, give it another dose and come back days rather than hours later.

Try to move it. If there is any sign of a shift, you are winning; give it another soak, more time and bit by bit it will come. Rush it and it will snap.

Stubborn, well rusted nuts and bolts holding cycle parts together call for another method. If they are too far gone for further use, if they hold solid sections and if the parts are none too strong don't try to undo them. You can easily do real damage to nuts, bolts, the major parts and your fingers, either with the spanners or the saw if you try that method. You won't be able to hold the fixing still to saw it so it will damage the parts.

The answer is to just do them up. For once get out the $\frac{1}{2}$ in. drive socket and wind it on until it goes bang. If the bolt is largish, drill a hole up its centre first, but don't try this on bolts fixed to tapped holes – ever.

Timing cases often respond well to an impact driver but if you go that route two rules apply. First is that the blade must fit the screw and second is to hit it good and hard. A series of taps is no use, it has to be one good blow. One of the very best motorcycle men I have known told me once that this distinguished the pro from the amateur. The latter would tap at a puller to jump a taper apart and either shift nothing or damage parts. The pro would decide it was tight, select a four pound club hammer and hit it once, good and square as direction is as important as the force behind the blow.

It always pays to think before playing the heavy hand as often parts won't part because you have not undone all you should have. Particular care is needed when dealing with castings or mouldings as both are brittle and respond in the same way if put under a bending strain. They crack. So if it's stuck check against the parts list as this may indicate a screw you have missed, either because it is hidden down a dirty counter-bore or due to it assembling from the other side to the rest of the fittings. The two screws in the mouth of the Triumph crankcase are a classic example and leaving them in has broken many a case.

Checking

At this point you really start to find out how much work you have let yourself in for. You need to go over each part to establish if it can still be used, if it needs mending and if it needs finishing. More lists I fear.

Whether a part can still be used will depend on what it is, its material and whether it is bent, cracked, broken or worn badly. If in any or all of these conditions it will need mending or replacement. Bent parts will have to be straightened using heat and a press on occasion, cracked and broken ones may be welded and worn ones reclaimed.

It is while you are checking parts that you will find the bodges that have been done over the years to keep the machine running. Often these are the greatest problem and you are left to think that if only the owners of the past had just repaired the model your troubles would be minimal.

Mending

You are thus left to return parts to their original standard and it can often take all your ingenuity to deal with the past horrors. Some of the worst concern studs and threaded holes, the first often broken off in the second. Removal means making a drill bush, drilling into the stud and using an extractor to wind it out.

One thing with cover screws is that if all else fails you can drill the head off and by this means release the cover which will expose enough screw for it to be easily removed.

Threaded holes in castings or the frame are another source of problems and thread inserts can be one solution. Normally there is enough material available to accommodate them but for success the maker's instructions must be followed carefully.

Mending also includes getting joint faces flat. To do this all the studs will need to be removed and it is worth checking round the hole that each screws into. Often the metal will have pulled up a little so needs to be counter-sunk and then the whole surface made flat. If you have to machine it keep it to a minimum as modern gasket sealants can help a good deal in keeping oil where it should be.

Welding or heating equipment is often vital for

dealing with the cycle parts which need to be warmed up before being straightened. It also allows holes to be filled up and redrilled where really needed so is very handy for some rear mudguards. It is not unknown for several sets of holes to exist for various pillion pads of the past, all long gone so the holes need removal as well.

It is possible to take parts to a shop for welding as individual items but the need for a heat source in your own workshop may be emphasized if some assembly is out of line. Getting everything straight really can call for the parts to be in place and this makes it difficult for the job to be taken elsewhere other than to a restoration specialist.

Finishing

Once you are satisfied that a part is correct and will assemble as required then it needs to be finished. This may be as simple as a coating of oil to prevent rust for engine and gearbox parts. Or it can be a complex sequence of plating, painting and lining for a tank.

Castings may be vapour blasted or polished, cycle parts are mainly painted, details are plated and in many cases parts will need to be masked to protect threads and holes.

The specialist electrical assemblies and others of the same delicacy all go through their own special processes as detailed later but their basic mechanics may need the same mending and finishing as everything else.

Then all you have to do is to put it all together again.

Note

From now on I will assume you are either starting from a complete machine or have loosely hung your basket job together and have collected most of the major parts needed. This is to avoid needless repetition of this assumption together with the notes relevant to it and already mentioned.

Using a timing disc plus dial gauge to measure valve movement of engine well clamped by vice

3 The engine

Most people start with the engine because it is of the greatest interest to them, and it is also likely to be the easiest area to restore.

The exact procedure you follow will depend on whether you have a unit or pre-unit model and on your working style. The first job is to take the engine, or engine unit, out of the frame and then to dismantle it. Before removing it a decision needs to be made about the large, tight nuts that are used in various places.

The purist approach to large nuts is to use a suitable tool to hold the part they are attached to and undo them. However this can be a problem in the number of special tools that may be needed and it may govern the sequence of operations.

At this stage all that is needed is for the nuts to be loosened and common practice is to do this with the engine in the frame and connected to the rear wheel and brake. With the machine in top gear, each nut is attacked in turn starting at the engine and working through the transmission to the rear wheel. A combination of jammed on brake and clouted spanner will usually prevail unless the clutch slips.

This method means that the timing cover has to come off at what is really too early a stage in order that the pinion and cam gear nuts can be slackened. The alternatives are less messy in their approach and enable parts to be dealt with as desired. The first is to use tools to hold parts still and a further option, given the equipment, is to use an impact spanner. If you do go that latter route do ensure that all the parts will take the shock.

Engine types

Triumph engines divide into two basic forms, pre-unit and unit construction, with further variations in detail construction and capacity. The pre-unit type dates from 1938 in the 500 cc size and this ran to 1959. It was joined by a 650 cc version in 1950 which was continued up to 1962 and there was also a 350 cc model built 1946 to 1951. This last had a good number of internal differences from the others although the basic concept remained unchanged.

The first unit construction engine came in 1957 as a 350 cc and was quickly joined by a very similar 500 cc version. Both were later produced in sports models and were joined in 1963 by a 650. This used a different crankcase and was stretched to 750 cc in 1973 but from first to last all engines shared many common features.

These include high mounted gear driven camshafts placed fore and aft of the engine, twin plunger oil pump for the dry sump lubrication, twin rocker boxes (except on the 3T model), pushrod tubes front and rear, and a very characteristic line. Variations were changes from magneto to coil, dynamo to alternator, to shell big end bearings, to alloy cylinder heads throughout, to crankshaft construction and a myriad of detail points and parts.

Removing the engine

The procedure depends on the basic engine type and your lifting strength. The unit engines weigh over 100 lb for the smaller and more for the 650 so removal complete is really a job for two or entails the use of some form of lifting tackle. The pre-unit engine is lighter and will come out by itself or complete with gearbox but the latter is preferably a two man job and the former a struggle for one.

For many the solution is to take off some of the heavier items while the engine is still in the frame. It is easy enough to remove the top half of the engine, the primary transmission and the gearbox internals which reduces the weight to manageable proportions. Of course, you will have to reverse the procedure on assembly which may not be quite so tidy as building complete units on the bench.

Whichever way you go, start by draining the oil from both the tank and the sump. Then replace the sump plate as you are bound to stand the engine on it. Also drain the primary chaincase and gearbox while you have the trays to hand. During your first steps you should have detached the control cables and wiring, if you have not then now is the time to do so. The dynamo, where fitted, can easily be removed but the other electrics can stay in place.

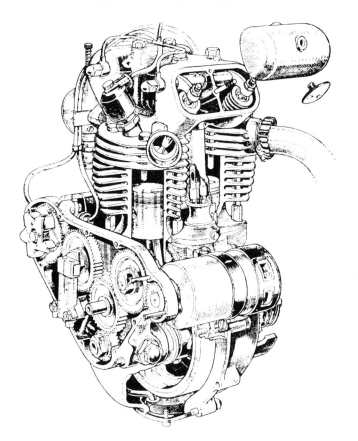

ABOVE *The 3T engine in earlier form with through bolts for cylinder head and one piece valve covers*

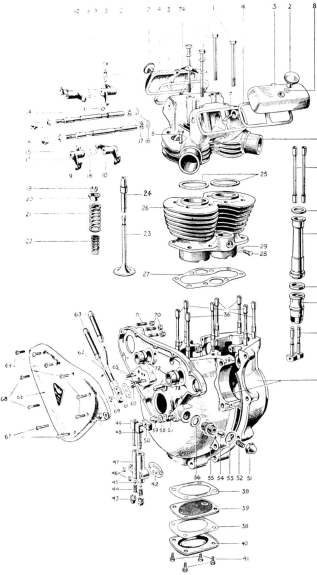

RIGHT *Parts list drawings for the early 3T cases, block, head and valve gear*

The external oil pipes can come off with the main ones being the connections between oil tank and engine. Also remove the rather small pipe that feeds the rocker gear and take care when undoing the acorn nuts that hold it to the rocker boxes. It is all too easy to find that the nut has stuck to the pipe union and is carrying it round with it to put a nasty kink in the pipe. You must hold the union to prevent this. Store the pipe with care so it does not get distorted.

You will have already removed the exhaust pipes and silencers so can now take off the footrests and rear brake pedal. On rigid frame models also remove the battery carrier at this stage.

The primary transmission is the next area on pre-unit engines unless you are removing everything as one lump. With the outer case off you can undo the engine sprocket nut using a close fitting socket and jarring it undone. The clutch spring nuts need a thin

blade under their heads to lift the springs away from their locking nibs and their removal releases the clutch plates. You then have to undo the clutch centre nut, some have a locking washer and to hold the centre still will either have to rely on the rear brake, use an old clutch plate with handle attached or lock the clutch centre and drum together with a plate of each type bolted to one another. You can use a piece of bent steel strip to form a scotch but this is not recommended as it puts all the load in one place.

Having got the nut off the shaft you can remove the centre and drum to just leave the hub. This is threaded internally and an extractor to pull it off was included in the toolkit up to 1970. Use it, don't try to remove the hub with levers or a multi-leg puller as you will break it. If it is too tight do the extractor bolt up firmly and then hit the bolt head squarely with a hammer.

Remove the inner chaincase and make a note of any

distance tube behind it on the pre-unit models. There is usually one on the footrest rod and if you leave it out you can easily crack the case on assembly. Also check it is the correct length and does fit the space it should.

You are now ready for the big heave. Remove the engine torque stays, slacken all the fixing bolts and studs, slide out all the minor ones and then support the engine weight with either a box or a jack. Pull out the remaining bolts in turn to remove all the distance pieces and note their position. A diagram and their length will help. Then pull the bolts and take the engine out. Note that with the early rigid frames this may allow the frame halves to move and collapse so watch out for this and if necessary arrange for the weight to be taken by another jack or hung from a girder in the roof.

Pre-unit dismantling

Hold the engine in the vice by its front mountings and add a support at the rear if this is needed. Make quite certain it is really secure and the unit is held firmly. You can now take it apart but don't rush it and do observe as you go. It is well worth checking the valve timing before you remove anything in case the markings are missing or the assembly wrong. Use a degree disc clamped to the drive shaft, set the valve gaps as prescribed and make your notes. Also check the ignition timing on full advance and retard while you have the disc in place.

The engine will come apart easily enough and on anything unknown the golden rule is to check everything, assume nothing and take it all apart. It may seem less trouble to leave a crankshaft in one but only full examination will show if it is really fit or just on the point of failure because the sludge trap is full.

Start at the top and remove the rocker box caps and, where fitted, the oil drain pipes, taking care not to strain them. Remove the rocker boxes by undoing the small nuts, the small bolts and then the bigger bolts remembering that at least one valve is open and could lean on the box. Turn the engine to minimize this effect and catch the pushrods and their tubes as the boxes come off.

Now, take out the remaining head bolts which will release the cylinder head and note which way up the gasket is. On the 3T only the rocker boxes are cast in one with the head which comes away after the removal of all eight bolts. Leave the head assembled for the time being as it and the rocker boxes reduce to a good few parts, many small and easily lost.

The timing cover is next but before shifting it at least slacken the oil pressure release body and the gallery bolt. Undo all the cover screws using an impact driver if necessary and remove the cover watching that the timing gear idler does not come off with it. Take the oil pump off and then inspect the timing gears for alignment marks in mesh and keyways. Make notes of what you have.

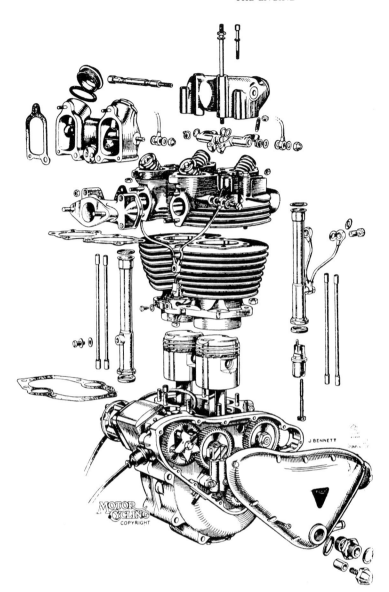

The first 6T engine in 1950, very much based on the Speed Twin and to continue in sports form for many years

Mark the block as some are reversible and there is no point in getting the pistons back correctly if you turn the block round. Then undo the block nuts, loop rubber bands round the tappets to stop them falling out, run the pistons up to top dead centre, give the block a sharp blow with a rubber mallet to break the joint and lift. Pack rag in the gap to catch debris and protect both rods and pistons. Lift off block and gasket.

Remove the circlips and put in a bag labelled 'used'. Don't use them again but keep them in case you need a

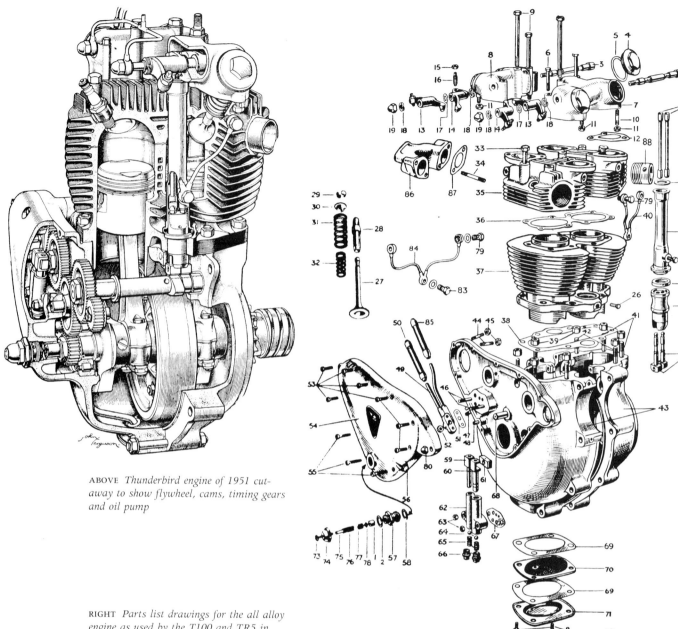

ABOVE *Thunderbird engine of 1951 cut-away to show flywheel, cams, timing gears and oil pump*

RIGHT *Parts list drawings for the all alloy engine as used by the T100 and TR5 in 1951*

pattern when looking for new ones. Mark the inside front of each piston L and R so you know you have it right before they come off. To remove the gudgeon pins it is best to use an extractor and this is essential if Triumph solid skirt pistons have been fitted. These are heated prior to the assembly of the pin and the same method of removal is to be recommended. Your butane torch in one hand and an oven cloth to hold the piston with will make the job easy. Split skirt pistons can have the pins drifted out but need to be supported so an extractor is better.

You can now lock the crankshaft using a good clean bar through the small ends and supports placed across

the crankcase mouth after it has been wiped clean. Undo the nuts holding the timing pinion on the crankshaft and the gears on the camshafts. Use a good socket noting that the cam ones have left-hand threads. Also undo the magneto gear nut.

Where an automatic advance unit is fitted the fixing bolt also acts as an extractor so will pull the pinion off the shaft as it is undone. Manually controlled magnetos have the gear held on a taper by a nut and the gear is threaded so the clutch hub puller will fit and can be used to remove it. Coil ignition models have the gear held by a cross-pin and a circlip.

Removal of the camshaft and crankshaft gears

requires the use of special pullers. There is no way round this and something will break if you don't use the correct ones. The camshaft ones can be left in place as they do not prevent the crankcase being parted but their removal is essential if the camshafts need changing or the bushes inspecting. Best to take them off unless you know the history of the engine. The crankshaft pinion must come off.

You are now ready to split the cases and start by removing the two screws in the case mouth. Many don't and fracture the casting. Next remove the sump plate and filter and then all the other studs and bolts. Drive the cases apart by striking the drive side of the crankshaft with a rubber mallet or on a block on the floor. Lift out crankshaft, camshafts and the breather valve behind the left end of the inlet one.

You now have the major parts ready for your attention.

Unit engine dismantling

In the main the unit engine comes apart in the same way as the pre-unit without the gearbox intruding to any real extent. In essence it is carried within the right crankcase half as a unit but cannot be fully removed until the clutch is off.

The main change in construction comes from the electric with all models being fitted with an alternator within the primary chaincase. The ignition system was by coil and points and up to 1962 or 1963, the latter were housed in a distributor mounted behind the cylinder block and the points cam was driven from the inlet camshaft by skew gears. From 1963 and on all 650 cc twins the points plate was mounted in the timing cover and the cam driven by the exhaust camshaft. Removal of the later mechanism is by Triumph puller or by using a bolt screwed into the cam spindle and an impact puller on that.

The timing side is stock Triumph with gear driven camshafts and up to 1970 the cam gears were screw cut for a puller as they had been since 1938. In the maelstrom of changes of the early 1970s this feature went to be replaced by two tapped holes in each gear to suit a stock form of puller. On the smaller twins the cam bushes went and the shafts, with an increase in diameter, ran directly in the crankcase and were retained by outer plates.

Aside from the presence of the gearbox, whose large nuts should have been slackened, and the ignition electrics, the engine can come down as a pre-unit. The top half details vary a little, the pushrod cover seals vary a lot, but taking it apart changed little over the years.

Details altered with the sump plate becoming a filter cap on the smaller twins and a screwed in assembly on the 650, both being fitted to the underside of the timing side case. The timed breather, driven by the inlet camshaft, went after 1969 and was replaced by a vent via the chaincase. Duplex primary chains were

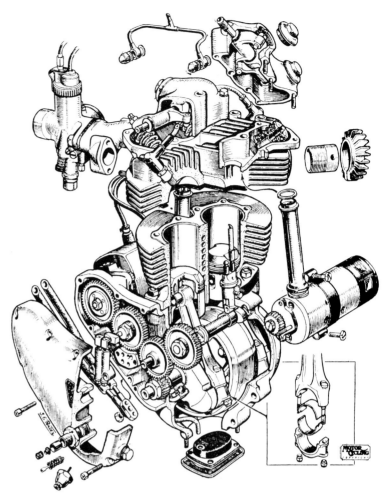

The 650 cc engine fitted to the T110 and TR6 in 1956 with light alloy head, revised pushrod tubes and big ends with bearing shells

fitted and equipped with a tensioner on all except the very early unit 350.

Thus, the engine comes down as for the pre-unit as regards the top half and the timing side. The primary transmission follows the same lines down to clutch hub removal and with that out of the way the gearbox can come out. This leaves the crankcase to split and again it is vital not to forget the two screws in the case mouth. Check round that all the bglts, screws and studs have been removed and then split as before.

Again, the major and minor parts await your attention.

Crankshaft

Three basic types of crankshaft were used in Triumph twin engines and all have the crankpins at 360 degrees. The differences affected the assembly of the

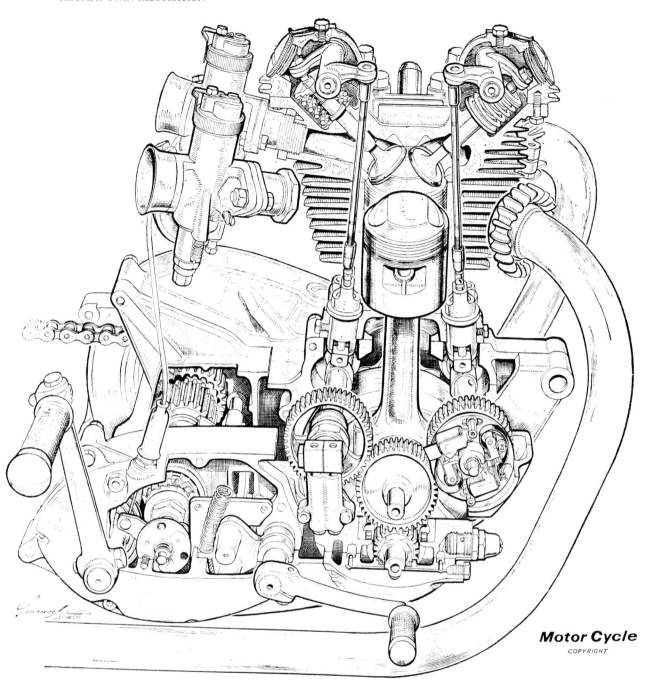

*The unit construction 650 cc engine and gearbox in its 1963
form as used by the T120 with twin Monoblocs*

parts while the flywheel and its fixing was to suit the
method of construction of the crankshaft. The balance
factor varied over the years in an effort to combat the
vibration. All engines have white metal big ends with
most using replaceable shells. Early twins and the
model 3T had the connecting rods metalled and were
meant to be replaced when worn.

The original crankshaft was built up from two
halves which clamped to each side of a central
flywheel with six nuts and bolts holding the assembly
together. All unit construction and pre-units from
1959-on, have a one piece crankshaft forging with the

ABOVE *1969 Bonneville with Concentrics, balance pipe and twin horns*

ABOVE LEFT *Drive side of 1947 Tiger 100 with iron engine and lovely lines*

LEFT *Exploded 1951 6T engine. Every part and all the nuts and bolts need to be cleaned and checked*

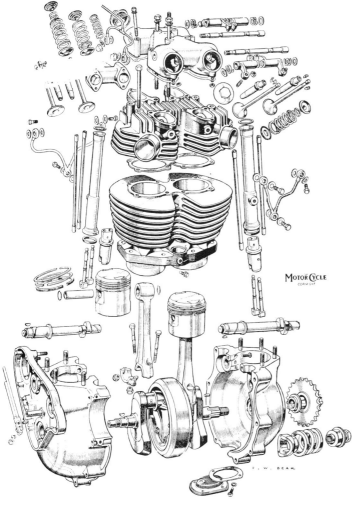

MOTOR CYCLE
COPYRIGHT

F. W. BEAK

flywheel shrunk on and held by three radial bolts. The 3T used a clamping system which allowed one piece rods to be assembled onto the crankpins which were then pressed into the flywheel where they were clamped.

In all cases mark and note exactly how the parts are assembled. On the 3T check that the alignment holes in the three sections are in fact in line and see the separate notes on that crankshaft. For all the others mark and remove the connecting rods to leave the bare crank assembly.

The crankpins must be inspected for wear and damage. It is feasible to remove light scores, marks and even surface rust with fine emery cloth but if they are worn they will need regrinding. A micrometer or vernier is an essential here but some idea of the degree of ovality can be obtained using calipers and feeler gauges to detect variations.

If the crankpins need grinding the reduction in diameter was in 0.010 in. steps from the nominal to a maximum of 0.030 in. The finish and end radii are important and have a bearing on big end life and crankshaft reliability.

The mainshafts also need to be inspected as they must be a good fit in the main bearings and their threads must be in good condition. If there is any sign of trouble its cause must be located and remedied. The shafts of the unit construction engines require a further check. On the 650 the timing side end runs in an oil seal in the cover. If this is damaged it can be ground down 0.020 in and a special seal fitted that accommodates the new diameter. Pre-unit twins had a bush in the timing cover to do the same job of ensuring that oil was fed into the crankshaft. On the smaller unit twins it was normal practice up to 1968 to grind the timing side main bush diameter at the same time as the crankpins and fit a new bush to suit. This stopped when a ball race replaced the bush but on an unknown crank all diameters should be checked in case this policy was not carried through.

On all crankshafts you must clean out the sludge trap and make sure that all oilways are unimpeded from entry to exit.

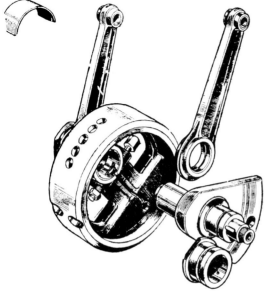

ABOVE LEFT *Front view of early 3T engine with its own style of timing cover and release valve*

LEFT *The 3T crankshaft, built up with half shafts, one piece rods and flywheel with clamp bolts. Dowel hole aligns and bush is timing main*

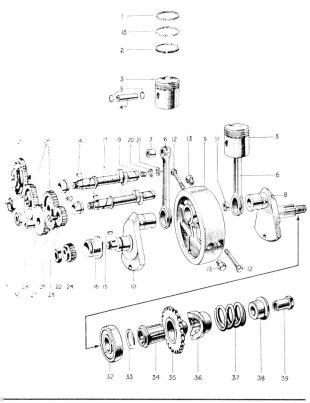

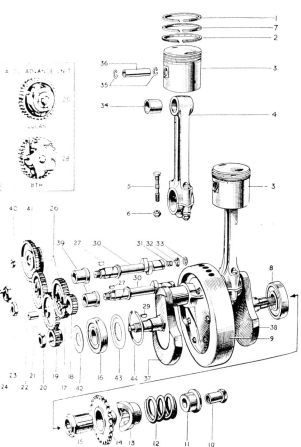

Pre-unit crankshafts to 1958

These are held together by six nuts and bolts which must be renewed with genuine parts. They are made from a 55 ton high tensile steel and nothing else will do. The bolts have ground shanks and should be a close fit in their holes. If they are not the holes will have to be enlarged and special bolts in the correct grade of steel made up to fit.

It is possible to interchange just about any 650 and pre-unit 500 crank assembly although the change in timing side main in 1954–55 will affect this. To complete any change it may be necessary to alter the bearing and maybe add a spacer or two. 650 unit cranks will also go into the pre-unit cases so inspect and check any unknown engine.

Part of the reason for this is the similarity of engine strokes at 80 mm and 82 mm which make it easy to swap over and hard to check when buying. There were also other alterations over the years and it is important to collect the correct items. Not a problem if you start with a complete machine but potential trouble with a basket case.

The 500 cc model was built in three forms as the 5T, T100 and TR5 and all used the same crankshaft halves up to 1949. For 1950 the method of manufacture changed to leave more material on the crank cheeks and less in the flywheel so both items changed. They remained as they were until 1953 when the drive side was altered to accommodate the alternator on the 5T and a sprocket without shock absorber on the others.

For 1954 the 5T was left alone but the T100 and TR5 had a new timing side crank half to suit the larger main bearing. At the same time they changed to a larger diameter crankpin so also had a new drive side. The timing one was modified to accommodate an oil tube for 1955 and the two crank halves also fitted to the 5T which thus gained the bigger main and crank pins. The 500s remained unchanged until 1959 when the T100 alone changed to the three bolt design.

The 650 followed a similar course with the halves unchanged until 1954 when the introduction of the T110 brought the increased shaft diameters. Again there was a change for an oil tube for 1955 after which it stayed the same for those two models and the TR6.

The flywheels also varied with a common one used

ABOVE LEFT *Parts list drawings for 3T engine rotating items*

LEFT *Engine internals as shown in the parts list for 5T, 6T, TR5 and T100. These and 3T may differ from model to model*

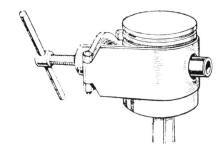

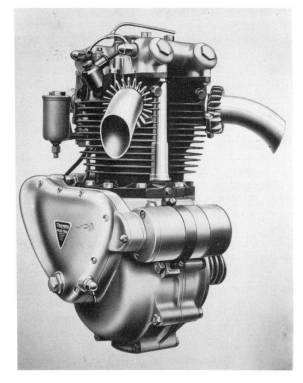

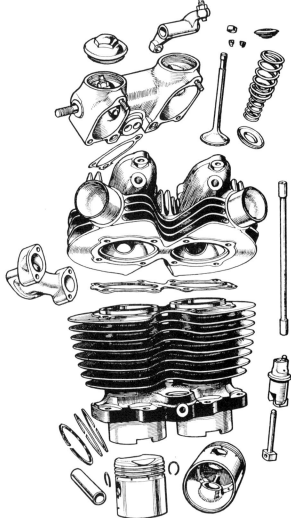

for the 500s until 1950 when they changed and the T100 used a modified version. Both altered for 1951 and in 1953 the T100 reverted to the 1938 5T wheel. It and the TR5 changed again for 1954 and this new wheel went onto the 5T for 1955. The 650 engine began with one wheel and changed for 1954 to that used by the T100 so this became standard for the range from 1955 to 1958.

To work on this series of crankshafts clamp the flywheel in the vice and remove the six bolts. Clean very thoroughly and reassemble. Where an oil tube is fitted this should be located into the timing side with its cutaway engaged with the oil hole plug. This will ensure that the hole in the tube points to the centre of the crankshaft so is as far from any sludge accumulation as possible.

Assembly should be with new nuts and bolts tightened to 250 lb. in. Pessimists also use Loctite and centre pop the threads to make sure.

The standard balance factor, which varies, should be kept to and it is normal practice to check this if

ABOVE *Top half of the 1939 Speed Twin engine*

LEFT TOP *A gudgeon or wrist pin extractor in use*

ABOVE LEFT *The 5T engine in its 1946–48 form with front dynamo and internal oil drains from the valve wells*

ABOVE RIGHT *Cut-away Tiger 100 all alloy engine on show at Earls Court late 1951, so 1952 models on view*

the crankshaft is ground or the flywheel changed. Triumph practice was to do this by clipping a weight on to each crankpin when checking. These varied, as did the balance factor, so work to the correct shop manual.

The man with a 3T has no problems with part variations as nothing changed in the crankshaft assembly during the model's life. His problems come in a different way due to the use of one piece connecting rods with white metal liners. This led to the special crankshaft construction with the crank-pins an interference fit in the flywheel. The snag is that if the pins are ground due to wear the flywheel has to be changed for one with a smaller hole in it. Easy for the works to arrange in 1946, rather harder now.

It may mean that the pins have to be built up by metal spray and then ground to standard size. Metal spraying is a process where minute metal particles are heated and directed onto the hot surface of the parent part so they fuse to it. The process requires special

equipment and skill to achieve the right result but it can save parts otherwise damaged beyond repair.

Assembly of the 3T crankshaft takes some care. A press is needed to push the pins into the flywheel and a 0.500 in. bar for the alignment holes. The oil tube must go between the cranks, the pin must be assembled dry to the flywheels, the rods must be the right way round as marked and the correct rod side play of 0.015/0.020 in. must be left. It must also be in line before the clamps are tightened.

Once assembled all crankshafts should be primed with oil to make sure there is no obstruction to its flow to the crankpin.

Unit crankshafts, 350 and 500 cc
The one piece crankshaft with flywheel held by three radial bolts first appeared in 1957 in the 3TA. The same stroke was used in all versions and sizes of this engine and will fit all engines to 1968. For 1969 it was given Unified threads and a change of main bearings which it retained to the end.

47

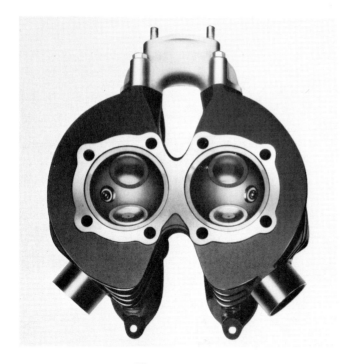

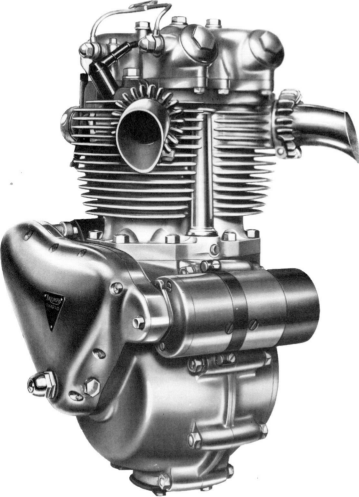

The first crankshafts had a plug at each end of the crankpin with an oil tube between them but for 1959 this was changed to a single plug on the right. For 1969 the threads on each end and those for the flywheel bolts altered. The flywheel changed once only in 1965 when it gained a notch to register tdc.

The oil tube sludge trap must be cleaned out in all cases and all the oilways checked for free oil flow. To remove the trap drill out the locking punch mark and unscrew the plug using an impact driver. Remove the nearest flywheel bolt which locates into a hole in the tube. Remove the tube using a large tap or Easiout as it will be tight, and clean everything to perfection. Unless the flywheel has to come off the bolt can go back and locate the tube but otherwise leave off, remove the other two and press the flywheel off after marking it.

Renovate the crankshaft as for the early pre-unit and reassemble. The flywheel has to be heated to get it to fit and 80 degrees C should do the trick. Wear oven gloves to handle it and remember that it will stay warm for ages. Make sure all three bolts go in properly and then fit each using Loctite and torque to 350 lb. in. Dispense with any washers as Triumph went over to Loctite from 1964 on these engines. If you have to replace the bolts remember that they changed for 1969 to match the crankshaft thread. Finally, refit the plug using jointing compound to seal it and lock by centre punching.

Pump oil through the crankshaft.

Three bolt crankshafts, 650 cc and late T100

The same construction was used on these engines so the same renovation methods apply. There were however rather more changes. The T100 missed these as it was only built for 1959 and then was replaced by the T100A.

The pre-unit 650 started out with a flywheel giving the traditional 50 per cent balance but for 1962 was changed for one giving 71 per cent. This only lasted for some 1250 engines for from D17043 another wheel with 85 per cent was fitted. This continued for 1963 when the crankshaft was amended to fit the unit crankcase and the oil seal in its timing chest. It stayed in this form until 1972 when the fitting of metric main bearings meant a change of mainshaft diameter. Such crankshafts should be stamped with an M to denote the metric sizes.

ABOVE LEFT *Tiger 100 cylinder head, most likely from 1939 but 1950 the same*

LEFT *The 1956 650 cc engine with alloy cylinder head used in the T110 and TR6*

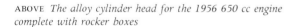

ABOVE *The alloy cylinder head for the 1956 650 cc engine complete with rocker boxes*

RIGHT *Engine unit of the 1957 350 cc model 3TA, also known as the 21. First unit construction*

The flywheel continued with its changes. For 1965 it received a tdc slot and in 1966 shed 2.5 lb although it retained the 85 per cent balance factor. At the same time the flywheel bolts were changed for longer ones. 1968 brought an ignition timing slot in the flywheel and during 1969, from engine NC 02256, a heavier wheel went back on to smooth out the running.

For 1971 there was yet another new flywheel complete with its own bolts and the latter changed again for 1972 when Unified threads were adopted and the crankshaft altered to suit.

Otherwise it is dealt with as the smaller unit twins and pumped full of oil when finished.

Crankshaft stud
Crankshafts from 1953 onwards, other than for the unit 350 and 500 cc models, have a stud screwed into the drive mainshaft end. This item was never altered and the fitment of a new part enables the thread to be easily reclaimed. As it holds the rotor and engine sprocket in place it should be fitted using Loctite.

Connecting rods
Most Triumph rods are forged in RR56 light alloy with separate caps and shell big end bearings. Exception are the one piece 3T rods and those fitted to the 3TA and T90 up to 1966 which were steel stampings. All had a white metal bearing surface and from engine

75103 built in 1956 shells were fitted. Prior to that the rod and cap themselves were white metalled.

All connecting rods must be carefully handled at all times and not allowed to knock against other items. This includes the crankcase mouth when working on the engine. All must be carefully inspected for any signs of damage which should be polished out. The rods may also be inspected for alignment if there is any chance they are out and if there is any doubt about a rod it should not be used. A snapped rod will totally wreck an engine and is not worth the risk.

For the early engines with white metal bearings repair is a specialized job best farmed out along with the crankshaft so that can be ground first and the rod bearing them made to fit. On the 3T the problem is compounded by the need for the pin to fit the flywheel and this aspect must be dealt with first.

One solution for the other early engines is to bore the rod and cap out to accept a normal shell bearing. This is a job that must be done to high standards of accuracy and the shells need cutting away to clear the big end bolts but it does work. To do it you need good facilities.

For later engines the normal practice is to fit undersize shells after grinding the crankpins. For most years these were offered in minus 0.010 in. and 0.020 in. forms but for the 3TA two further grinds were possible.

It is good practice to renew the rod bolts even on the cooking engines and mandatory on the sports ones. If you do intend to use the existing bolts check them with care for any signs of stretching or thread distortion. In all cases fit new nuts. Those should be done up evenly and in steps to the torque figure or until the bolt stretches 0.005 in. Figures are 27 ft lb for the pre-unit 500, 28ft lb for all 650s up to 1968, 22ft lb from then on for the Unified threads and 18ft lb for the 350 and 500 cc unit rods.

Rod types

The 3T rod is easy to recognize as it is the only one piece one and was not changed during the model life. The 5T and T100 began life with a rod whose cap was formed with integral fixing studs which were secured by nuts and split pins. This design was used postwar in 1946 but was joined by a revised type with separate bolts fitted with their heads under the rod cap. This was used up to 1949 and for the early TR5 model.

During 1950 the rod was altered so that the bolt went in from the rod side and the nuts held the cap in place. At the same time locking nuts were adopted and the split pins deleted. For that first year the 5T used a different rod to the 6T and the T100 had the 5T rod but polished. From 1951 they all used the 6T rod

including the T100 which continued to have that little extra attention given it.

This continued up to 1954 for the 5T but that year saw a change in big end diameter for the other models and thus a new rod which the 5T adopted for 1955. For 1956 all models received big end shells and this rod form remained in use up to 1965. The advent of the unit 650 saw the TR6 and T120 fitted with the same rod but polished and this continued until the change to Unified threads for 1969.

The cap nuts and bolts remained unchanged from 1950 until the 1969 thread change although the nuts were later modified in 1970 and 1972. The big end bearings were unchanged from 1956 onwards for all these models.

Of the smaller unit twins the 350 cc models began with steel rods but from 1967 went over to alloy. All the 500 cc rods were alloy and one type was used for most models up to 1969. Before that in 1968 the T100R and T100T models adopted a revised rod and in 1969 changed again to a rod without small end bush which was amended for 1971.

The cap nuts and bolts were not changed until 1971 and up to then the nuts were as used since 1950. The bearing shells remained the same for all models and years.

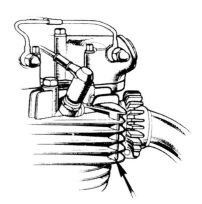

ABOVE *The vertical rib added to each side of the 650 cc cylinder head for 1961 to reduce resonance*

LEFT *The 1964 5TA engine unit of 500 cc and much as the 350*

RIGHT *6T engine unit from 1964, the tourer with a skirt*

Small end bush

There are only three bush types to cover all applications. The 3T and 3TA series used the same bush, the 5TA series another which left one more to cover the rest from 1938 to 1972.

If worn they can be pressed out using a new bush but line the oil hole up first. Then ream to give a nice slide fit on the pin. Avoid reaming by hand if possible as a guided machine reamer will do a much better job. Check the oil holes again and put to use.

Pistons

Before worrying about the condition of the pistons you should see if the block needs boring as if it does you will fit new ones anyway. If you plan to keep the existing ones they do need to be closely inspected. They must be examined for cracks in the skirt or around the gudgeon pin bosses while the ring grooves must be in good condition as must be the pin holes and circlip grooves.

There are a number of pistons that were available for each engine size and while many remained constant during their production life the existence of options means that a check should be made if there is any doubt. Check the compression ratio by measuring the combustion chamber volume and doing a small

sum. Also compare the valve head diameters with the cutaways in the piston crown to see if they are compatible as this may provide further evidence.

Due to the variety of pistons used they have been listed in an appendix with the nominal compression ratio they gave and their use as a standard fitment. Most were available around the same time as an option for other models and nearly all could be obtained in a range of oversizes.

If you replace the piston use a quality make and keep to the standard compression ratio for your model. Any attempt to raise this could bring a major disaster in its train as the middle aged or old engine objects to the added loads. Should you find yourself with a sports engine fitted with the touring cast iron cylinder head go for the touring pistons otherwise the engine will overheat.

If you keep the existing pistons expect to renew the rings in which case you may need to remove the glaze from the bores with a specialist tool or medium to coarse emery cloth. Check the gaps on the new rings and do fit the taper ones the right way up or you will have a plug oiling problem.

The same gudgeon pin was used in all 500 and 650 engines from 1938 to 1966. For 1967 a short pin was used in the 500 and T120TT models and continued in

the smaller machines. The other 650 adopted a longer pin up to 1969 but from 1970 on all 650s used the same short pin as the 500. Circlips were unchanged from 1938 to 1966 and then changed. They reverted to the original type for the 650s in 1972.

The 350 cc models shared a common pin and circlips for the 3T and from 1957 to 1966. The 1967 style items were then used up to 1969.

The pins should be checked for ridges and changed if not in really good condition. The clips you change as a matter of course.

Cylinder block

This needs to be checked for damage and wear as either may have occurred. Damage may be to the fins, the top and bottom mating surfaces or to the threads. Wear occurs in the bore. On 650s from 1966 the oil feed to the exhaust tappets also needs to be checked to ensure it is free of obstruction. Finally the block may need to be finished to restore its appearance.

Damaged or broken fins may be repaired by welding or brazing but it is not easy to get back to the original appearance. If you have the broken part this will help but it is a tricky job to do. If a middle fin has gone you may have to cut others away first and then refix them once the broken one is fixed. Be careful about heating the block and let it cool slowly. Do all this work before any rebore or machining that may be needed.

Check the gasket surfaces for burrs and distortion. At the base these may only cause an oil leak but at the top could lead to a blown gasket which could mean burn damage to both head and barrel. If extensive it may need machining to clean up but this must be kept to a minimum. However it must be done or the trouble will reoccur. If high compression pistons are fitted it may be prudent to check the piston to valve clearance when you assemble the engine.

Nearly all blocks have eight or nine tapped holes in

TOP LEFT *1964 Bonneville. Note wire locking of float chamber screws and twin switches on side panel*

CENTRE LEFT *T90 in the same year, 1964, with similar switch arrangement*

LEFT *The twin carburettor head adopted in 1972 by the T120 with rocker box covers in place of caps*

their top surface. These should be inspected to ensure that the threads are in good condition and not pulling up around the holes. If it is it must be machined flat, the holes lightly countersunk and the threads cleaned up.

Bore wear is best checked with a Mercer gauge which will provide exact measurements. An idea of the position can be gained by feeling the wear ridge at the top of the bore but judgement as well as an oily finger is needed. Alternative methods if you don't possess a Mercer or an internal micrometre are available. One is to use an internal bore gauge which can be set to the unworn diameter at the bottom of the bore and used with feelers to find the wear at the top. Internal calipers can do the same job but a more delicate touch is needed to get accurate results without measuring caliper spring. More homespun techniques are to use the piston and measure the skirt clearance at several points or a piston ring and check its gap in the same way.

If the bore is worn it will have to bored and before this is done two other points need attention. First you must establish whether it is on standard or oversize at the moment. This will indicate what you have to go out to. Second you *must* get the new pistons before having the bores machined in case there is a supply problem.

All blocks can be taken out to plus 0.040 in. but no further or there is a chance that the base flange will pull off. The alloy T100 with close pitch fins and the matching TR5 can have their liners replaced but not the early TR5 with square fins as theirs were cast in place.

Finishing

When the block is mechanically fit for use it needs to be finished. This process will have begun with the cleaning it received before work began but this now needs to be completed. The block will need to be

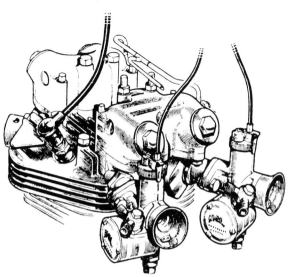

masked and if in alloy either bead or vapour blasted to get an even matt finish. Iron barrels will most likely need sand blasting to get all the dirt out of the crevices between the fins.

It then needs to be painted either black or silver and stove enamelling is to be preferred to get the tough finish needed. An alternative is a modern air drying paint but to get between the fins a spray gun is needed. A trick that sometimes will work is to use a piece of felt, stiffened with wire, but a brush is most awkward to use for this job so is best forgotten.

Let the paint dry fully and then remove the masking and check carefully for blasting grit in all holes. If you have masked properly there won't be any but make certain.

Block types

The first check on determining which block you are holding is the bore size. Standard figures were 55 mm and 63 mm for the pre-unit 350 and 500, 58.25 mm and 69 mm for the unit versions and 71 mm for all 650s. If you find 75 or 76 mm you have the 725 or 744 cc T140 block and anything similar may equally be part of a big bore kit. These have been sold for many years and the Morgo especially is likely to crop up.

The 3T block was one of its few parts to change in its short life. In its first form it was clamped down by the head bolts screwing into extended crankcase stud nuts so just has clearance holes in it. From engine 89333 this changed to fall into line with Triumph practice with tapped holes in the block top and a machined flange at the base for the nuts.

The 1938 5T block is unique in only having six studs to hold it down. It was changed to eight for 1939 and also used by the T100. For 1946 the block was modified to include extra holes to drain the oil from the rocker boxes but these went again for 1950 when the external lines reappeared. The 5T then kept that block until 1956 when it was changed for one that would fit the 6T crankcase.

The TR5 was introduced with the square fin alloy barrel with the cowling bosses in its sides also used by the Grand Prix racer. For 1951 it joined the T100 with a new die-cast, close pitched fin, alloy barrel but up to 1950 the T100 used the iron 5T block. Both models changed for 1956 by reducing the spigot height into the head from $\frac{3}{16}$ in. to $\frac{1}{8}$ in.

The 350 cc and 500 cc unit blocks were unchanged from their introduction until 1969 when the base fixings were altered to 12 point nuts.

The 1957 splayed head for the Tiger 100 was able to accommodate twin Monoblocs. The older parallel design was less easy to equip

The 650 blocks are all in iron and the first was used by the 6T up to 1955. It was joined by another in 1954 for the T110 which was produced by a shell moulding process which gave an improved finish to the fins. This block was adopted by the 6T for 1956 and the T120 for 1959 and used up to the end of the pre-unit series in 1962. The TR6 which came in 1956 used the same block finished in aluminium.

The unit 650s had a new block with nine head fixing holes from the start in 1963. For 1966 it was modified to provide an oil feed for the exhaust tappets and to take new tappet guides but was otherwise unchanged to 1972.

Tappet guide

These seldom wear to any extent and an idea of the condition can be found by rocking the tappet and measuring that for wear. Guides should be examined for cracked or broken ears and if replaced must be pressed out and in. The screw is for location, not to hold, and its hole must be aligned before pressing the new part in. Don't try to turn the guide in situ. On the 1966 and later 650s the oil feed passage should be checked for blockage.

The same cast iron guide was used in the iron 500 and 650 cc blocks from 1938 to 1965. The 3T used its own type. The alloy TR5 used a similar guide in light alloy with a body that was circular along its full length unlike the 5T one. This was used by the TR5 up to 1954 and the T100 for 1951 only. For 1952 the T100 reverted to the 5T guide shape adapted to fit its alloy barrel and this guide also went into the TR5 from 1956 on.

ABOVE *The T120 for 1967 still on Monoblocs. Bolt in crankcase behind barrel blanks off timing hole when not in use*

LEFT ABOVE *A year earlier, the T120 in 1966 with rev-counter driven from exhaust camshaft*

From 1966 the 650s changed their guides with the exhaust drilled to allow the oil to flow from the block feed to the tappets. For 1969 both changed again to suit the pushrod cover seal and the exhaust one gained an O ring to seal it into the block.

The smaller unit engines used a common guide up to 1963. It was then changed to suit revised pushrod cover seals and gained an O ring seal for 1969, its last year of use. For the T90 only in 1969 a new guide was fitted and this was used by all models from then on.

Cylinder head

You may find this a victim of misguided enthusiasm with valve seats cut back due to years of keen but unnecessary valve grinding. Each owner may have done this 'to put the sparkle back' with the result that the valve heads are now well masked. The only answer will be an insert – a job for a specialist.

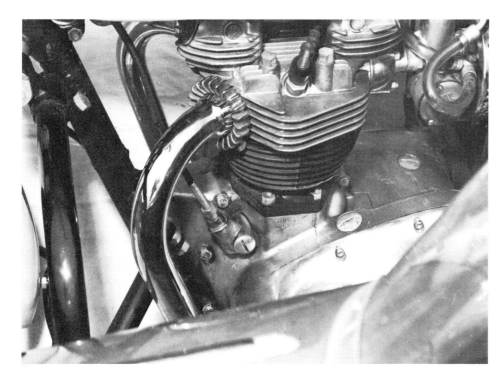

1966 single carburettor TR6, also with rev-counter and coupled to a sidecar in this instance

The first job with the head is to remove the valves and clean it thoroughly. If iron this can be done using a caustic soda solution but *never* use this for aluminium parts. These can be done in a hot house-hold detergent. After immersion in either case the head must be well washed with hot water, dried off and the iron or steel items oiled or greased to prevent rust.

Inspect the valve guides. If they are worn or cracked they must be replaced and this is best done with the head evenly heated. Unless the valve seat has been damaged the fitting of new guides is normally the only occasion when the seats need cutting. Even then a *light* cut only is needed followed by a minimum of valve grinding with the valves it is intended to fit.

Check the plug thread and fit an insert if it is in poor condition. Check all the other holes and fit inserts if required. Make sure the internal oil drains are clear. Inspect the head joint area for any signs of gas leakage and the top for damage. Deal with this. On alloy heads make sure that the exhaust port adaptor is fully home. For production racing these would be locked with a small cross screw and if you can add this it won't do any harm and could avoid major damage and expense. On the pre-1955 TR5 alloy heads check the port thread and ensure that the pipe nuts can screw in properly to hold the pipe firmly in place.

Finally complete the head in the same way as the block in either natural or paint finish.

Cylinder head types

The 3T had two types of head for when the block fixing changed at engine 89333 so did the head gasket and the head spigot. Thus it became a new part but it kept the same valve guides throughout and these were common for inlet and exhaust.

The prewar 5T head was modified to internal rocker box drains for 1946 and then changed to external for 1950. It remained in this form from then on and can be recognized by the tapped holes for the drain pipe banjo bolts. The valve guides remained the same from 1938 until they changed for 1950 and from then on. Inlet and exhaust guides were never the same part.

The T100 head was not the same part as the 5T in 1939 and was also available in bronze. Postwar it used a modified form of the 5T head up to 1949 with internal drains and with external ones for 1950 while still cast in iron. 1951 brought the die cast alloy head and this was continued with just an alteration in the spigot depth for the block from 1956. Valve guides were as for the 5T.

The TR5 head first appeared with square fins and parallel exhaust ports. For 1951 it adopted the T100 head but modified in the exhaust port to accept the pipe nuts in lieu of the normal port adaptors. From 1955 it was fitted with the T100 head and like it changed its spigot depth for 1956. Valve guides were as for the 5T with the later type being fitted from the first, a year ahead of the other models.

The 6T head was in iron from 1950 to 1960 but did alter for 1957 in a minor way. For 1961 and 1962 it was fitted with the alloy head then in use on the T110 and TR6. The first T110 model had an iron head similar to the 6T for 1954 and 1955 but with an extra cooling fin and it and the TR6 were both fitted with alloy ones from 1956. Due to a change of pushrod cover they altered again from engine 80599 that year and then

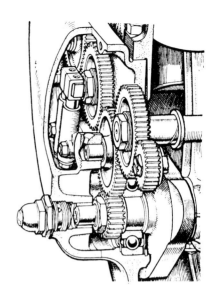

ABOVE *Pre-unit timing gears, oil pump and pressure indicator*

LEFT ABOVE *Pushrod tube end. Holes must clear rods so tube must be aligned or the pierced washer removed*

LEFT *The TR6 for 1967, very clean with points in the timing chest*

again for 1958. At this point the exhaust valve diameter was reduced slightly to enable the material thickness to be increased at one point to minimize the chance of cracking. They continued in this form to the end of the pre-unit series. Valve guides were again as for the 5T.

The T120 head differed from the others in that it had splayed inlet ports with screwed-in tracts locked with large nuts. The valve guides were also different from those fitted to other models. Such heads had been available from 1956 as options for both 500 and 650 cc engines and were preceded by twin carburettor kits as part of the race kit available from 1951 to 1953 and also fitted to the T100c in 1953. For 1961 the casting had the outer fins joined by a vertical runner just ahead of the plugs and it continued in this form for 1962.

The small unit engines began with the 3TA which changed its head for 1959 and for 1964 there was a further change to suit the pushrod covers and for 1965 a new casting with smaller ports.

The 5TA came in with the revised fins in 1959 and changed for 1964 as the 3TA. The T90 began much as the 3TA but with bigger valves. It was modified to suit a change of compression ratio for 1967 and again in 1969 to suit revised pushrod covers and Unified threads. The early T100 used the 5TA head from 1960 with its change for 1964 plus a valve guide change for 1966.

Revised heads were brought in for 1967 for the single and twin carburettor engines. They changed for the pushrod covers and to Unified threads for 1969 and for 1970 both fitted the 1969 T100S head. This continued for the 1971 twin carburettor models while the singles changed to iron valve guides. 1972 brought further changes to both to suit yet again revised pushrod covers.

All valve guides of the small unit twins are located by a circlip unlike all pre-unit and all 650 which use a shouldered guide. The guides were common from 1957 to 1966 with the T90 and T100 models changing that year to a guide that remained common to 1972 except for the T100C in 1971 and 1972.

The unit 650 cc engines all have a nine bolt head fixing from 1963 to 1972 and were all of a similar pattern. The 6T and TR6 were common up to 1966 when the 6T went from the range and the TR6 was modified to accept T120 exhaust valves for 1967. For 1969 it gained Unified threads, for 1971 a change to suit new head bolts, rocker boxes and box dowels and for 1972 push-in exhaust pipes.

The T120 was changed to bigger ports for 1964 and then mimicked the TR6 from 1969. The T120 TT had a head modified in the ports from standard.

Valve guides continued from the pre-unit engines with the T120 ones different from those used in the 6T and TR6. There were no changes.

Inlet manifold

These are cast in light alloy and are often polished. They should be examined for damage, flatness of the mounting faces both in and out, and for the condition of the threaded holes that take the carburettor studs. When twin carburettors were fitted they went on separate steel stubs, and if connected by a balance tube, this and its fitting should be checked for leaks.

Nearly all models were fitted with a single carburettor and one into two manifold. Most had a common form with the head studs one above the other and the carburettor ones side by side. This applies to all 5T models which changed their manifold for 1956.

The T100 was of the same pattern up to 1950 after which its head studs took a form with the upper ones spread out further than the lower. The TR5 copied this and the two shared a similar part from 1951 although they were not identical. From 1955 they used the same part.

The 6T used a manifold similar to that of the 5T from 1950 but for 1952 changed to an SU carburettor and this dictated a new part with the studs one above the other. For 1959 it reverted to the earlier layout with a manifold already in use on the T110 and TR6 and this part remained with these models up to 1966. For 1967 the TR6 alone continued with the manifold revised to suit a larger Amal and for 1970 it was fitted with studs of Unified thread.

The T120 always had twin Amals on stubs from its inception in 1959. For 1964 these became handed to accommodate a balance pipe and were locked by a revised nut. For 1969 they took a Unified thread so the balance pipe adaptors also changed. New locking nuts were also listed from 1970. For 1972 bolt on adaptors were fitted.

The 3TA manifold copied the old T100 layout and was continued with an enlarged manifold from 1959 when the 500 came in. For 1966 only it reverted to its original part. The T90 had its own part in the same style as did the T100 series. From 1968 these were held in place by cap bolts but from 1970 the upper pair were replaced by bolts.

The twin carburettor T100 models used handed adaptors with a balance tube. They were not the first 500 cc Triumph to be so equipped for back in 1951 a twin carburettor flange had been listed as part of the race kit and for the 1953 T100c. It was again listed in 1956 and for 1957 a 500 cc head with splayed inlet ports and stub adaptors was available. It was joined by a 650 cc version for 1958 but this went the following year with the arrival of the T120 Bonneville as a standard machine.

Valves

Unless these are in very good condition they should be replaced, especially the exhaust which has a hard time. Grind the new valves in lightly without taking too much from the valve seat.

Valves did not change too much over the years. All postwar 5T have the same fitments. The T100 and TR5 copied the 5T on exhaust but increased the size of the inlet when the 1951 alloy head came in. The 3T never changed.

The 6T was the same for a decade but for 1961 changed to the T110 valves with its alloy head. The T110 came in in 1954 with a bigger inlet valve and the 6T exhaust which was increased in size for 1958. The TR6 followed suit so from 1961 all three used the same parts and this continued up to 1966.

Meanwhile the T120 had begun with the same parts from 1959 to 1963 and then had an increase in size which lasted it to 1972. From 1967 the TR6 used the T120 valves.

For the smaller unit engines the 3TA kept one valve size through its life as did the 5TA and the T90 which used the 3TA exhaust valve and its own inlet. The T100 used the same parts as the 5TA to 1966 and changed for all versions on the inlet side from 1967. On the exhaust the single carburettor models kept the 5TA valve for 1967 while the twin versions used a new valve. This became standard for all from 1968.

Valve springs

These should be replaced as a matter of course. Over the life of the twin they remained little changed for many models and thus the 5T, T100, TR5, 6T, T110 and TR6 all used the same inner and outer springs on all engines from 1938 up to 1961 for all bar the 6T

ABOVE LEFT *Twin carburettor T100T of 1967 with rev-counter drive and single switch in side cover. Float connection missing*

LEFT *The 1968 Bonneville with Concentrics and plain side cover*

RIGHT *Be careful when moving the arrowed nut to avoid distorting the oil pipe. Easy to do and awkward to correct. Still the 1968 T120*

which used them to engine D11192 in 1961. The 3T had its own springs as did the T120 and the latter were used by the TR6 in 1962 while the 6T had a new pair from engine D11193.

This arrangement continued to 1965 but for 1966 the 6T springs became standard for all 650 engines and the inners stayed that way to 1972. The outer was changed once more for 1968 and on.

In the small unit engines one pair of springs were used for the 3TA until changed in 1966. The 5TA followed the same pattern and its outer remained as common to all models with the new inner.

Valve caps, cups, cotters and collars

Caps were only fitted prewar and most of the other items changed little over the years. Split cotters were the same from 1938 to 1969 and for 1970 took a new part number while continuing to fit the same valves and collars.

The top collar was the same item for all pre-unit engines except the 3T and continued in use on all unit 650s. The smaller unit engines had their own part which was unchanged for all models.

The story was the same for the spring cup with all pre-unit engines except the 3T using the same part which continued in the unit TR6 and T120 up to 1965. It was then changed to a thicker item to allow for the shorter springs and continued with this part to 1972. For the 6T a new cup was introduced from 1963. The smaller unit engines used a common part until a change was made for all for 1969 to the cup that had been fitted to the twin carburettor models from 1967.

All these small details require cleaning and careful inspection for any signs of damage or cracking. Replacement is the only answer if there is any. Be sure there is no sign of collar collapse or cotter pull through.

Rocker boxes

On the 3T alone these are integral with the cylinder head but their detail parts are dealt with in the same way as for the other models. For them there were two rocker boxes each with a pair of rockers on a common spindle.

It is possible to inspect the boxes without dismantling them which is acceptable for servicing but not a full restoration. For the latter a full check is necessary so everything must come apart. Note carefully the sequence of washers and check that it is as it should be. Normal practice is two thrust washers between each pair of rockers, a spring or thackeray washer outside each rocker and a second thrust washer outside them with the one on the threaded side of the spindle a smaller diameter.

From 1953 the rocker spindles were fitted with O rings which may need renewal. They will need help to compress them into their holes. The spindles should be inspected for wear and their oilways checked for obstructions. The rocker boxes need to be checked for cracks or damage, faulty threads or poor mating

59

surfaces and these items refurbished as required. The rockers themselves need the same treatment together with their ball ends and adjusters.

Rocker box types and details

Most of the detail parts remained the same for much of the life of the engines. The spindles and rockers were common to all the pre-unit series, except the 3T, and the unit 650. The smaller unit engine had its own type. This also applied to the adjusters and locknuts except that the 3T used the common part in this instance.

The rocker ball pins were common from 1938 to 1968 with the smaller unit engines having their own part. The action of the pushrod on the ball should be checked in case the rod end contacts the rocker arm. If it does the ball pin should be changed and any wear marks stoned away. During 1968 the pin assembly to the rocker was altered to cut off the oil supply to it to benefit other parts. For 1969 the parts were undrilled except for the TR6 which caught up for 1970. The T90 pin for 1969 differed from the T100 and went with that model at the end of the year.

The rocker box caps had hexagon heads and no locking for all pre-unit engines. The unit 650 had a cap with a cross in its surface for fastening and a serrated edge for a locking strip. This was used up to 1971 but

for 1972 the design changed to a single flat cover for each pair of valves. The smaller unit caps were similar to the unit 650 but without locks at first. From 1964 they used the 650 cap plus their own style of lock and continued in this form to 1972.

The rocker boxes were always handed as inlet and exhaust although very similar. The first 1938 pair were modified in 1947 for the T100 and used for all 500 and iron 650 engines from 1952 to 1960. The arrival of the 650 alloy head in 1956 for the T110 and TR6 brought new boxes without locations for the pushrod covers. These continued in use for these models, plus the 6T for 1961, until 1962.

New finned boxes came in for the unit engines in 1963 and continued in this form until 1971 when an extra fixing hole appeared plus access plugs on each side. This changed again for 1972 when the single

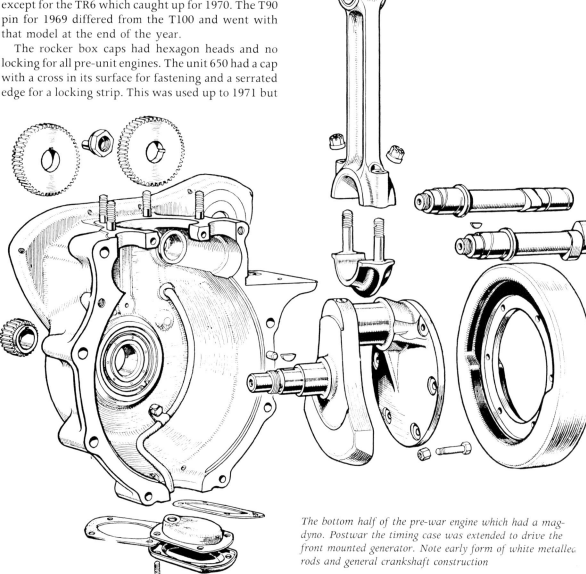

The bottom half of the pre-war engine which had a mag-dyno. Postwar the timing case was extended to drive the front mounted generator. Note early form of white metalled rods and general crankshaft construction

finned cover appeared on each box. On the smaller engines one pair of boxes were used for all models until 1971 when they were modified with access holes in each side.

Rocker box drain pipes

These were fitted to the very first twins with one pipe running from the front of the head to the pushrod cover and the other from the head side to the inlet cover. The pipes need to be examined for cracks or obstruction and their bolts and washers checked.

The pipes were not fitted in the early postwar years as their work was done by internal holes but they appeared in 1949 on the TR5 and on the 5T, 6T, and T100 for 1950. They went onto the T110 in 1954 but came off again for 1956 when the alloy head was fitted. They remained in use on the 5T, T100 and TR5 to their

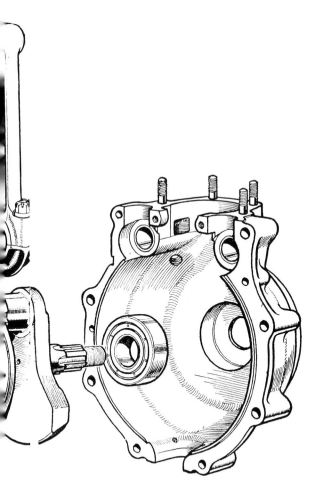

end and on the 6T while it retained the iron head up to 1960.

Tappets

These should be examined for wear at the foot and their fit in the guide block. The oilways in the later ones should be checked for any obstruction.

All pre-unit engines fitted the same tappets which received one change for 1951. At that time they gained hard tips induction brazed in place to reduce wear but were fully interchangeable from the first 1938 twin. This form continued on to 1965 in the unit 650s and for the 6T and TR6 inlet side for one more year.

For 1966 the exhaust changed to tappets with oilways while on the T120 went bigger foot radius tappets, again with oilways on the exhaust side. From 1967 these T120 parts became common with the exhaust being modified from 1969 to give a timed oil feed. The tappets with oilways have the milled flat on the outside to suit the supply in the guide.

On the smaller unit engines the tappets for the 1957 3TA were still in use in 1972. The only models to fit anything else were the T100R and T100T from 1967 which had ones with a larger foot radius.

Pushrods

These need to be checked for straightness by rolling them on a flat surface such as a sheet of glass. Examine the ends for cracks, undue wear or any signs of looseness on the body of the rod.

The prewar 5T had steel rods but nearly all others were alloy with pressed on ends. The one used for the T100 prewar continued in that engine while it was in iron and in the 5T, iron 6T and T110. For the TR5, alloy T110, TR6, T120 and 6T from 1961 there was a composite pushrod and this remained in use for all unit 650s.

The smaller unit engines had a different form of pushrod with a cup formed at the top only. The lower end was simply rounded to fit the cup in the top of the tappet. One size went into all 350s and another in all 500s.

Pushrod covers

These should be cleaned and the ends examined for distortion. Those with a tapped hole for the rocker drain pipe should have that thread checked. Finish was chrome plated so this may need to be redone and if so again check the thread as the banjo bolt that goes in it won't like much strain.

The covers and their seals changed little over the years of the pre-unit engine but varied a good deal on the unit engines in an attempt to seal them completely. The early tubes had a reduced diameter for much of their length with the drain pipe boss low down on the larger part. 1946 brought tubes of the same form without boss which were used up to 1949. For the TR5 of that year a new tube with boss came in and was

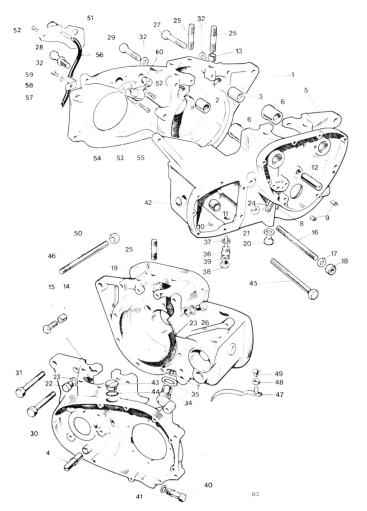

used on that engine up to 1954 and by the T100 in 1951 only. The T100 copied the 5T to 1949 and both plus the 6T went back to the 1938 type for 1950 to 1960 as did the TR5 from 1955.

The T110 used this same cover for 1954 and 1955 but from 1956 fitted a new type without boss to suit the alloy head with its recess for the cover which no longer had to extend to the rocker box. Both head and cover were modified from engine 80599 and the new cover was used from then on for the T110, TR6, T120 and 6T from 1961. It continued on the unit 650 engine to 1965.

The cover seals on the pre-unit engine were simply a thin washer at the top which changed from 1955 and a thicker one below which remained the same throughout. They need about 0.06 in. compression to stop leaks as with less they leak and with more they distort and leak.

This arrangement continued on the unit 650s until 1966 when the cover became a parallel tube with collars top and bottom. At both ends went the existing top seal with a supporting cup beneath the lower one. This continued to 1968 with a seal change from 1967.

For 1969 a new cover appeared with castellations at the top and a pair of O rings to seal it. The top ring was changed for 1970 and the whole assembly for 1971 although the existing rings were retained. The cover was modified to drilled holes at the top in place of the slots and the lower O ring was backed by the reappearance of the 1967 seal and a supporting cup beneath it.

On the smaller unit twins the cover was similar to the pre-unit engines and used their top washer and its own style of lower. From 1964 the cover became a

ABOVE LEFT *Two views of each crankcase half for the 1971 650 cc engines and typical of the unit construction*

LEFT *Single carburettor T100S for 1968 with access cover in chaincase for strobe ignition timing*

RIGHT *The T100T for the same year, 1968, with 12 sided cylinder block nuts. Note gear indicator on top of crankcase*

parallel tube with a common washer at each end supported by a cup under the bottom one. For 1969 a similar design to that of the 650 appeared with castellations at the top and this with its two O-rings stayed in use, with a change to the top ring for 1971. For 1972 the O-rings continued with cover tubes with holes at the top in place of the slots.

Camshafts

There are many varieties of these but in all cases they need inspecting for wear on the cams and the bearings. Make sure the keyway and nut thread are fit and there is no obvious damage.

Camshaft types are more legion than cam forms for one of the latter was often used on several of the former, the best known being the 3134. This does exist as a camshaft but also appears in many other places. The picture is further confused by the existence of many performance cams from Triumph and others. The only way to be certain as to what you have is to check the timing it gives and normally this is done with the gaps set at 0.020 in.

Generally run what is specified for your model and set it to its correct timing for the year. The exception is the use of the later nitrided shafts in earlier engines in order to combat wear.

The 3T has its own camshafts which were one with breather valve slot and one without until 1950 when the slotted one became common.

For the 500 both shafts began as the same in prewar days but the inlet was slotted for the breather drive for 1946. When the TR5 came in it had the slotted shaft at both positions and this was done for the other engines for 1950. Up to that time all ran with valve

gaps at 0.001 in. except for the TR5 at two and four thou. For 1951 this applied to the T100 also.

In 1953 the ramp cam appeared and engines so fitted were stamped with a wheel mark alongside the engine number. All had 0.010 in. gaps and were used on the 5T to 1957, T100 to 1959, 6T to 1960 and TR5 to 1954.

With the arrival of the T110 came the performance 3325 cam set at two and four thou. This went into the TR5 for 1955 and the TR6 the next year.

The 3134 camshaft first appeared in the T100 race kit of 1952 and in the T100c of 1953. It reappeared as the inlet camshaft of the T120 for 1959 along with the 3325 as the exhaust one. For 1961 the 6T adopted the T110 cams along with its alloy head but changed again in mid-year. New camshafts were adopted for the unit engines with one pair for the 6T and another for the TR6 and T120. These changed for 1967 when they were copper plated, 1969 when nitrided and for 1970 when the breather drive went and Unified threads appeared.

For the smaller unit twins the same pair of shafts were used by the 3TA and 5TA until 1963 after which the exhaust one changed. The T100A came in in 1960, changed for 1961 and became the T100SS with a 1961 inlet and 1960 exhaust from the T100A. The T90 copied it but both changed for 1964 and the 5TA used the same shafts in its last year in 1966. For 1969 the T90 and single carburettor T100 shared a new exhaust cam while the twin carburettor models used another. All three had the same inlet. For 1970 the inlet lost its breather drive and the exhaust gained a threaded tachometer screw drive hole. The exhausts continued to differ between the single and twin carburettor models.

All small unit twins run the right end of the camshafts direct in the crankcase and locate them with bolted on plates behind the driving gears. These plates and their fixing screws were changed for 1969.

Timing gears

Perhaps the most important point with these is not to damage them during removal or installation. The cam gears are held by left-hand thread nuts and require the correct puller. The crankshaft nut is normal thread and the gear needs the correct tool to remove it. For the 3T and smaller unit engines this is the cam gear puller as the crank gear is screw cut in this instance.

You will have noted carefully the marks on the wheels and which keyways were in use while taking the engine down. The parts need to be cleaned and inspected for wear.

The bush in the intermediate gear may need replacing but otherwise wear should be minimal. If the gear teeth do show signs on the teeth a full new set are likely to be needed as changing just one will reduce it to the same state as the others very quickly. Originally the gears were selectively assembled and a

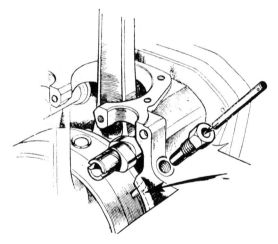

ABOVE *The timing tool in use to lock into the flywheel slot to hold the crankshaft at top dead centre*

BELOW *Typical Triumph timing marks. Don't copy, use the right diagram for your engine*

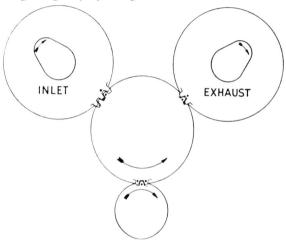

STANDARD VALVE TIMING MARKS (ALL MODELS AND CAMSHAFTS EXCEPTING T100T/T100R)

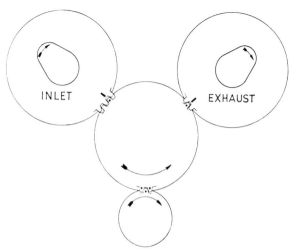

VALVE TIMING MARKS (T100T/T100R ONLY)

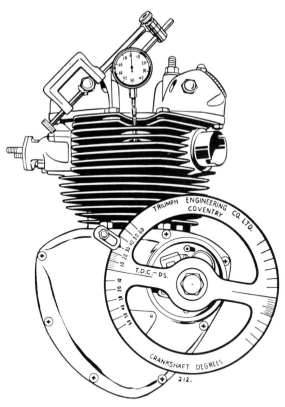

ABOVE *Checking ignition timing with disc on camshaft after using dial gauge to establish tdc. With this set-up ignition can be checked on full advance or retard for both cylinders*

random pairing may produce whine or clatter.

Much of the timing gear remained the same for many years. There were no real changes on the pre-unit models and some details continued on to 1972. The crankshaft gear changed for the unit 650 for 1963, 1964 and 1966 due to variations in shaft clamping. Its nut was new for 1963 and did not change again until 1972.

The cam wheels had two letter suffix changes to their part number during pre-unit days and new types were fitted for 1963. The only change that mattered in the early days came in 1951 when wheels with three keyways were adopted to give vernier adjustment to the cam timing and a further problem to some owners. The 1953 wheels continued until they were revised for 1971 to take a different puller. Their nuts stayed as the pre-unit on the inlet and new from 1963 on the exhaust until 1970 when the threads became Unified.

The intermediate gear was revised for 1963 and modified for 1966 but continued with the same bush and spindle as had been used in 1938. The magneto gears varied according to whether they drove a mag-dyno, Lucas or BTH magneto and whether the machine had manual or automatic advance.

The 3T had its own set of gear wheels but used the pre-unit fixings. Its crankshaft gear was threaded for pulling off. The same gears reappeared in the small unit twins with the nuts changing to Unified for 1969 on the crankshaft and 1970 for the cams. Some other details were common with the unit 650.

Timing cover
This needs to be inspected for flatness, clear oilways and good thread condition. Most owners polish to a high degree as well. Check for cracks and the condition of the bush on the pre-unit and oil seal on the unit engines which runs on the crankshaft. These control the oil supply and are important.

If it is necessary to remove the patent plate this should be done with care as the holding drive screws are harder than the plate or the cover.

The cover was altered for the postwar engines to include the dynamo drive. This type remained in use up to 1959 but was joined by another from 1953. This was used that year by the 5T, on the 6T the next and for the remaining models from 1960. All covers had the same bush fitted but the fitments varied with a release valve in the side from 1946 with a connection for a gauge from the front. For 1949 this became a blanking bolt and the release valve gained an indicator button.

The 3T cover was plain as were the smaller unit engines at first. For 1963 on the T90 and 1964 for the others the cover changed as the points were mounted in it and a recess, oil seal for the drive shaft and a cover added. For 1969 this was altered to add the crankshaft oil feed via a second oil seal, an oil switch and a change of points plate mounting.

The unit 650s had this design of oil feed from 1963 plus points in the timing cover. For 1968 the points cover changed while for 1967 only there was a metering dowel, jet and filter fitted behind the timing cover in the supply to the exhaust tappets. From 1969 the oil gauge point was fitted with a pressure switch instead of the blanking plug, Unified threads were adopted and the points plate mounting revised.

In addition to the standard covers are those modified to accept a rev-counter drive. This is taken from the exhaust camshaft and the gearbox is built into the cover. Early machines had a normal drive box bolted in place of the dynamo with its gear meshed to the exhaust camshaft one but the alternative cover became available in the late 1950s to suit production racing. It should be checked over in the same way as any other plus a check on the gears, their mesh and the bearings they run in.

Gaskets
The cylinder head gasket should be examined for distortion or burning but if in good condition can be used again if annealed. This is done by heating it evenly to a cherry red and either allowing it to cool or by quenching it in water which may produce a slightly softer material. Make sure the gasket fits over the head bolts cleanly and that continued re-use has not reduced its thickness materially.

Block and rocker box gaskets should be renewed or replaced with a modern silicone jointing compound but keep it clear of the oilways. These gaskets did not alter too much and changes were to suit modifications to other parts.

The head gaskets were also seldom changed with the iron 500 using the same one from 1946 to 1958. The alloy engines differed as did the 650 which changed in 1956 to suit the alloy engine and again in 1963 for the nine-bolt head. The 3T began with two ring gaskets but from engine 89333 changed to a flat one piece type. Each size of small unit twin had its own gasket which changed for 1964 on.

Crankcase
These will need cleaning well and checking for damage, cracks, poor threads and obstructed oilways. To remove or refit main bearings the case around them should be evenly heated after which they should drop out. The usual way of checking the temperature is to split on the bearing housing. If it spits back its ready. A ball or roller race must be completely cleaned before checking and is best renewed. A bush is less likely to need to be changed but if they do the oil holes must line up and the bush may need reaming after installation.

The internal oil scavenge pipe must be secure and oiltight. Check for cracks as any leak may stop the pump scavenging which means a full engine strip to rectify.

The main bearings will benefit if held in place by Loctite and replacement ones must be wiped clean before being dropped into place in the hot case. Don't forget any washers or shields that go with some mains, also the circlip used to locate some pre-unit timing side races and the location tab fitted to some smaller unit twins.

Crankcase types
The first pre-unit cases only had six block stud holes and changed to eight for 1939. Postwar they were modified to accept the front mounted dynamo and were joined by the similar style 3T cases and in 1950 by the 6T cases.

For 1953 the 5T changed its cases as the dynamo was replaced by an alternator but the others were unaltered until the next year. For 1954 the T100 and TR5 had revised cases to take the larger timing side main. The 6T had a new case to accept the alternator while the T110 had the new main but kept to a dynamo. For 1955 the 5T changed to the bigger main and for 1956 to the 6T cases. That year the TR6 came in

ABOVE *1969 TR6 with Concentric and exhaust balance pipe*

TOP *T100S also from 1969 and with the same features. Note also the tank badge*

with T110 cases and was joined by the T120 in 1959. For 1960 all 650s used the 6T cases as they all went over to an alternator.

The 650 cc unit construction cases were changed for 1965 by the addition of the tdc location slot hole and for 1966 with the tappet oil feed. For 1968 a hole was added to take the fixing for the chain guard blade and in 1969 they went over to Unified threads. For 1970 a new breather system was adopted, which meant holes appeared in the left case to connect into the primary chaincase, for 1971 a Unified thread oil pressure valve and for 1972 a metric timing side bearing, all of which meant changes. The last should be stamped with an M to indicate the metric dimensions.

The smaller unit cases changed for 1960 when a primary chain tensioner was added and for 1964 when the points drive moved. 1966 brought a tachometer drive hole and 1969 a change of mains to a ball race on the timing side and roller on the drive. 1970 brought the revised breathing system.

Main bearings

These were in two sizes for much of the engine's life but with detail variations of their use. The 3T was alone at first with a timing side bush. On the drive went a MS10 ball race with dimensions of $1 \times 2\frac{1}{2} \times \frac{3}{4}$ in. For the 500 the same race went in the timing side with a circlip to locate it and a disc inboard of it. On the drive side went a MS11 ball race with dimensions of $1\frac{1}{8} \times 2\frac{13}{16} \times \frac{13}{16}$ in. That remained in that location right through to 1965.

On the timing side went a roller race of MS10 dimensions from 1949 with a chip shield outboard of it and this remained so up to 1953 generally and 1954 for the 5T. For other than the 5T 1954 brought a second MS11 ballrace without circlip, inboard disc or chip shield but with a clamping washer between race and timing gear. This arrangement was adopted by the 5T for 1955 and remained in use for all pre-unit engines. On the drive side an oil seal was added from 1958 outboard of the race and inserted to face the primary chaincase.

For owners who wish to fit the later crankshaft to an earlier engine a race to LS11 dimensions of $1\frac{1}{8} \times 2\frac{1}{2} \times \frac{5}{8}$ in. will marry the two parts but will need a spacer to fill the gap.

The unit 650s continued with two ballraces to 1965. They used a clamp washer and timing side crank location for 1963, switched to drive side location for 1964 and reverted to the timing side once more in 1966 when the washer reappeared after missing the two previous years. For 1966 the drive side bearing was changed to a single lip roller of the same size but longer life and this arrangement stood until 1971. Well worth changing to on older engines. The oil seal was fitted up to 1970 and for 1972 the timing side ball race was changed to a metric one measuring 30 × 72 × 19 mm.

The smaller unit engines fitted that same ball race on the drive side from 1957 to 1968. From 1969 it became a roller of the same size and was joined by a ball race in the timing case. This was $35 \times 72 \times 17$ mm and replaced the previous bush. An oil seal was fitted on the drive side until 1969 and went when the new breather system came in.

Camshaft bushes

The same bushes were used for all postwar pre-unit engines and all 650s to 1969. The smaller unit twins had their own pair at the left end only and all models had a change for 1970 when the new breather was fitted.

Assembly

Generally to be done as set out in the manual with some alteration to acknowledge the use of modern sealants and fitting compounds and the sequence to be used to lock up the larger nuts.

Slow and steady is the guiding rule so you make sure everything is well at one stage before going on to the next.

Start by laying out the first components needed and check that all your tools are clean. Fit the crankshaft to the drive side case and the camshafts with the breather valve under the inlet one. Paint jointing compound onto the case face and fit. If it does not go home easily find out why. Fit all the screws and Loctite the pair in the crankcase mouth to make sure. Check that everything goes round.

Fit the timing gears and set the timing to the marks if this is already established. Then lock the crank and tighten the nuts in the timing cover. Fit the pistons, warm, followed by the block. Grease the head gasket and fit the head followed by the rocker boxes with the pushrods and their cover tubes as dictated by the engine type.

If the valve timing has to be set from scratch you should build the engine up without the timing nuts or pushrod covers. Then set the timing using a degree disc, remove the block and tighten the nuts. Refit the block and continue with the head and rocker boxes.

Fit and time the magneto or distributor except where the points are in the timing cover. Prime and fit the oil pump, paint jointing compound on the timing cover, bolt up and add points when applicable.

Complete the assembly by adjusting the tappets and fitting the covers. You will have oiled parts during assembly and with pump and crankshaft charged with oil this should look after the surfaces while you deal with the rest of the machine. Don't seal it completely if you have to store it for any time and do turn it over occasionally.

ABOVE *1970 T100T Daytona with two Concentrics. Note breather pipe rising from the top rear of the chaincase*

TOP *Other side and a year older, 1969 T100T. Inlet manifolds also have a balance pipe*

4 Transmission

The transmission covers all the mechanical parts from the engine crankshaft to the rear wheel sprocket. It thus encompasses two chains, four sprockets, a clutch and a set of gears. Included with the gears is the kickstart mechanism and ancillary to them are the gearchange mechanism, clutch lift and the gearbox shell.

Attention

Articles on the restoration of a machine often state that the owner has not stripped the gearbox but is using it as found. In many cases it is apparent that the box history is not known and this practice must be condemned.

Unless you check you cannot be certain that a gear tooth is not about to fail or an errant part about to jam the gears. In the timescale of a restoration the period spent on inspecting the gears is minimal and even on a straight rebuild the time will be well spent if you make sure the box is not going to lock up on you.

Triumph transmission

All models covered had a four-speed gearbox with footchange pedal and kickstart lever on the right. For 1972 only there was a five-speed option also available. Primary and final drive was by chain and a multi-plate clutch was used. At first the transmission shock absorber went on the crankshaft but the advent of the alternator meant that it had to move into the clutch body.

Early models had a separate gearbox but from 1957 unit construction began to be adopted with all models using this from 1963. For many years both wide and close ratio gear clusters were available to replace the standard set and these were on occasion fitted to the more specialized machines such as the TR5 or T100c.

Engine sprocket

The first twins had this mounted together with a shock absorber but from 1953 this item moved to the clutch and one by one the models were fitted with an alternator. Until this arrived those without carried a distance piece.

All pre-unit engines had a single strand primary chain and all unit ones a duplex. After 1972 came triplex chains. Sprockets need to be checked for their fit to the crankshaft, the condition of their teeth and the smoothness of the oil seal rubbing surface. If healthy, continue to use but if in doubt change along with the chain.

All the pre-unit models adjusted their gearing with the engines sprocket so a range running from 17 to 24 teeth was available from 1938 to 1949 and with a 25 tooth from 1950 on. The unit ones came in one size to suit the fixed centre application.

The 1938 sprocket was common to the range of singles and all changed for 1939. They were altered again for 1949 and to their final form for 1953 when they lost the shock absorber cam. The unit sprockets only altered with the addition or removal of dowel holes which locked the alternator rotor for ignition timing purposes. On the 650 a further change occurred for 1971 with the removal of the oil seal face and machining to allow the use of shims to set the chain alignment.

Shock absorber – engine

This system was only used up to 1952. With it the engine sprocket ran free on a sleeve splined internally to the crankshaft and on the outside for a slider. This and the sprocket had matching cam ramps and were held together by a spring. If the sprocket turned on the sleeve the ramps forced the slider along the splines against the spring to provide the absorbing effect.

Most of the details remained unchanged but the slide was modified for 1939 to match the sprocket change. At the same time the spring changed but the 1938 one reappeared in 1946 fitted to the 3T. A new spring went onto the TR5 in 1949 and the rest of the range for 1950. The spring used in 1938 and for the 3T was $1\frac{11}{16}$ in. free length and the other $1\frac{13}{16}$ in. If they have shortened they should be replaced as should any other parts showing signs of wear. Minor damage may be stoned out but check that this is not finishing off the hard surface or that it will make one ramp bear more load than the other.

ABOVE *The early Triumph gearbox in use on a 1947 Tiger 100. Adjustor, clutch arm rubber and filler cap are all typical*

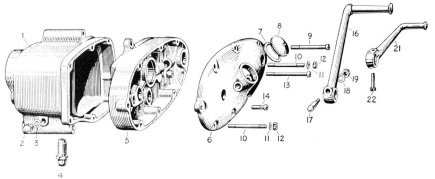

RIGHT *Parts list drawing of the main gearbox castings and control pedals*

Shock absorber – clutch

This was built into the clutch centre and comprised a spider with vanes which lay inside the centre and its vanes. Between the metal parts went drive and rebound rubbers and the assembly was encased by front and rear plates secured by countersunk screws. The assembly should be checked and the rubbers changed if they seem at all hard.

The first design had four vanes on the spider and a total of eight rubbers with the drive ones fatter than the rebound. The rubbers were changed for 1957 and the same design went into the 3TA that year. The four vane design continued to the last pre-unit engine and to 1963 in the smaller units. The introduction of the unit 650 brought in a three vane centre of the same form and this went onto the smaller models for 1964.

For 1968 the spider was modified and for 1972 the front and rear plates changed to a through bolt design, this arrangement going into the 650 first during 1971.

Primary chain

Expect to change this unless you find it in perfect condition. The sizes used were 0.5 in. pitch × 0.335 in. roller diameter × 0.305 in. between inner plates on all pre-unit engines, otherwise known as $\frac{1}{2} \times \frac{5}{16}$ in. The unit engines all used $\frac{3}{8}$ in. duplex chain with dimensions of 0.375 × 0.250 × 0.225 in.

The number of links of the pre-unit models ranged

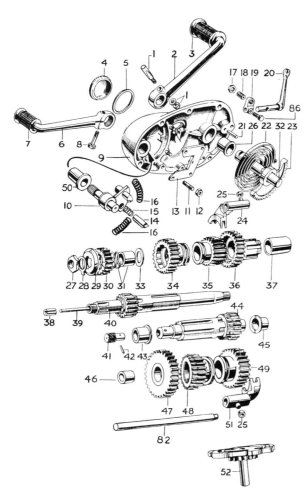

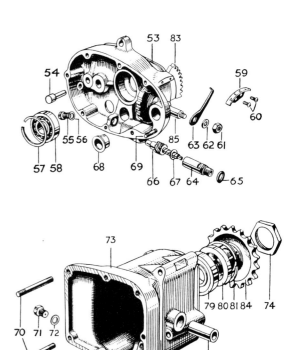

ABOVE *Parts list drawings of the gearbox adopted from 1950 for the pre-unit models and only changed in detail from then on*

BELOW *The mechanics of the Triumph gearbox as shown in the 1948 sales brochure*

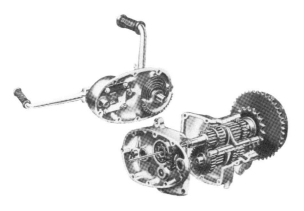

from 70 to 80. For the smaller unit engines it was 78 and for the 650s it was 84.

Primary chain tensioner

This is only found on the unit engines and first appeared in 1960. The tensioner blade and its trunnion of the smaller engines was changed for 1966 but the latter reverted to the earlier type in 1968. The unit 650 used a similar design which had detail changes in 1966 and 1969.

Clutch

In essence all Triumph twins are fitted with the same type of clutch and one or two piece parts did remain unchanged over the years. The detail design varied, first with the introduction of the shock absorber in the centre and second with a change from four to three springs which affected the number of vanes in the absorber.

The clutch parts should all be cleaned and examined for wear or damage. Normal wear points are the tongues of the plates and the slots in the drum, the hub rollers and the springs which may tire. Plates should be checked for flatness and the clutch nuts for the locking nib under the head.

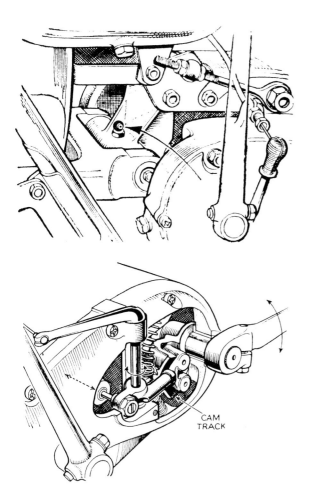

CAM
TRACK

For most parts replacement is the normal course of action. On some models the housing race can be pressed out and renewed but will need grinding once in place which requires an engineering workshop. Expect to replace the rollers which are $\frac{1}{4}$ in. diameter with black, not ground, ends. Fit a new lockwasher on all models that have one which is up to 1967. Fit new springs if they are much below the normal free length.

The clutch springs must be adjusted so that the pressure plate lifts squarely and turns truly. If it does not the clutch will drag and spoil the gearchange. It is for the same reason that the plates must be able to slide sideways in the slots and be free of burrs or notches.

Clutch hub

This is fixed to the gearbox mainshaft on a taper and located by a key which remained common to all models for all years. One hub was used for all pre-unit models but new ones went into the unit models with a thrust washer added on the 650s from the start and in 1964 on the smaller machines. These washers had location tabs for some years but as they sometimes broke the design was changed for 1970. From then the washers were without tabs and the hub without location holes.

The hub was held by a nut which was changed with the introduction of the shock absorber in the clutch for 1953. A plain washer was fitted from the start and joined by a lock washer in 1946. The first only varied for 1953 but the latter altered twice before adopting its final 1953 pattern. For 1967 and from 650 cc engine DU48145 a locknut was fitted and the locking washer dispensed with on all models while at the same time a new plain washer was introduced.

Sprocket and housing

These two items are riveted together with the bearing race pressed into the centre. The part is prone to wear on the sprocket teeth and in the housing slots and in either case repair or replacement may be necessary.

Care is needed when replacing as the depth of the housing varies according to the number of clutch plates fitted aside from any other alterations. This aspect affects the clutch centre, spring cups and spring pins. Sprockets are to suit the primary chain fitted and except for this and depth little changed.

Springs, cups, pins and nuts

Either four or three of each are fitted depending on the clutch. The nuts only changed once from first to last with the alteration coming for 1968. The spring pins generally come in one of two under head lengths which are $1\frac{19}{32}$ in. and $1\frac{27}{32}$ in. but there is another shorter one used on the 3T only. The longer ones go in the clutches with more plates.

Spring cups have the same kind of variation while the springs come in various free lengths and strengths. Some confusion is possible as there may be more than one spring available for one free length so wire diameter and number of turns also matter.

Plates

These come as plain driven, bonded or inserted driving and pressure. Numbers of the first two vary depending on the power to be transmitted with a maximum of six of each. Early driving plates had cork inserts but from 1956 bonded ones were fitted and can be used in the earlier models. The driven plates were altered at the same time and from then on the same pair was used for all models.

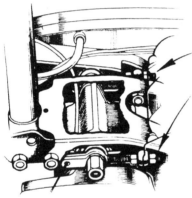

ABOVE *1957 Tiger 100 fitted with the optional splayed cylinder head. Gearbox as from 1950 to 1957 and before 'Slickshift'*

LEFT *Twin primary chain adjusters appeared in 1961 for the pre-unit models*

The pressure plate was modified for the TR5 in 1949 and the rest of the range the next year and continued in this form for all pre-unit models. All machines have a hardened button in the centre of the plate and this remained the same throughout.

The arrival of unit construction brought new pressure plates with an adjusting screw and locknut in the centre. Those fitted in the smaller twins had four holes for the springs up to 1963 but from then went to three as on all 650s. Both types were fitted with a bigger adjusting screw for 1966 so it is necessary to ensure you have a matching set of plate, nut and screw.

Clutch mechanism

This is the area that connects the clutch cable movement to the pressure plate and it goes under the outer gearbox cover and includes the clutch pushrod.

While various types were used they all come down easily enough and should be checked over for wear or damage. The pushrod must be straight or the clutch will feel very heavy. Grease the load points of the

mechanism on assembly so that the action is smooth and easy.

Pre-unit models have a lever mechanism and from 1938 this had a long vertical outer lever forged in one with a horizontal shaft which turned in the outer gearbox cover. Inside, a short arm was added with an adjuster screw to move the pushrod. The operating cable swept across the top of the box with an adjuster screwed into a lug on the top of the inner cover and its end covered by a rubber cap from 1939 on.

For 1958 the design was modified to provide the 'slickshift' system of semi-automatic clutch operation linked to the gear pedal. For this the lever mechanism was swung round so its pivot shaft was vertical and the cable arm moved in an arc across the gearbox top. Inside went a modified short arm with a roller added to impart the gear pedal movement to the clutch. Slickshift models also have a shorter clutch pushrod with a chamfered end. In 1960 the rubber cap came back while the slickshift was not used on the T120 or the TR6 from 1961.

The 3TA used a completely different system with a

quick-thread screw. For 1961 the lever and screw part was modified and for 1962 changed again so the cable connected via a spoke to the lever instead of directly.

For 1964 the mechanism changed to a three ball ramp type but the cable attachment remained as it was. Alternative cable adaptors appeared for 1966 and the cable abutment was Unified for 1969. The same mechanism with some common parts was used for the first unit 650. From 1968 the cable was directly attached to the ramp lever which was modified to suit. A Unified abutment came in 1969, a modified ball thrust plate in 1970 and for 1971 a new ball part number although the item remained a $\frac{3}{8}$ in. diameter ball bearing. For 1972 the ramp lever was altered to improve the clutch action.

Chaincase

On pre-unit models this comprises an inner and outer with fittings but for the unit engines the crankcase forms the inner with just an outer casting separate. As with other engine area castings they need to be cleaned and carefully inspected for cracks, damage, poor threads and irregular joint faces. Check that the footrest distance piece behind the pre-unit inner is in place and does fill the gap it should. It is often left out and the case cracks when the footrest nut is done up so that area is one that is suspect.

The detail parts should also be checked over and renovated as necessary. Many changed little over each series of models which can ease the spares problem and some were common to all unit engines.

Chaincase types

There were quite a number of changes to the chaincases over the years so if parts have to be

ABOVE *Primary chain tensioner as used by the 350 and 500 cc unit construction models*

RIGHT *The gearbox as featured in the 1938 brochure with gear indicator but no clutch arm rubber*

obtained some care is needed to ensure they match the model. The very first cases for 1938 lacked a chain oiler screw so differed from those of 1939. They continued for 1946 but were joined by a shorter version for the 3T and the outer from this also went on the early TR5 which used its own special inner.

Nineteen fifty brought the 6T which used 5T parts and for 1952 the oil retainer plate lost its centre boss to become a simple disc. 1953 brought a new case pair for the 5T to mount the alternator stator in the outer with an access cover. This went on the 6T in 1954 while the TR5 continued as it was. The T100 and T110 received new cases which can be recognized by two changes on the inner. First the breather pipe boss is forward of the footrest hanger rod and second the cast guard around the gearbox shaft is no longer at a constant radius and semi-circular but shaped a little.

For 1955 new cases went onto the 5T and 6T with the stator mounted to the inner. These were common but the outers were not as they carried the model name. Neither had the earlier access cover fitted. The TR5 adopted the Tiger parts which were also used for the TR6 in 1956 and the T120 in 1959.

In 1960 all models had alternators which meant a 6T type inner case for the T110 and a variation for the TR6 and T120. The outers also varied with the 6T continuing with its existing part and the other models getting a new one. For 1962 the 6T outer was changed to give more stator clearance.

The original 3TA case was only used up to 1960 and that year a new part went onto the 5TA and T100A. This gave more clearance to the clutch and provided the mounting for the chain tensioner and its adjuster. The same parts went onto the 3TA the following year and were not altered until 1968 when a rotor cover was added. The case changed again for 1969 with Unified threads and then remained as it was.

For the unit 650 the story was the same with a rotor cover in 1968 and Unified threads the next year.

Gearbox

In 1972 machines with five-speeds were available but in all other years the twins had a four-speed gearbox. All have positive stop footchange with the pedal on the right with the kickstart lever. Gearbox design is

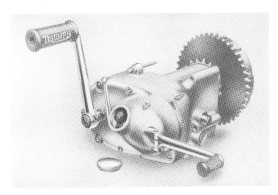

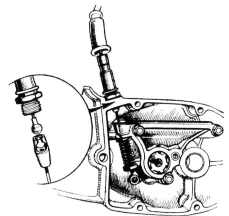

ABOVE *A 1960 Bonneville showing the gearbox end cover change which occurred to suit the slickshift. Device never fitted to T120 but cover is common*

LEFT *Revised clutch cable attachment brought in for 1962*

conventional English with sleeve gear carrying the output sprocket concentric with the mainshaft and clutch. All early models have a separate box with unit construction being adopted from 1957 for the 3TA to 1963 for the 650s.

Dismantling the gearbox is straightforward and with pre-unit models best done with the box clamped in a vice by its bottom lug. Check on the mesh between the camplate and the quadrant as you go, don't muddle the selector forks and don't lose the rollers that fit on their pegs. During assembly the same points need watching and the operation of the box and its gear selection must be fully checked out on the bench. On the smaller unit models life is easier as the whole assembly of shafts and gears can come out as one.

Gears

These must be carefully inspected for signs of wear or damage on the teeth and the driving dogs and splines.

Replacement is usually the only answer if things are bad although it is possible to build up and machine or grind back to original if the dogs are worn. Not at all easy to get right and very specialized.

There have been a good number of gears over the years so if parts are needed it is most important that they match. It is good practice to replace them in pairs as an old gear can easily wear out a new one. Before shopping consult the tables so you know the number of teeth on the gears you need as a starting point.

The pre-unit gearbox of 1938 was offered with either standard or wide ratios. From early 1946 the mainshaft second gear was changed and the sleeve gear and its bush altered. 1947 brought a close ratio gear set and a speedometer drive box which bolted to the box for use when a sprung hub was fitted. This was available from frame TL9153 for the 3T and TF19577 for the 5T or T100.

Nineteen forty-nine brought the TR5 with its own set of gears giving the stock wide ratios. This only lasted for the one year for 1950 saw the 6T arrive and with it a need for a stronger box. The design of layshaft and its gears altered and new sets of gears offered in standard, wide and close ratios. At the same time the speedometer drive was taken from the end of the layshaft with a pinned on pinion driving a gear coupled to the speedo cable. An alternative gear pair were available to suit the wide ratio box while by 1953 a plug was listed to blank off the drive when a close box was in use.

A year earlier in 1952 the layshaft second and top gears were altered, except for the TR5 model, with attention to the mating dogs. A year later in 1954 the close ratio mainshaft and third gear were also modified. 1955 saw the TR5 fall into line with the rest of the range and fit standard ratios while 1957 brought new sleeve gears and attendant bushes for all ratio types. This change was done to extend the bush into the primary case boss to reduce oil leaks when parts wore. Finally in 1961 for the 650 cc models the layshafts were changed to suit needle bearings.

The smaller unit twins had their own style of gearbox when introduced in 1957. For 1961 needle races were brought in for the T100 models at the left end of the layshaft and for the T90 and the right shaft end in 1963. The touring models continued with a bush and for 1964 the complete gear set was changed. In 1966 a wide and a close ratio set were added as options for the T90 and T100 only with the wide set fitted as standard to the Eastern T100C built for the USA.

For 1967 the mainshafts were changed to a Unified thread and all layshafts ran on needle races as the touring models had been dropped. 1968 saw new sleeve gears which extended into the oil seal in the back of the primary chaincase and a new gearbox sprocket nut to suit while 1970 brought another new gear set with the same ratios as before.

The unit 650 gearbox began with a new layshaft modified to suit the speedometer drive of the machine and all the other old gears. For 1964 the sleeve gear splines changed and in 1966 the speedo pinion was deleted with the advent of rear wheel drive for the instrument. At the same time wide and close ratio gear sets were listed, using the older parts again, and the wide set was fitted as standard to the Eastern TR6C sold in the USA.

Nineteen sixty-seven brought a mainshaft with Unified threads from engine DU48145 on plus a suitable nut to hold the kickstart ratchet together. In addition its length went from 10.984 in. to 11.297 in. In 1968 the layshaft lost its speedometer pinion hole and the sleeve gear was extended into the oil seal in the back of the primary chaincase. For 1969 the third gear pair was modified, for 1970 a new gear set fitted with revised third gear ratio and for 1971 four of the gears were again modified and new sets introduced for the close and wide ratios. With all these changes great care is needed to ensure that all the correct parts are to hand.

Finally in 1972 came the five-speed gearbox which was totally new and available in all models.

Shafts

These should be inspected for damaged splines, poor threads, bearing surfaces and the condition of the clutch rod bush. Replacement is normally needed if all is not well and, as with the gears care is needed to ensure the shafts are compatible with all the other items.

The first pre-unit design used up to 1949 was unusual in that the layshaft was plain without splines, dogs or gears. It ran in bushes and on it ran a gear sleeve carrying other gears while a further gear ran free on the layshaft. From 1950 a more conventional layout was used with changes as indicated in the

The 21 or 3TA in 1964 showing the way the clutch cable runs into the casting. Skirt, nacelle and points position are also to be noted

section above. Thus the pre-unit layshaft went onto needle races in 1961 as did the unit T100 models. Again the changes in the later models are mentioned to emphasize the importance of using the correct parts.

Bushes and bearings

Ball and needle races need to be completely clean before they can be checked. If there is any doubt as to their condition they should be renewed. Some play is normal for ball races but there must be no rough spots.

Bushes are used for the layshaft and in some of the gears. If worn they can be renewed and Triumph parts were sized so that when fitted they did not need reaming as a pressing allowance was made during manufacture.

The bearings remained the same size for all models other than the smaller units. The sleeve gear turned in a ball race $1\frac{1}{4} \times 2\frac{1}{2} \times \frac{5}{8}$ in. and the mainshaft in $\frac{3}{4} \times 1\frac{7}{8} \times \frac{9}{16}$ in. The part numbers changed for 1971 and the five-speed gearbox has a roller race for the sleeve gear but otherwise the bearings and their locating circlips stayed as they were with the sleeve gear oil seal appearing for 1950.

The smaller unit twins used metric bearings of $30 \times 62 \times 16$ mm and $17 \times 47 \times 14$ mm. Layshaft needle races were brought in on them for 1961 for the T100 models and fitted to the right end of the shaft from 1963 and on the T90. They were used on the pre-unit 650s from 1961 and on all the unit 650s.

Shell and covers

All models have an inner and outer cover and the pre-unit ones have a shell which for the unit engines is incorporated into the right crankcase. Attention to these parts is as for any other alloy casting with checks for cracks, damage, threads and joint faces.

The first pre-unit shell was modified in 1947 to accept the speedometer drive gearbox and was changed for 1950 when the stronger box was introduced. In 1954 the shell was revised for the T100 and T110 in the new swinging fork frame and lost the gear indicator pointer and scale. This shell went onto all models from 1955 and was modified for 1961 to accept the layshaft needle races.

The pre-unit inner cover was changed for 1950, again in 1954 to lose the indicator scale and in 1958. The last added a filler hole in the top face and deleted the cable lug on top of the casting. In 1959 a boss was added just behind the layshaft bush housing while for 1961 the cover was modified to accept a needle roller layshaft bearing.

The pre-unit outer cover was changed in 1950 to suit the revised gearbox but retained its characteristic knurled filler cap. For 1958 it was altered to suit the revised clutch arm so gained a vertical hole for that item and at the same time a small access cover held by two screws.

On the smaller unit models the inner was un-changed until 1969 when it became Unified and was altered again in 1971 to accommodate a circlip change. The outer began with a slot for the clutch cable but for 1962 this became a tapped hole. The interia was modified for 1964 to suit the ball ramp clutch mechanism and the part changed to Unified threads in 1969.

The unit 650s changed the inner cover in 1966 to delete the speedometer drive hole and in 1969 to Unified threads. For 1971 it was altered again to accept the two bolts holding the camplate leaf spring. The outer was altered for 1964 to add an oil seal on the kickstart shaft and for 1968 with a filler cap in the side. For 1969 Unified threads were adopted.

Gear-change mechanism

This starts with the rubber on the gear pedal and runs through to the selector forks which move the gears. There are a number of wear points that need to be checked and the sides of the forks is the area most likely to give problems. The various springs need to be changed if tired and the whole mechanism must operate smoothly.

The basis of the design did not change at all but its arrangement did to suit the unit engines while some detail parts changed from year to year. The first occurred in 1939 when a revised camplate and plunger were fitted. No gear pedal rubber was listed for 1946 but it was back the next year and the revised gearbox for 1950 brought a modified mainshaft selector fork and a new layshaft one. In 1954 the gear pedal was altered to suit the Tiger models and a heel-and-toe alternative offered for the 5T and 6T. For 1955 the Tiger pedal was standard for all models as was the option of the heel-and-toe one. At the same time the 1938 plunger went back in.

1958 brought a change to the assembly to which the pedal attached to add the Slickshaft cam track and 1958 saw a revised heel-and-toe pedal option. For 1960 the T120 adopted its own plunger spring and in 1962 the Slickshift and its camtrack went. It was always possible to remove the feature by taking the roller off the clutch arm.

The smaller unit engines had their own form of change mechanism which was first modified for 1959 with a change of the plungers which moved the camplate round. At the same time an O-ring was added on the pedal spindle. 1964 saw a brace added to the top of the camplate to stiffen the track form and new parts in the positive stop mechanism to suit the adjacent clutch ball ramp housing. In 1968 the gear pedal rubber changed and lost its 'Triumph' legend to become an anonymous black part and an O-ring went onto the camplate spindle which carried the gear indicator finger. 1969 brought a new camplate plunger and spring while 1971 saw a new camplate.

The unit 650 began using all the pre-unit parts and its only early change was in 1964 to the quadrant

spindle which lost a groove and a threaded end. 1968 saw the new pedal rubber appear along with a new camplate and an optional heavy duty spring for it. For 1969 there was a new gear pedal and also new camplate plunger, spring and holder with the last machined so its spanner hexagon was no longer cutaway for much of its length. 1970 brought a new camplate and spring together with a new mainshaft selector fork and shorter selector rod. Finally 1971 saw the introduction of aluminium bronze selector forks without rollers on their pins and the leaf camplate index spring.

Speedometer drive – gearbox

This was introduced in 1947 for use when a sprung rear wheel was fitted which prevented the use of the standard wheel drive box as fitted to the front wheel prewar and to the rear one postwar. From 3T frame TL9153 and 5T or T100 frame TF19577 the gearbox drive box was available with a 28 tooth pinion and a 23 tooth gear. From 1950 the drive was built into the gearbox with a pinion fixed to the layshaft driving a mating gear. For all standard gearboxes the pinion had

1966 TR6 unit 650 to show its clutch cable entry and gearbox end cover

ten teeth and the gear 16 while if a wide ratio gearset was fitted the speedo drive was changed to 8/15 teeth. The same design was used in the unit 650 from 1963 to 1965 but the gear pairs were 10/15 solo and 9/15 sidecar. Note that the two 15 tooth gears were not the same item as the helix angle has to suit the mating pinion. Beware when buying a layshaft with fitted gear.

Kickstarter

All pre-unit and all unit 650 cc models have a similar system with a quadrant meshed with a ratchet gear on the end of the mainshaft. The smaller unit models have a pawl and ratchet working inside the end layshaft gear.

Parts need to be cleaned and examined for wear.

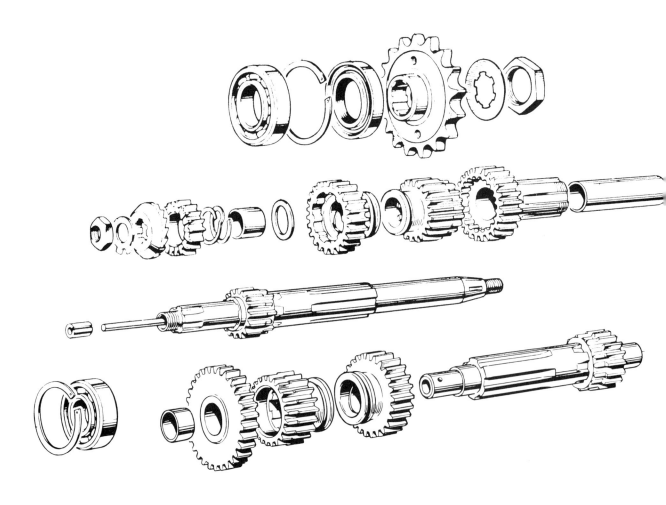

Gearbox internals as shown in the 1966 parts list for 650 cc models

Replacement is normal when needed and many items remained common over many years. For the pre-unit model the ratchet and gear were changed for 1946 when a lockwasher was added to the mainshaft nut. 1949 brought the TR5 and for that model a folding kickstart was produced. In 1954 a new cotter was used on the T110 only and in 1955 a new folding kickstart was fitted as standard to export Tigers going to the USA. That year the ratchet spring and sleeve were also changed and the associated thrust washer deleted.

In 1956 the TR6 came with the folding kickstart held in place by the T110 cotter. For 1957 a new cotter was fitted to all models. In 1958 a sealing rubber was fitted onto the kickstart spindle outside the cover and in 1961 the folding pedal became standard for all models.

This design continued without change onto the 1963 unit 650 but for 1964 the kickstart lever was modified as the 1958 sealing rubber was changed for an oil seal fitted into the outer cover in a housing. 1965 saw the ratchet spring and sleeve revert to its pre-1955 design with new parts including a thrust washer. For

1966 the kickstart lever was made longer to ease the starting force needed. In 1968 the mainshaft nut and lockwasher changed to suit a Unified thread and the pedal rubber was moulded so its hole went all the way through and was no longer blind. Another new kickstart lever came in 1969 with a Unified clamp bolt while for 1971 the quadrant and the lever cotter pin both changed.

On the smaller unit models the first change came with the fitting of a revised spindle with needle race bearing for the layshaft in 1963 on the Tiger models. For 1964 all models were fitted with a folding pedal and in 1967 an oil seal and housing added in the gearbox cover. The kickstart lever was changed for 1968 and the pedal rubber lost its 'Triumph' legend at the same time. The lever was altered again for 1969 when its threads were Unified.

Sprocket cover plate

This item seals the back of the primary chaincase on the unit models only and its removal gives access to the gearbox sprocket. It needs to be checked for damage in case the rear chain has attacked it at any time and cleaned up to remove the grease and road dirt that accumulates on it. Expect to change the oil seal which has to work hard in that environment.

The cover and seal used for the unit 650 in 1963 were not the same items as had been fitted to the smaller twins since 1957. In 1968 they both changed to common parts when the sleeve gear was extended to form the seal running surface which called for a larger seal which in turn meant a bigger hole in the cover to take that seal. The parts fitted to the five-speed machines in 1972 were different again.

Gearbox sprocket

This is likely to need renewal. Look for worn or damaged teeth, tired splines that don't fit the sleeve gear well and rough oil seal surface. Fit a new oil seal unless the existing one is perfect. The same one was used for all pre-unit models from 1950 and all unit 650s. Earlier pre-units had a dust seal and the smaller units their own size which remained unchanged.

The pre-unit sprocket was modified slightly in 1947 but otherwise remained the same with 18 teeth up to 1962. Its nut was unaltered from 1938 and continued in use on the unit 650. The sprockets for that model range were available with from 17 to 20 teeth for 1963. In 1964 their splines were strengthened and two tapped holes added. For 1965 only a felt washer appeared next to the sprocket nut and in 1966 a locking washer was fitted and sprockets with 15 or 16

teeth made available. The advent of the five-speed gearbox in 1972 brought a new 19 tooth sprocket to fit plus its own nut, washer and oil seal.

The smaller unit models began with an 18 tooth sprocket, added a 17 and 20 in 1959 and a 19 in 1960. As with the 650 a felt washer was fitted in 1965 only and a lockwasher from 1966 on. In 1968 the sprocket nut was altered.

Rear chain

Bound to need renewal on any rebuild. The size is the same for all models with 0.625 in. pitch × 0.400 in. roller diameter × 0.38 in. between inner plates and better known as $\frac{5}{8} \times \frac{3}{8}$ in. Pre-unit chain lengths vary from 90 to 101 links, the smaller units from 100 to 104 and the unit 650 from 102 to 106.

Assembly

This is a straightforward job but the details need to be checked as you go along. Bearings should be held in place with Loctite as an added security and joint faces can be sealed with the traditional gasket or a silicone rubber compound. As always this should be used sparingly.

Work to the manual and check each stage for correct operation. Make certain you have the selector forks in the correct positions and engaged in the proper cam tracks with the small rollers fitted to most. Double check the gear selection as a mistake can be traumatic on the road. If you leave the main nuts until you have the machine assembled so you can use the brake to hold the shaft make sure you cannot forget by some means or other.

Remember to fill the gearbox and primary chaincase with oil before using the machine. A tie-on label on the filler or the gear pedal may help.

5 Carburettor and exhaust

These are two areas that can give the restorer considerable problems unless the parts are simply replaced. The difficulties arise as the first wears and the second corrodes all the time the machine is in use and so their condition changes continuously. Both affect the performance of the machine, especially the carburettor, and both are important to the final appearance of the model.

Except for the 6T from 1952 to 1958 all Triumph twins had Amal carburettors and the standard models used type 6 to 1954, Monoblocs from 1955 to 1967 and Concentrics from 1968. The racing GP was offered with the optional splayed inlet port cylinder head in 1958–59 and listed by Amal for the T100 for 1955 and 1957. The 6T used an SU carburettor for its years away from the Amal fold.

A variety of exhaust systems were fitted to the twins over the years with the most common being a separate exhaust pipe and silencer mounted low down on each side. The early competition models adopted a two-into-one system with single silencer carried high on the left side. In the early 1960s siamezed pipes were used for a year or two with the silencer low on the right while the mid-1960s brought more variety for the US market. From 1969 balance pipes were adopted.

The Amal number system

Amal stamp all carburettor bodies with a number sequence that is their method of stock control. This is the build standard and up to the late Concentrics is unique as to the internal settings of the instrument. Thus if *any* setting was changed the assembly received a new part number and was stored accordingly. In this manner they could easily check that they delivered the correct unit to their many customers and they in turn could readily check them into their stores and in time out again onto the correct machines.

The type six carburettors are stamped with the basic type number followed by two letters, an oblique line and a further three digit mark. The type number is 275 for units up to $\frac{7}{8}$ in. bore, 76 or 276 for those of $\frac{15}{16}$ to $1\frac{1}{16}$ in. and 289 for $1\frac{1}{8}$ in. The two letters give the

build standard of the settings while the final series indicate the float chamber which goes with the unit.

Monobloc carburettors have no need for this last and are stamped with the type number followed by a two or three digit build standard number. The first can be 375, 376 or 389 with the same size limits as the type 6. This carburettor also exists in pairs with one float chamber body cut off for use in twin carb. installations for models without splayed inlet ports and with both cut off for the T120 when a separate float chamber is fitted. In the first instance the unmodified unit acts as float chamber for both.

The Concentric carburettor uses the same system for the 600 and 900 series and the units are numbered R or L for right or left-hand, followed by a six or nine plus the bore in mm, to give 626 or 928 for example, with the build standard to finish.

The effect of this system can be shown by taking as an example the type 376 Monoblocs fitted to the 5T and T100 in the years from 1955. Both are of $\frac{15}{16}$ in. bore with the same slide, needle position and needle jet. However, the main and pilot jets are respectively 200 and 30 or 220 and 25 so the assemblies are numbered 376/25 and 376/35. Thus it is easy to check that the correct item is fitted.

A perfectionist would seek to fit a carburettor with the correct number stamped on it but otherwise there is no obstacle to just changing the settings to the correct ones for the machine in question.

Amal restoration

The instrument has to be taken apart and checked over. New fibre washers, float needle and seating are normal practice and a new needle and jet may not come amiss. Checking the mounting flange for flatness, its holes for clearance and all the internal passages for obstructions is also usual with any rebuild. Pilot screw damage is common.

The problems arise from body and slide wear plus doubtful threads, especially the one for the top ring. Most of the other threads can be repaired or reclaimed with an insert, even in some cases by a thread change with a new mating part made from scratch. The top

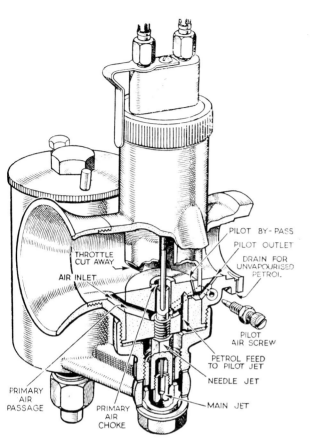

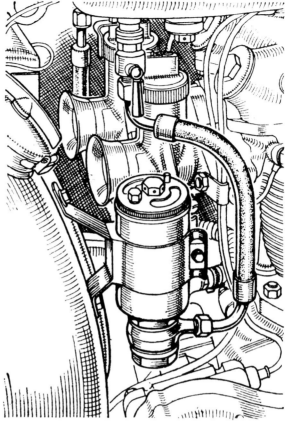

ABOVE *Float chamber mounting on oil tank front used for road T100 model with twin carburettors and fitted with a battery*

LEFT ABOVE *Cut-away of Amal type 6 carburettor with its detachable float chamber*

ring, or mixing chamber cap, is more tricky and often the chamber thread will be found to be damaged or worn away to a taper. It is possible to cut it deeper and make a new ring but it is a tricky engineering job needing good equipment.

The wear problem can be dealt with by sleeving the body and again this is a tricky job which must be done to a high level of precision. As with all carburettor work it must be tackled with a delicate touch as the parts are fragile and easy to break.

If you can find replacement parts it will be easier than repairing an old carburettor and the notes about Amal numbering should help. The type six units were handed so you must check that you have the correct item with the throttle stop and air screw on the right when looking into the bellmouth. Exceptions were the prewar models which had these items on the left while the race kit and the T100c used one of each as a matching pair.

The prewar float chambers went on the right but postwar they moved to the left and all were of the bottom feed type. As the mixing chamber was at seven degrees downdraught the arm of the float chamber was cranked round to suit and thus the pre- and postwar chambers cannot be swapped over.

Chambers and their floats require normal inspection but usually it is only the needle and its seating that wears. Make sure the float in a Monobloc

can move freely on its pivot as a tight spot can cause confusion. Check all floats for leaks.

Assemble the instrument with care and make sure the petrol feed area is as it should be. It is well worth connecting this up to a tank and checking that it holds a level and does not flood. Better to find out before it goes back onto the machine and drips all over the magneto.

The finish of the earlier Amal bodies was in a silver grey paint specially developed to resist petrol. This is no longer available as no-one is prepared to order the required large quantity, so a problem exists. Do not be tempted to use any other paint without a trial first as it may react with the fuel to produce a dreadful mess that is more a sludge than anything and a full clean out

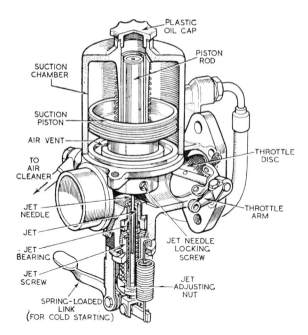

PLASTIC OIL CAP

PISTON ROD

SUCTION CHAMBER

SUCTION PISTON

AIR VENT

TO AIR CLEANER

JET NEEDLE

JET

JET BEARING

JET SCREW

SPRING-LOADED LINK (FOR COLD STARTING)

THROTTLE DISC

THROTTLE ARM

JET NEEDLE LOCKING SCREW

JET ADJUSTING NUT

LEFT *The SU carburettor fitted to the 6T from 1952 to 1958*

BELOW *Exploded drawing of SU showing its piston, butterfly throttle and cold start arrangements*

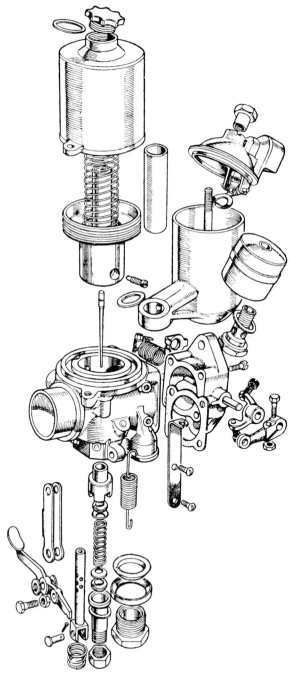

will then be needed. Better to go for vapour blasting which gives a very similar result but do check every passage afterwards in case it was not correctly masked.

SU restoration

This follows the same lines as for the Amal with attention given to the butterfly spindle which may wear the housing a little and itself a lot. The various seals are likely to need replacement as will the float needle and its seating. It is important that the jet needle is straight and that it can drop straight down into the jet. If it won't it must be centred. The piston must rise and fall easily and the cold start mechanism function correctly.

Make sure the float chamber vent is clear or you may have a power fade at three quarter throttle. It is best to completely assemble the carburettor on the bench as this will allow an easy check to be made of the piston movement. It will also prevent the needle being bent when fitting piston and chamber top on the machine which is awkward as space is tight and a mistake easy to make.

Petrol pipes

Flexible pipes were used on the twins from the start and postwar this practice continued. The detail style varied a little over the years but in general each pipe comprised a good length of flexible material swaged onto short lengths of copper tubing carrying the end fittings. Nuts on the pipes connected these to the petrol tap and the float chamber.

Around 1952 the flexible section became transparent plastic but otherwise the construction was the same with the plastic held to the copper pipe by a ferrule crimped in place. Unfortunately this plastic is

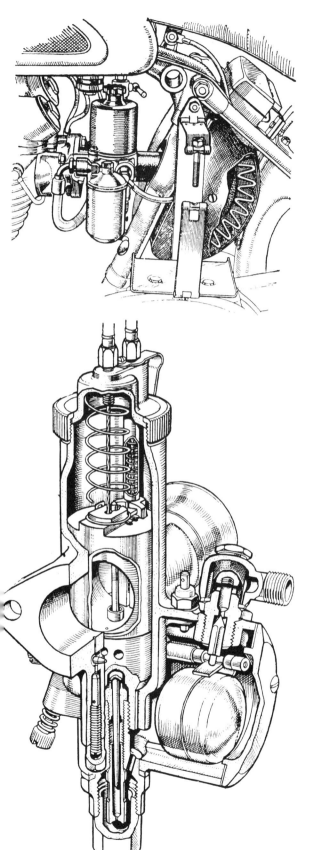

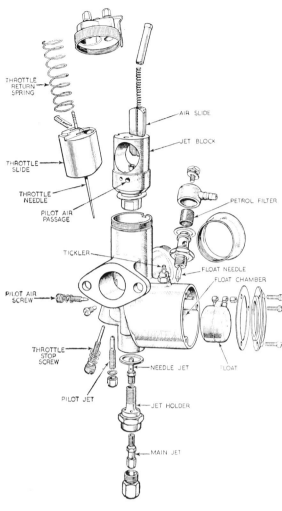

THROTTLE RETURN SPRING

THROTTLE SLIDE

THROTTLE NEEDLE

PILOT AIR PASSAGE

AIR SLIDE

JET BLOCK

PETROL FILTER

TICKLER

FLOAT NEEDLE

FLOAT CHAMBER

PILOT AIR SCREW

THROTTLE STOP SCREW

NEEDLE JET

FLOAT

PILOT JET

JET HOLDER

MAIN JET

ABOVE *Exploded drawing of Monobloc as used by Triumph for many years*

LEFT ABOVE *The SU as installed on the 6T for 1952 when it had a rigid frame which was modified to allow the hose to the filter to pass through*

LEFT *Cut-away drawing of Monobloc. Correct assembly and a free moving float are both important to avoid flooding*

very prone to hardening and may then split. Replacement really is essential on safety grounds and in 1960 Triumph themselves changed to a black tubing for the T120 at least. Other models kept to the transparent plastic and this should always be checked.

The pipe end fittings need inspection to make sure they seat and seal as they should and that the nut threads are in good order. Older pipes can take a set and are often very stiff so they will pull on the tap or the carburettor which is not a good idea.

If new pipes are needed and total originality is not required then modern black neoprene is to be recommended as it has a long life and holds onto the fittings well even without any clips. It also remains very flexible even in cold weather which is a good point. When making up pipes ensure they are long enough not to pull at the ends or kink, that they lie naturally and avoid vertical loops which can cause air locks.

Air filter

The element should be washed, dried and re-oiled or renewed according to type while the body needs to be repaired and finished as any other sheet steel component. The hose connecting the filter to the carburettor must be carefully checked for cracks which could cause air leaks.

A filter was listed as an extra prewar but not at all from 1946 to 1948. In 1949 it reappeared sandwiched between the oil tank and battery carrier in box-like form. At the same time the old style bellmouth continued as an option with appropriate corrections to the carburettor settings. In 1952 a new filter appeared with the shape of a letter D and this was used exclusively from 1955 while the bellmouth option continued.

The T120 arrived with bellmouths and in 1960 the 6T and T110 reverted to a box shaped filter while the TR6 kept to a D. This continued for the pre-unit models to 1962. For the unit 650s 1963 brought round filters for the 6T and TR6 and in 1964 the TR6 adopted its own pair with a coarse felt element while the 6T stuck to felt and the previous year's body.

1965 saw both with new bodies and 1966 brought another body and a paper element for the US version of the 6T plus yet another body and the same paper element for the US TR6. For the Western T120 a single chamber and element were used which stretched across the frame to feed both carburettors. In 1967 the US TR6 kept its filter while the T120R and T120TT adopted two of the type fitted to the TR6. This continued for the TR6 alone the next year.

In 1969 a new body appeared using the previous element and this changed again for 1970. The T120 adopted its own round body in 1969 with the same element as the TR6 and also changed for 1970 but again to a different body. Finally in 1971 the filter

ABOVE *Cleaning out the Monobloc float chamber of a 1961 6T*

TOP *The air filter installation and connection as used on the 3TA in 1957*

arrangements were completely altered to two side boxes each with an element which combined to feed one or two carburettors as called for. Rather too many mouldings appeared to deal with the two applications.

The smaller unit twins had a box type filter from 1957 to 1961. During that year this was altered to provide a renewable element while the T100SS adopted a round filter with felt element. The body was modified in 1964 and 1965 and joined in 1966 by a version with paper element for the USA. 1967 brought another type with coarse felt element for the T100R and T100T twin carburettor models and for 1968 the element was changed to a cloth type. It changed back again for 1969. In 1970 a single body type was adopted and the 1968 cloth element fitted into it and this combination remained in use until 1972.

Exhaust system

This comprises the pipes and silencers plus the clips, brackets and stays which hold them to the machine. The parts are steel, chrome plated, and this finish often suffers from both heat and corrosion which detracts greatly from the machine's appearance.

Fortunately replacement with pattern parts is possible for these popular models and it is worth paying a sensible price for the items rather than looking for the cheapest. The pipes and silencers are an important facet of the looks of the model so well worth getting right for the sake of a little extra money. Quality parts will also fit better and last longer.

If the pipes, clips and brackets are in good order it may be feasible to clean and polish them for further use. Before the final polish they should be checked for their fit to the machine mounting points and to the cylinder head. Most models clamp the pipes to adaptors screwed into the exhaust ports but late models have push-in pipes and some early ones use pipe nuts. For the first you may need to swell the pipe to ensure it is a snug fit in the port and heat plus a wooden wedge may be needed to do this. The second type are tricky as the pipe must fit squarely into the port and the nut must be able to run in true into the threads without trying to damage them. If any parts are distorted real care may be needed to get everything back into line.

The brackets and clips should be easy to repair and re-finish if this is needed as most are simple parts. The correct nuts, bolts and washers plus the D section parts used with the clips should be checked and

RIGHT BELOW *Also of 350 cc but a Tiger 90 from 1965 showing the correct 376/300 Monobloc*

BELOW *Monobloc, filter and feeds of 1964 TR6. Also note the splash shield on the filter and twin switches*

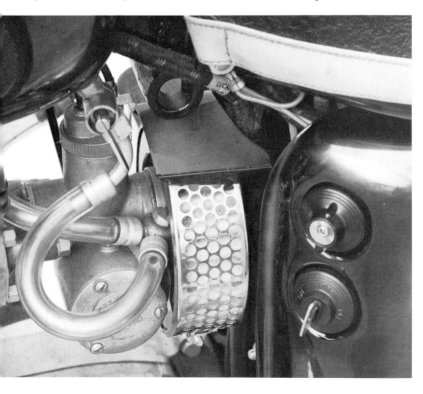

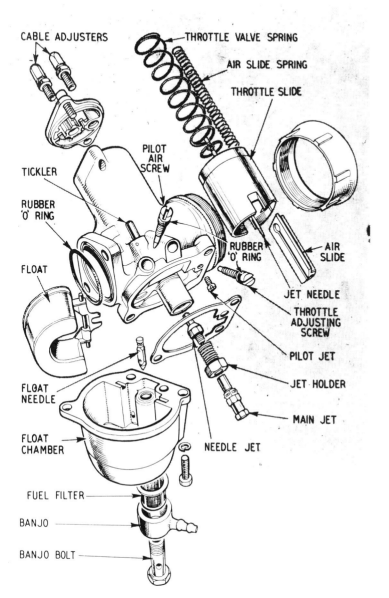

CABLE ADJUSTERS

THROTTLE VALVE SPRING

AIR SLIDE SPRING

THROTTLE SLIDE

PILOT AIR SCREW

TICKLER

RUBBER 'O' RING

FLOAT

RUBBER 'O' RING

AIR SLIDE

JET NEEDLE

THROTTLE ADJUSTING SCREW

PILOT JET

JET HOLDER

MAIN JET

FLOAT NEEDLE

FLOAT CHAMBER

NEEDLE JET

FUEL FILTER

BANJO

BANJO BOLT

ABOVE *The Concentric Amal shown in exploded drawing form*

RIGHT ABOVE *Monobloc and filter as installed on a Tiger 100 in 1966*

RIGHT *Two Monoblocs with air brushed filters as on the T100T in 1967*

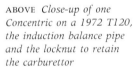

ABOVE *Close-up of one Concentric on a 1972 T120, the induction balance pipe and the locknut to retain the carburettor*

RIGHT *Air filter box with outer cover removed as on 1972 T120*

refurbished as necessary. On some models heat shields were fitted and these need similar treatment.

The silencer body is much more of a problem if you wish to re-use it and it is not in good condition. Often the thin outer shell will have corroded from the inside which makes repair a skilled metal working job. A further problem is the plating for firms that undertake such work will not want to put a dirty silencer in their tank and it is just about impossible to fully clean it.

Thus the existing silencer can only really be used if in good order and the practical alternative has to be a pattern part unless you are lucky enough to locate an unused original.

Exhaust pipe types

There is variety here and it is important to get the right one or you can have problems. The sequence starts with the pair used by the 1938 5T and these remained on that model up to 1952. They were plain pipes with no welded on brackets, just slit at the port end for clamping and bent to shape. The right pipe ran straight back but the left one had a small kink just aft of the footrest to raise the level a trifle. These pipes were also fitted to the 6T from 1950 to 1952 and the T100 from 1946 to 1950.

For 1939 the T100 was fitted with shorter pipes to suit its silencers and in 1951 the pipes gained small lugs near the front for the attachment of support brackets and were to suit the new alloy cylinder head. For 1954 they changed again to suit the swinging fork frame but continued with the small kink in the left pipe.

In 1953 the 6T kept its existing pipes and the 5T the right one but on the left the pipe ran down a little lower to tuck under the alternator and thus had more of a kink to return to its normal level. The kink was

ABOVE *Speed Twin in 1947 showing its right side exhaust pipe and silencer*

TOP RIGHT *The mechanics and exhaust system of the 1957 Thunderbird*

SECOND RIGHT *Same for 1960 T100A, also showing part of bathtub*

THIRD RIGHT *And siamesed system as used by the T100SS in 1963 when it still had its skirt*

FOURTH RIGHT *Left side exhaust system fitted to the TR6 in 1966*

BOTTOM RIGHT *And finally the T120 in 1968*

FAR RIGHT ABOVE *Parts list drawing showing the variations for 1951*

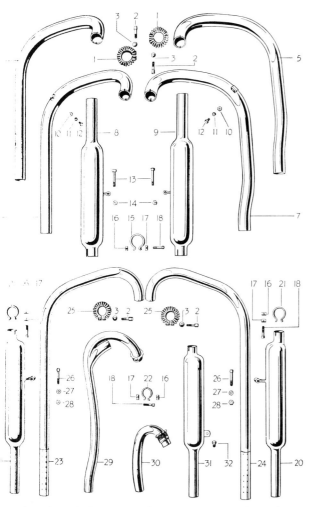

until 1955 when the frame changed. The cylinder head became as the T100 with screwed in adaptors so the pipes changed to clamp fixings onto these. Otherwise the pipe run continued in the same place to the end.

The TR6 appeared in 1956 with the same style system as the TR5 but not the same pipes. It was modified for 1960 to suit the change to an alternator chaincase and again for 1961. That year the model format changed from trail machine to sports tourer, a single carburettor T120 in fact, and the exhaust system became a twin silencer one as on the 6T. For 1962 it copied that model with a siamezed system low down on the right using the same pipes.

The T110 came in with pipes much as the T100 with small lugs for stays. As with the other models the left one had a kink in it but for 1958 both pipes were changed for ones with a small bend in place of the kink which tilted the silencers up a touch. For 1960 the left one was altered to suit the alternator chaincase.

The T120 used the T110 pipes for 1959 and like it changed the left one for 1960.

The unit 650s had new pipes in 1963 for the 6T and T120 but the TR6 continued with its siamesed system using the 1962 left section with a new right one. For 1964 it was changed to the same type as the others and for 1965 all three were altered. The single lug to the frame on the straight part went and was replaced by another further forward on the lower bend. A bracing strip went across the machine between the two lugs and a second one joined the pipe to silencer clips together.

This design continued for the home market models until 1969 when a balance tube was added and the front cross brace strip changed to two angle brackets. The first balance tube was held in place by a split clamp with two bolts at either end but was quickly changed for another with single bolt clips. 1971 brought two new pipes using all the old clips, brackets and balance pipe. These changed again to push-in pipes for 1972 but still retained the same detail parts.

For the USA there were other systems in 1966. The 6T, TR6R and T120R all used the home market pipes but not the other models. The Eastern TR6C had a pair of pipes each of which ran along at crankcase top level to a silencer. For the Western TR6C the pipes were open ended and both ran above the primary chaincase with the right cylinder one above the left. The ends were stylishly cut off at an angle. For the T120TT yet another form was used with two open pipes running down and under the engine unit closely tucked in to finish just aft of the rear pivot spindle.

The open systems on the T120TT continued for 1967 but the TR6C received a new style. This began for the Western TR6C with both pipes run at waist level on the left but continued on each to its own silencer. There was no connection between the two systems.

thus about half the pipe diameter or twice what it had been. For 1954 both models changed both pipes for a new common pair shaped much as the 1953 5T type. They both changed again for 1955 with the addition of lugs for stays which linked them to the engine plates and remained in this form for the 5T to the end and on the 6T up to 1961. For 1962 only a siamezed system was used on the 6T with the left pipe crossing over just above the engine plates to join the right which swept down to a single low level silencer.

The 3T kept to one pair of pipes throughout its life. These were longer than on the 5T and extended well into the silencer body. The tube ends were perforated and the pipes supported at port and silencer alone.

The first TR5 had a rather nice system with the right pipe running over to join the left which ran along the top of the chaincase to the silencer. The pipes were fitted with castellated nuts which screwed directly into the exhaust ports so correct alignment was essential and this was made easier by the ports being parallel.

This only lasted for two years as 1951 saw the new alloy head on the TR5 which meant two new pipes to suit the splayed ports. This new design continued

TOP *A 1968 T100C showing the twin waist level exhaust systems it used*

ABOVE *A T100T in 1969 with low level exhaust systems and balance between pipes*

The next listing was not until 1971 and repeated the style of the 1967 TR6C but with changes. The two pipes were run into a connection section which joined the two together and then went on to a pair of silencers. To the assembly was added a wire mesh guard built up from four vertical wires and a dozen horizontal ones. This continued for 1972 with the pipes altered to the push-in type.

The smaller unit models began with a low level system on each side with the pipe stayed to the engine plates. The pipes were changed with the introduction of the 5TA in 1959 and remained in the lists from then to 1967.

However, in 1962 all models except the T100A were fitted as standard with siamesed systems and the silencer went low down on the right with the left pipe crossing over. This continued in 1963 for the T90 and T100SS but the 3TA and 5TA went back to their two separate systems. For 1964 all were back on twin systems with a new and smaller pair of pipes for the T90. These were adopted by the 3TA in 1965 and the T100R and T100T in 1967.

In 1968 the stay lug moved from the start of the straight section to above the lower bend and two pipe sizes were used, one for the T100S and the other for the T90, T100R and T100T. Only the T90 continued with the same pipe for 1969 as the T100 models all gained a balance pipe which, like that on the 650, was soon revised. 1971 brought new pipes for the T100R during the major model revamp and these were altered again for 1972.

Again the US models differed and the 1966 T100C machines for east or west used a system much like that of the old TR5 with the right pipe passing over to join the left which ran back at waist level. The T100R used the normal pipes. For 1967 the T100C copied the TR6C with twin pipes and silencers all mounted at waist level on the left but without inter-connection. Small pipe guards could be clipped to each tube.

The same parts were used for 1968 but for 1969 the model adopted the connection section and wire mesh guard seen in 1971 on the TR6C. This continued to be listed for the T100C in 1971 and had changed pipes and brackets for 1972.

Silencer types

The first 5T had a pair of tubular silencers held by a single bolt to the frame. As with all such systems the silencer should be pushed well onto the exhaust pipe before its clip is tightened to make sure it is not trying to push the pipe away from the engine. The reverse is better if it can be achieved. The 5T kept these silencers for 1939 but the T100 of that year had a special pair styled as megaphones with rounded ends and tailpipes. To enhance the image the end could be removed by undoing three screws to just leave the megaphone on the end of the pipe.

Postwar both 5T and T100 adopted new silencers

The balance pipe adopted by most models in 1969 and here shown on a T120 of that year

for 1946 according to the parts list but went back to the 1938 items from 1947 on to 1953 for both models plus the 6T from 1950. The 3T had its own pair and these differed in that the mounting lug was about one third of the way along the silencer body instead of being in the middle while the pipe end was offset down and not central to the body.

For 1954 the 5T, 6T, T100 and the newly introduced T110 adopted a new style of silencer with a body that tapered down slightly from front to rear. For 1957 the lug design changed from a strip of metal that rose up to roll round the bolt and back again to a flat lug welded to the side of the silencer body. This was used only for the 5T and 6T in 1958 and 1959 while 1960 brought a revised design with a mute in the tail for the 6T. This silencer was changed for 1962 when the siamezed system was fitted on the right only.

The T100 and T110 adopted a new pair of silencers for 1958 which were changed again for 1959 and adopted by the T120. In 1960 they were altered again with the fitting of the mutes in the tailpipes and once more for 1962.

On the TR5 a single silencer was fitted on the left and this had an offset inlet and a mounting lug near the tail of the body. For 1954 only this was altered to a style with the body tapered from front to rear but still with its small mounting lug on the top and near the rear. In 1955 the use of the new frame changed the lug to something longer, a little further forward and positioned below the body which continued with its offset inlet.

This silencer went onto the TR6 in 1956 and continued in use until a new one of similar appearance arrived for 1960. This changed completely for 1961 when twin silencers were fitted and again for 1962 when a siamezed system and single silencer was fitted, the same as fitted to the right side of the T120.

New silencers appeared for the unit 650s in 1963, two for the 6T and T120 and a single for the TR6 with its siamezed system. In place of the welded support lug was a strip held to the silencer body by two bolts. The TR6 had two for 1964 and this type continued for the home market until 1969 when a straight-through absorption type was adopted, this having first been seen in 1966 on some US models. For 1971 the style was changed completely to a megaphone shape with reversed cone end and this type was held by two bolts whose heads fitted under a bracket on the silencer body.

Meanwhile in 1966 the 6T, TR6R and T120R were all fitted with the absorption type silencer while the Eastern TR6C with its waist level pipes had a special pair of silencers with welded on mounting lugs. In truth the left one was that used by the TR6 in 1960 and the right one came from the 1961 export T120 which could have waist level pipes.

For 1967 the TR6R and T120R continued as they were while the TR6C adopted twin pipes and silencers. The two bodies were mounted one above the other and hung from a single strip clipped to the frame. In 1971 this style re-appeared with a connection piece interposed between pipes and silencers which now hung from a more complex bracket.

The smaller unit models began with a pair of tubular silencers which remained the same up to 1968. The T100A had a different form fitted with a mute which continued to be listed as an option for all models up to 1967.

When the siamezed systems appeared in 1962 a revised silencer was fitted and this continued for the T90 and T100SS for 1963. In 1964 all models were back on the 1957 silencers again. For 1969 the design was modified when the balance pipe was added and for 1971 the home market models adopted megaphone style silencers while the export ones had the support brackets changed.

The silencers fitted to the range for 1969 were used earlier on the T100R from 1966 to 1968 and for the USA something else again was used. For 1966 only the T100C had a single silencer on a siamezed pipe and used the one fitted to the TR models from 1955 to 1959. For 1967 it changed to two separate pipes and silencers, one above the other and hung from a single strip. This strip was modified for 1968 to curl under the lower silencer and changed for 1969. That year a connection piece and two new silencers appeared and the silencers and mounting bracket were revised for 1972.

And a final reminder that the whole system must fit the machine without stress or strain to avoid fractures or parts coming adrift.

The T120 of 1970 showing its exhaust system along with its twin horns and twin leading shoe front brake

6 Lubrication

All Triumph twins have a dry sump system and most a separate oil tank mounted on the right side of the machine beneath the saddle or front of the dualseat. In 1971 the oil tank became part of the frame for the 650 cc models only but the 500 retained its separate container. A twin plunger pump driven by the inlet camshaft gear nut was fitted inside the timing chest which was drilled to pass the oil as needed. A pressure gauge, indicator button or switch was fitted in this area along with a pressure release valve.

Filters were provided on the feed line in the oil tank and in the base of the sump on the scavenge pipe. The rocker gear was lubricated by a branch taken from the return line near the oil tank except on prewar models which were pressure fed via a flow adjuster. The accumulated oil either drained back to the sump via external pipes connected to the pushrod tubes or internal drillings. Late unit 650s have an added pressure feed to the exhaust tappets and the rear chain is looked after from the oil tank on some unit models.

Up to 1969 a timed breather was fitted at the left end of the inlet camshaft. This connected to a passage that led to the outside world via a tube and extension rubber pipe. For 1970 the design changed so the engine breathed into the primary chaincase via holes and from this to the outside via a stub and pipe bolted to the back of the chaincase above the gearbox sprocket.

Oil pump

As this works in oil there is seldom much wear on the plungers or in the bores. The most likely wear point is the drive block which is easy to replace. Below each plunger is a ball, spring and retaining plug. It is possible that the ball is not seating correctly in which case a tap after the parts have been cleaned should do the trick. Only in extreme cases will the ball seat need cutting but if this is required a drill will do the job if sharpened to suit. The spring may tire and need renewal and it should be $\frac{1}{2}$ in. long. The same one was used for all pumps.

The plug that holds the spring changed for 1952 but otherwise the real changes only affected the plunger diameters and thus the body. The pre-unit engines all have the feed on the left as you look into the timing cover and at first this was $\frac{5}{16}$ in. diameter and the scavenge $\frac{7}{16}$ in. In 1950 the feed went up to $\frac{3}{8}$ in. and these sizes remained in use up to 1966.

Before then in 1957 for the smaller unit and 1963 for the 650 the plungers were reversed so the scavenge was on the left and this layout applies to all unit engines. For 1967 the scavenge plunger was increased in size to 0.487 in. and this pump continued for all the smaller models. On the 650 only the feed was increased to 0.406 in. for 1970.

Release valve, indicator, gauge and switch

The first of these is a spring loaded valve that controls the oil pressure that reaches the engine. If this level is exceeded excess oil is dumped back into the sump. The other three are assurances that all is well and the oil is circulating.

The valve is positioned in the timing cover or the timing chest area of the crankcase. It may be dismantled, cleaned, inspected and re-assembled. The parts seldom give trouble.

A pressure gauge was fitted in the tank top instrument panel from 1938 to 1948. This would normally read about 30 psi at 30 mph in top gear and higher when the engine was cold. Hot, this reading could and does drop to zero but this is not necessarily cause for alarm. At speed the oil is centrifuged out of the crankshaft so fast the pump is hard pressed to keep up with the demand from that quarter without bothering with gauges. And, if the oil is pouring out of the big ends, there will not be much pressure which was one reason why Triumph stopped fitting the gauge as too many owners sent in worried letters. Also they changed the tank design, added a small tank top rack and moved the instruments to the nacelle, awkward for an oil gauge pipe.

So in 1949 the release valve gained an indicator button which came out to show signs of pressure. This continued unaltered and went onto the 3TA in 1957. For 1960 it was modified but only in respect of the end

ABOVE *The T100c of 1953 showing its oil tank, oil pipes, release valve and indicator among other features*

ABOVE *The elements of the twin plunger oil pump used by Triumph as shown in a 1950 drawing*

cap which was fitted with a seal for the indicator rod. This design also went onto the unit 650 engine until 1964. From 1965 to 1968 no indicator was provided but in 1969 a pressure switch was fitted to the engine using the tapped hole that had been provided for years for a pressure gauge for checking. At the same time the release valve was Unified and for 1971 became a single assembly. This continued for the 500 but the 650 reverted to the 1969 design for 1972 while both sizes continued with the oil pressure switch.

Filters

There are two of these, one in the oil tank and the other in the engine sump, and both protect the intake lines to the oil pump. They are made from a metal gauze or mesh and need to be inspected for damage which cause the oil not to be strained. The mesh is either soldered or silver soldered in place so can be replaced or repaired with two provisos. First is not to restrict the oil flow and second is not to decrease the degree of filtration. Thus, do not replace a fine gauze with a wide mesh. Also check the parts for damage to the mechanical fixing and function.

The pre-unit engines all have a sump plate and matching filter through which the scavenge pipe

passes. The parts were retained by four bolts up to 1952 but from then on studs and nuts were employed. Check the threads as they tend to get mangled and the area is a natural for oil leaks.

The design was changed for the unit engines. On the 650 a large bolt with filter attached was screwed into the underside of the right crankcase so the filter body fitted round the scavenge pipe. The 1963 type was modified to provide more gauze area in 1964 and the thread change to Unified for 1969 but otherwise it remained the same basic design.

On the smaller models an assembly of cap, filter, spring and washers was used, again on the underside of the right crankcase. The only change over the years was to the cap which was Unified in 1969.

The tank filter was essentially the same on nearly all models but with detail changes from time to time. Pre-unit machines had one such for 1951 when the oil pipes changed to flared unions in place of soldered nipples but otherwise remained as they were from then to 1962. The 3TA came in with a similar style of union plus filter extending into the tank body. For the 350 and 500 cc models from 1959 to 1963 the union was extended to bring the feed pipe connection point lower down, no doubt to ease access under the

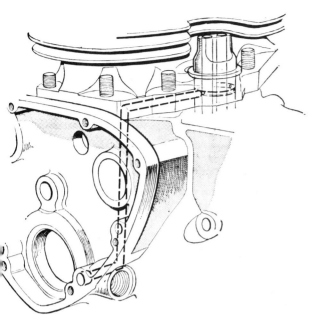

bathtub. From 1964 the original type was fitted and this also went on the unit 650 from 1963 to 1970.

In 1971 the 650 oil in the frame model was introduced and the filter was mounted on a plate at the base of the seat tube carrying the lubricant. This one piece assembly of filter and plate was quickly changed to two separate parts which continued for 1972.

Rocker box oiling

Prewar this was done with a pressure feed line from the release valve but postwar the feed came from the return line just before it reached the oil tank. The small bore pipe carried the oil up to the rocker box and internal drillways took it on to the places where it was needed. These all need to be clean and unobstructed with no kinks in the pipes or the oil won't get there.

The oil drained from the rocker boxes either through pipes to the pushrod covers or straight down them. Cleanliness is the need in these areas.

Pipes

The main ones were the feed and return that connected the oil tank to the engine. In addition there was the rocker box feed, the drains on some engines and vent pipes on others. All need to be inspected for any signs of cracks or leaks. Check carefully any flexible pipes. The material may deteriorate and either swell or break away and either fault could block the pipe. Also check for any loose area that could flap about and stop the flow once this begins but which would leave the pipe clear when inspected. A rare fault may be but confusing and expensive if it happens.

An important internal pipe is the scavenge that runs from the sump to the crankcase wall behind the oil pump. This must be secure and without leaks or cracks otherwise the pump will not empty the sump. Inspect closely in case there is a hairline crack which may widen under heat so that the pump will scavenge at first and then begin to fail to clear the accumulation of oil.

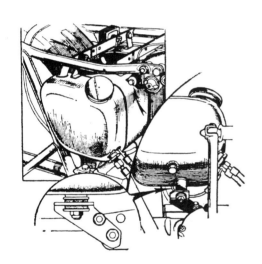

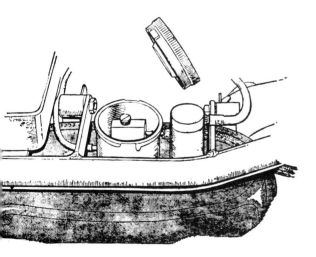

TOP LEFT *Line of the oil feed to the exhaust tappets adopted from 1966*

CENTRE LEFT *Rubber bush oil tank mounting as used by the TR6 and T120 models in 1962*

LEFT *Regulator screw for oil bleed to rear chain introduced on 1966 models*

Exhaust tappet oil feed

This was introduced in 1966 in an effort to reduce cam wear. It was modified with the addition of a metering dowel and jet in 1967 only but this went in 1968 when timed tappets were adopted. It was continued to 1972 but is not required when nitrided camshafts are fitted.

Breather system

This is an area that seems to give owners a headache if it has any problems. Perhaps the snag is that is consists largely of holes and as such cannot appear on a parts list.

Nearly all Triumph twins have a timed rotary disc breather driven by the left end of the inlet camshaft. It comprises a fixed disc with ports in it, a rotating one with ears that fit into a slot in the camshaft end and a spring which holds the two discs together.

The device is normally trouble free but can be jammed and broken on assembly. If this happens either the engine can breathe all the time and loses oil rapidly or it cannot breathe at all and the pressures generated will force their way out elsewhere and cause leaks. The latter trouble will also occur if the breather pipe, located in the back of the crankcase, is blocked in any way.

Prewar twins have a different system altogether with a diaphragm breather screwed into the drive side of the crankcase. This allows the crankcase to breathe out but not suck in. On occasion it needs to be cleaned in petrol.

For 1970 the twins of all sizes dropped the timed breather in favour of a system which used the primary chaincase as a second chamber. Thus three holes appeared in the case wall to connect the two and

LEFT ABOVE Adjusting the oil supply to the rear chain on a 1966 TR6. Oil tank and battery carrier mountings can also be seen

RIGHT ABOVE Oil pipe connections and lower tank support as in 1968 on a T120

quickly the drive side oil seal was deleted. This increased the breathing chamber volume and the gases then emerged from a stub bolted to the back of the primary chaincase above the final drive sprocket. Inside the case went a baffle plate and on the 650 this included a catchment area which collected oil and fed it down a pipe to the primary chain. It is this system that is recommended for competition use.

Good breathing is as important as good joints in cutting out oil leaks so it is vital that all the parts do their job correctly including all the holes that contribute to the system.

Oil tank

This container always sits in the same place except where built as part of the frame but comes in various shapes and sizes. Two basic forms were used to suit rigid and swinging fork frames but each can be found in several varieties.

Leaving aside the finish which is covered later, the tank needs to be cleaned and inspected. On a running

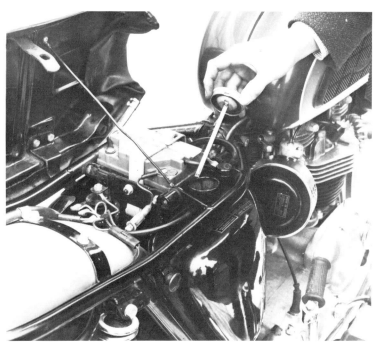

Filler cap with dipstick for a T120 in 1969. Battery strap and petrol tap have also changed since 1966

model the first part is, or should be, no problem but an unknown tank can be full of horrors. Oil tanks seem able to harbour more dirt, sludge, spiders and unknown substances than even the underside of mudguards; maybe it's the confined atmosphere. Whatever it is, you have to get it all out. It may take every solvent and detergent you have but clean it must be, both inside and out.

Only then can it be checked over. Look for cracks and split seams which will need to be welded up. Oil tanks are prone to this due to the combination of heat and vibration. Thus the mounting system and the actual fastenings need to be inspected to ensure they are not straining the tank or themselves. Correct as necessary. Also inspect all the pipe or union threads and any washer seating faces that may need cleaning up. If this has to be done it is worth fitting the parts and checking that paraffin won't seep through the joint even if you have to clean it out again. Better than finding an oil leak later.

Check the fit of the tank cap and its washer. Examine the breather, froth tower, rear chain feed or any other ancillary feature. For oil-in-frame 650s make sure the oil filter plate fits and seals to the bottom of the seat tube. After all it is effectively the bottom of the oil tank and a leak will not be easy to spot unless it becomes dramatic. Then it's Hobson's choice between a seized engine and an oily rear tyre.

Oil tank types

There are a good number of these as fixtures and fittings varied from year to year so take care when buying a replacement. Some changes may not affect the fit of the tank to the frame but others will. In

operation all do the same job so can be pressed into service if desired.

The first 1938 5T had a six-pint tank with a screwed cap with crossbar. In 1939 it was joined by the T100 which had an eight-pint tank with hinged filler cap. Postwar the return pipe on all tanks gained a T-branch to feed the rocker box and initially both 500 cc models fitted the same eight-pint tank. The 3T used the six-pint with screwed cap and this particular tank came from prewar days and the 3SE and 5SE singles. During 1946 the 5T changed to it and this arrangement continued for another two years.

For 1949 the T100 changed to the 5T tank and the TR5 appeared with its own tank and the 5T cap. In 1950 the 6T joined the range and used the common road tank. For 1951 all the models changed to tanks with a more angled filler and a plain screw cap without crossbar. The TR5 tank continued with its own tank which received the same changes.

At the same time the race kit was introduced with an eight-pint tank with hinged filler on the front face angled at about 45 degrees. Normally this was flanked by a remote float chamber for racing but this then occupied the battery position so a further tank was offered for riders who wanted to retain road equipment on their race-kitted T100. This had four blind tapped holes in its front face to take a bracket to carry the float chamber on the right.

For 1952 the road tanks all changed as did the race kit one while the TR5 continued as before. Only the race kit one changed for 1953 with further revisions to its mountings. The 5T, 6T and TR5 continued as they were for 1954 but the T100 and new T110 went into swinging fork frames and thus had new oil tanks. These changed in detail for 1955 and went onto all models including the TR5 which differed only in that its filler cap, bayonet fitting as the others, had a safety chain to prevent it being dropped on the ground.

The same tank and safety chain went onto the TR6 in 1956 and all tanks continued unchanged to 1958. In that year another eight-pint performance tank appeared to suit the frame type and it led to the new tanks used by all except the 6T in 1959. Two new types were introduced, both with an anti-froth tower, and that used on the new T120 differed from the one for the other models in the matter of the air filter cut-outs.

1960 brought two more tanks in different styles with one much as before for the TR6 and T120 while the other was designed to fit under the bathtub worn by the 6T and T110. The first had the anti-froth tower moved to the rear end of the tank top and the fixings altered. The top rear one was turned so its bolt lay horizontal along the machine's length and was a little forward of the tower. The top front remained much as it was and the lower front changed to an open ended slot. The TR6 continued with its safety chain.

The second tank was slimmer with its filler cap set to the rear of the top face. Two flat lugs were welded on for the top bolts which lay along the machine and the third mounting was at the base with the bolt across the model. The feed and return pipes were both positioned aft of the mounting lug and the feed one was furthest to the rear.

This tank style had first been seen in 1957 on the 3TA and this had a similar form, top mountings and cap. The base of the tank had no fixing other than the oil pipes and this tank differed from later ones in that the feed pipe was positioned at the forward lower corner as with older tanks and the drain plug went into the end of a short tube welded into the rear lower corner. For 1959 and the 5TA as well as the 3TA both models were fitted with the tank that was to go on the 6T in 1960 so there was no drain plug. This tank continued on the smaller models including the new T100A for 1960.

The 650s were unchanged for 1961 as was the 6T for 1962 but the TR6 and T120 were given anti-vibration mountings for that year, the last for the pre-unit models. The smaller unit twins continued as they were for the 3TA, 5TA and T100A but a new one appeared for the T100SS. This had the filler cap moved forward to between the two top mountings and an anti-froth tower added at the top rear corner in place of the old cap.

This continued to 1963 which was the year the unit 650s first appeared with a tank much as that of the

LEFT BELOW *Oil pressure switch as fitted from 1969 with warning light in headlamp shell. Here on a T120*

BELOW *The under seat area of a T100T Daytona in 1970*

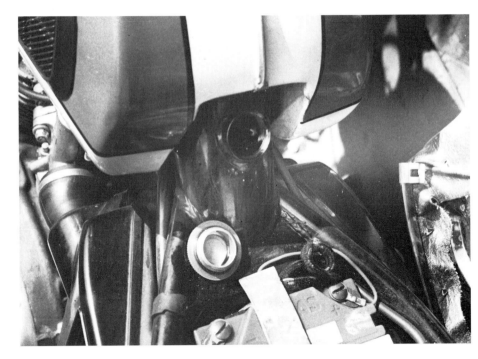

The oil filler and cap of the 1972 oil-in-frame T120. The air filter connection can also be seen

T100SS but with rubber top mountings. For 1964 it changed the lower fixing from a bolt to a rubber isolated spigot and a drain plug was added. The smaller twins all changed to this form in 1964 with a right-angle bracket welded to the tank base for the spigot to lock into. A drain plug also appeared and this one tank continued on all smaller models for 1965 while the 650s continued with theirs.

For 1966 the tank became common to all models although the spigot bracket continued to vary between the 650s and the others. The tank was new but its filler remained about halfway along the top. In its neck went a regulating screw for a metered oil supply to the rear chain taken off the return line. In front of the filler went an anti-froth tower with vent. The top tank mountings were changed to a rolled form, like a door hinge, and these went round rubber mounts bolted to the frame.

There is some confusion as to the capacity of the 1966 tank, also used by all models in 1967, with one contemporary report indicating an increase from five to six pints. The parts lists add to this as while the 650s are given as five pints, six US pints and, in one case, five US pints, all these are also quoted as 2.8 litres, other than one printing error. All this agrees as it should with only one tank being used. But the list for the smaller twins using the same tank quotes six pints and 3.5 litres or six US pints for the US models.

This discrepancy continued while the two ranges shared the same tanks until 1970 when the 650 is listed at $5\frac{1}{2}$ pints or the correct 3.125 litres, maybe in an attempt to cover both stools at once while the 500 was still listed at six pints or 3.4 litres.

The tank was changed for 1968 in respect of the

rocker feed in the return line and this tank was also used for 1969. For 1970 the tank capacity was increased as indicated by the various volumes given and changed again for the 500 in 1971 by the deletion of the adjustable oil supply for the rear chain.

The 650 range went over to the oil-in-frame arrangement in 1971 which reduced the capacity to four pints. With the new frame came a set of pipes and connections to suit.

Rear chain lubrication
This is taken from the primary chaincase on all models from 1939 to 1970. The pre-unit machines have an adjustable needle screw with locking spring at the rear of the primary chaincase. All models use the same parts which must be in good condition. The oil holes must be free from obstruction.

The unit construction models were fitted with a tube and jet from 1957 to 1965. The jets are common to all models and years but the tubes are different in the 650s. In 1966 the feed came from the oil tank return line with regulating screw in the filler orifice and this was used to 1970. After that it was down to the owner to deal with.

Engine oil grade
An area of myths and folklore over which owners argue well into the night.

In the beginning there were straight oils that were thick or thin. They had no additives and did not last over long. The grade of oil was classed by an SAE number, usually 20, 30, 40, or 50 and the rider changed to a thinner one for the winter and back again in the summer.

The additives were put in the oil to prevent oxidation, inhabit rust, improve the load level and many more to give monogrades. These still needed to be changed to suit the season but lasted longer and are especially suited to all ball and roller engines which many motorcycle engines are.

Finally there came multigrades which combined the merits of thick oil for hot running with thin oil for easy starting, even in winter. These had an unfortunate time when first introduced but those days are long gone and modern quality multigrades are excellent for engines with plain bearings. Without them cold starting would be very difficult indeed.

This leaves the Triumph twin owner well astride the fence as he has plain big ends and ball or roller mains in most cases but in fact the loading of the bearings is such that a multigrade is an easy choice. SAE 20W/50 is readily available and better for an engine with some rolling element bearings than the SAE 10W/40 used by oriental machines with their many plain bearings and consequent high drag at low temperature.

Many will disagree with the above and prefer to run on monograde which is their choice. In which case SAE 30 in summer and SAE 20 in winter were the Triumph recommendations with one grade thicker in hotter overseas climates. These heavier grades are recommended for home use by Triumph experts.

Transmission oil grades

Monogrades are more usual in these areas which are not subject to the same temperature range as the engine. SAE 20 goes in the primary chaincase with an alternative of SAE 10W/30 in the later unit engines. From 1970 the same grade of oil as is in the engine must go into the chaincase as the two areas are connected.

The gearbox is separate and an SAE 50 oil was specified for many years but as the power went up and heavier loads were generated on the gears this was changed to an EP90 gear oil. This has a similar viscosity to the earlier engine grade but is better able to cope with the stresses involved.

Checking the oil level of a 1972 T120 using dipstick provided. Note cramped electrics behind battery and minimal tool storage space behind that

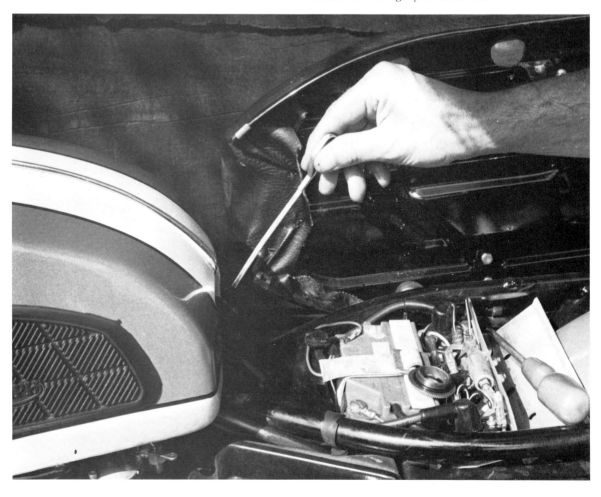

7 Electrics

This is an area which gives many owners considerable difficulties and even some very skilled engine fitters will own that it is all a big mystery. The problem stems in part because you never see the substance, only the effects. Also, like an oil leak, it can spread all over the place so easily without any obvious evidence as to where it comes from.

If you intend to do a restoration you have to accept that you must wrestle with the subject or it could defeat you. Fortunately real electrical faults are rare despite what you may think as nearly all troubles are caused by mechanical failures in some way or other. Most can be cured by correct assembly and settings. Remember the need to comply with current local legislation.

Things to remember that help are as follows. The system has two sides, one dealing with charging and the other with use. Although they may connect in operation and control they can be thought of as two distinct areas and dealt with accordingly. The most common fault is a poor earth which is simply a poor connection for the return of the current rather than its supply. Also very common is a poor connection in the supply leads. Finally buy the tools for the job which means lighter spanners or wrenches, smaller screwdrivers, pliers, cutters, electrician's soldering iron and a small multimeter. The last does not have to be anything special as continuity checks will be its main job but it will help a great deal. An old ammeter, preferably with centre zero, and reading 15 amps or so, is also worth having to check current flow in and out of the battery. Even if the machine has one it is not always convenient to use so a meter with leads can be better.

Triumph electric systems

The twins ran the full range of postwar possibilities with their electrics from magneto to coil and dynamo to zener diode control. They began with magneto ignition and dynamo charging with a separate control box containing regulator and cut-out. Prewar this was by a mag-dyno mounted behind the cylinders but postwar the two functions were split with the magneto remaining where it was and the dynamo mounting on the top front of the crankcase.

In 1953 the alternator first appeared on the 5T and a distributor with coil bolted above it replaced the magneto. This went onto the 6T in 1954 but the other pre-unit models continued with dynamos to 1959. For 1960 the 650s all had an alternator but only the 6T used coil ignition as the others retained their magnetos to 1962.

All unit construction engines were fitted with alternators and most had coil ignition. The early machines had the points mounted in a housing behind the cylinders but from 1963 or 1964 they moved to a housing in the timing chest. Some models had energy transfer ignition and later a capacitor discharge design powered from the alternator was available.

The models changed from 6 to 12-volt systems during the 1960s and with this came better control of the output using a zener diode. This simplified the wiring and improved the electric performance.

Magneto types

Both BTH and Lucas magnetos were used from 1946 to 1953 but prewar the twins used the Lucas mag-dyno unit. This had manual control of the ignition advance but this feature was not continued for the early postwar machines. These were built with either make of magneto and the automatic advance unit incorporated within the driving gear in the timing case. The Lucas design was by bob weights but BTH used five rollers in a shaped cage to give the same effect. The fixings of the magnetos were all by three nuts to the back of the timing chest and this never altered. All magnetos were of the anti-clockwise rotation type as viewed from the driven end.

In 1949 a manual advance BTH unit appeared on the TR5 and this was also fitted to the T100 in 1951. In 1952 a manually controlled Lucas magneto also became available for these two models and by the end of 1953 the 5T and 6T had changed to coil ignition. At the same time the use of BTH magnetos stopped as did that of automatic advance.

Thus for 1954 the T100, T110 and TR5 were all

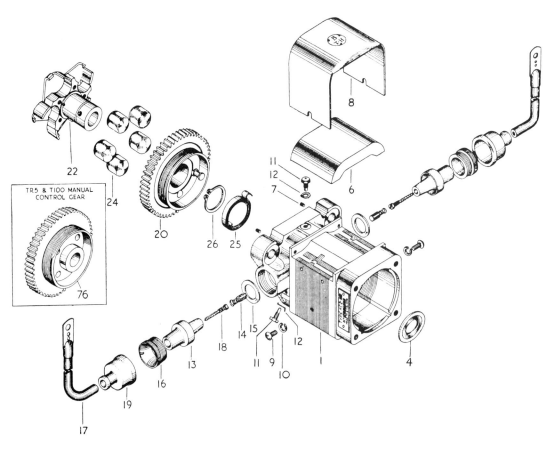

TR5 & T100 MANUAL
CONTROL GEAR

Parts list drawing of the BTH magneto used from 1946 to
1953. Similar to Lucas but preferred by many owners

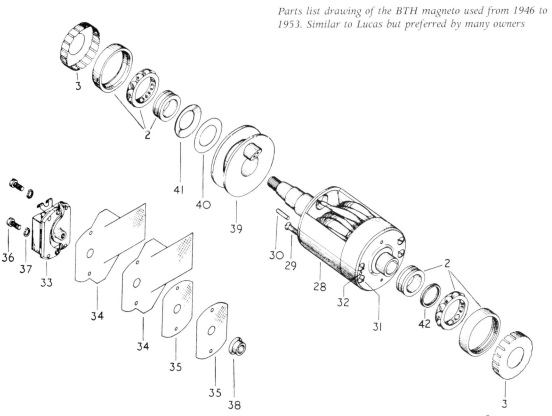

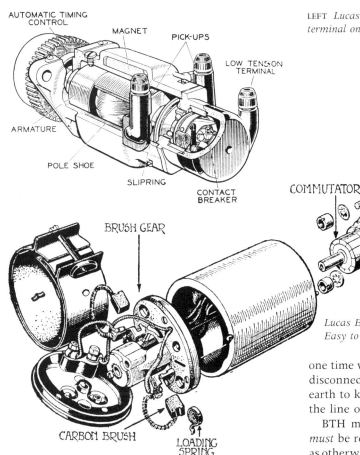

AUTOMATIC TIMING CONTROL

MAGNET

PICK-UPS

LOW TENSION TERMINAL

ARMATURE

POLE SHOE

SLIPRING

CONTACT BREAKER

LEFT Lucas twin cylinder magneto type K2F with cut-out terminal on end cap

BRUSH GEAR

CARBON BRUSH

LOADING SPRING

COMMUTATOR

STEEL PINION

ARMATURE

Lucas E3HM dynamo exploded to show its construction. Easy to work on

fitted with a manual Lucas magneto with either a clip held end cap or a screw-on one where the alternative Wader magneto was used. For 1955 these were joined by a racing magneto offered for the TR5 only while in 1956 only the Wader unit was used with the racing one an option for both TR models. This continued without change for two years but for 1959 the Wader was specified for the T100, T110, T120 and TR6 with four options for all. These were a version with modifications to end cap, advance control, armature and slip ring, this one and the standard one but with auto-advance, and a racing unit.

For 1960 the T100 and T120 changed to auto-advance but the TR6 remained on manual and both used variations of the same instrument. This continued as it was for 1961 but for 1962 both T120 and TR6 used the same magneto with auto-advance.

Magneto service

This concerns itself with the points gap which is 0.012 in. and the brushes. There are several of the latter for in addition to the high tension lead pick ups in each side of the body there is a brush in the rear of the points plate on the 1954 on magnetos and an earth brush. In many cases there is also one in the cap for the earthing lead and if the magneto fails to work this is

one time when a connection to earth is not wanted so disconnect it. In use it takes the low tension side to earth to kill the magneto and an intermittent fault in the line or the button can be a trial to deal with.

BTH magnetos have safety gap screws and these *must* be removed before any real dismantling is done as otherwise the slip ring will be damaged. All brushes need to be examined for cracks and checked for free movement in their holders and general good condition. If worn they should be replaced.

Note that some Lucas magnetos also have a safety gap screw and the same rule applies. Also that on occasion a brush or gap screw may be masked by a label so care must always be exercised.

Magneto renovation

There is not a great deal more that can be done with a magneto other than to clean it and maybe replace the bearings. Dismantling is straightforward but mark parts first as often they could be reversed. Once apart the details can be cleaned and inspected, especially for any cracks that could leak the high tension to earth.

It is a fairly skilled job to replace and set up magneto bearings and even more tricky to change a condenser or rewind an armature. Unless you are really competent in this work it should be sent to a specialist. This is especially true if the magneto has lost some of its magnetism and is therefore sparking poorly, if at all. Magnetizing equipment is complex and expensive so not really a practical proposition for any other than the professional.

Grease the bearings on assembly which should give no problems. Do make sure all the little insulating washers and bushes are in the right place. More ignition systems fail to work after a rebuild for this reason than any other. Fit the leads, clamp the magneto in the vice, earth the plugs to it and give it a spin. Anti-clock of course. Check that the earthing connection does its job.

Dynamo types

Prewar the dynamo was strapped to the top of the magneto and thus ran in a clockwise direction. All postwar models had the dynamo in front of the engine running anti-clockwise.

Only Lucas dynamos were fitted and from 1946–49 the type E3H was used. From 1950 the more powerful E3L went on all models having first appeared on the TR5 in 1949. During 1952 from engine 19706NA the electrical system changed from negative to positive earth and remained this way to the end of dynamos for Triumph twins in 1959.

Dynamo drive

Postwar this was by gear from the exhaust camshaft. The gear was held in place by a single bolt and was small enough to pass through the hole in the rear of the timing chest. Thus by removing the clamping band and one acorn nut the instrument could be withdrawn. For competition use this was a popular feature and a cover plate was available for some years to fill the resulting hole.

The prewar dynamo was driven by a gear on the magneto armature and built into it was a slipping clutch to protect the parts. This is a simple design and should be set to slip under a torque of 4–10 ft lb.

Dynamo testing

This can begin on the machine by disconnecting the leads to the dynamo. Then join the two terminals, D and F, and connect a voltmeter from the join to the dynamo body. Run the machine so the dynamo speed is up to 1000 rpm and look for the voltage reading to rise smoothly and quickly to ten volts. Don't run the dynamo faster in an attempt to push the volts value up. If there is no reading at all look to the brush gear, if it is about 0.5 volt the field winding is suspect and if between 1.5 – 2 volts then the armature winding is the likely culprit.

For any further work the dynamo will need to be dismantled.

Dynamo service

Mark parts before taking them apart and proceed with some delicacy as some items are rather brittle. Clean all the connections to reduce contact resistance and check that all wires are in good order and not frayed in any way. Examine the brushes and replace if worn down to about $\frac{5}{16}$ in. Make sure the brushes, whether old or renewed, can move freely in their boxes and that the brush springs are strong enough to hold them in contact with the commutator.

This last will need cleaning and if burnt may need machining to restore it to true round. Should this be needed remove the minimum of matErial and be prepared to undercut the commutator segments. Also examine the wire connections to the segments for any signs of overheating which may indicate problems in the armature. Clean out all the carbon dust as it can short out the insulated wires.

Armature rewinds and field coil replacement are best left to specialists. The first requires special equipment but the second can be attempted with fewer facilities. There are two problems to overcome. First is the single fixing screw which must be tight and second is ensuring the new coil is really home in the body. Service departments used a special driver for the first and an expander for the second problem but both can be overcome in the home workshop.

Grease the two ball races of the longer unit and the single one of the shorter. Lubricate the bush of the latter with thin machine oil but not too much or it will be all over the commutator. Reassemble with care to ensure everything goes back where it came from.

The finished result can be tested off the engine by connecting it to a battery so that it becomes an electric motor. This is done by joining the F and D terminals and connecting the join and the dynamo body to a six-volt battery. The body connection is to the normally earthed terminal and if all is well the armature will revolve. This is not as good a test as that with a voltmeter but is useful if the engine is by now apart and not to be available for some while.

Regulator unit

This is also known as the compensated voltage control unit or cvc and may be referred to as the automatic voltage control or avc. Not to be confused with the later cvc used for cars where the initials stand for current voltage control and the unit has three coils in its assembly under the cover.

The motorcycle cvc is simpler with just one control coil plus the cut-out under the lid. It has fewer connections than most cars with just four terminals in a row and these are usually connected to wires which plug in and are held by a strip secured by two screws. The wires are positioned by this strip and the screws are of different sizes to prevent a reversal of the connections.

The early twins used the MCR1 regulator up to 1949 but for 1950 the MCR2 was introduced. This differed in that the control resistor became a carbon disc fitted to the main frame behind the coils and can be recognized by a swelling in the back of the cover put there to clear it. On these two models the terminals were labelled FADE but for 1954 the unit was changed to a RB107 which had its connections in the order FAED.

The cvc is a delicate electro-mechanical assembly and must be treated as such. It can be set up and

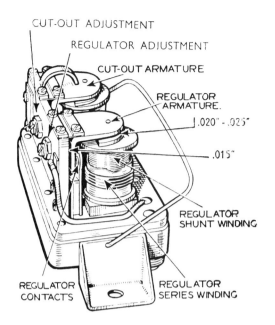

CUT-OUT ADJUSTMENT

REGULATOR ADJUSTMENT

CUT-OUT ARMATURE

REGULATOR
ARMATURE.

.020" - .025"

.015"

REGULATOR
SHUNT WINDING

REGULATOR
CONTACTS

REGULATOR
SERIES WINDING

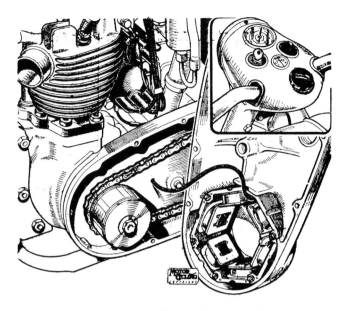

ABOVE *The alternator as installed on the 1953 Speed Twin plus distributor, coil and nacelle layout*

LEFT ABOVE *The Lucas cvc regulator type MCR1 as used up to 1949*

LEFT CENTRE *The RB107 regulator used from 1954 with rearranged terminal order*

LEFT BELOW *Lucas MCR2 used from 1950 to 1953 with carbon disc resistor as control element*

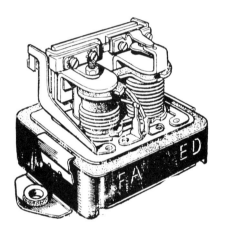

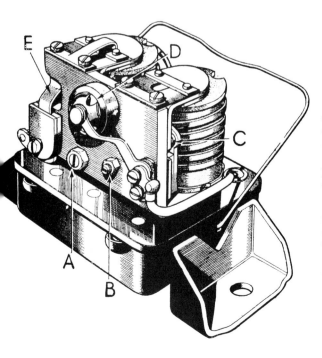

adjusted by the owner but this must be done precisely or the system will not work as it should. Really no different to valve clearances or ignition timing.

Regulator function

Two jobs are done inside the cvc unit. The regulator side switches a resistor into series with the field coil to reduce the field current and thus the generated output. It is in a state of vibration while doing this. The cut-out is simply a switch which disconnects the dynamo from the battery when needed to prevent it trying to motor it which would discharge the battery.

The confusion with the unit usually arises because

105

the theoretical circuit diagram, practical wiring diagram and the unit all look completely different. Further confusion arises in that the internal frame is used as part of the electric circuit but is not an earth. In truth it connects via the cut-out points to the battery supply line so is insulated from the mounting frame.

Regulator service

If you decide to work in the cvc trace out the electrical circuit first so you know where each part fits into the scheme of things. It will then be much easier to check each item for continuity or open circuit using your meter. In most cases the only problem will be the mechanical aspects of the contacts, their cleanliness and their adjustment. With these dealt with the circuits are most likely to all function as they should.

Looking at the coils, the one on the left is the regulator with a few turns of heavy gauge wire about its middle. The adjustments are first by moving the armature which is the bent steel part pulled by the coil magnetism and carrying one of the contacts. Next by bending the fixed contact on the MCR units and finally with an adjuster screw at the rear.

Air gaps are required between the vertical leg of the armature that carries the contact and the frame, also between the horizontal leg and the bobbin core on the MCR. The first should be 0.015 in. on the MCR1 and 0.020 in. on the MCR2. The second figure is 0.020 in. for both but with a tolerance of plus 0.005 in. on the MCR1 and minus 0.008 in. on the MCR2. On the MCR2, with the armature held against the bobbin core, the points gap should be between 0.006 and 0.017 in.

The RB107 has a different method of adjustment. The armature screws are undone, a feeler gauge 0.021 in. put between the armature and the bobbin and the screws done up. The contacts are then adjusted so they just touch with the feeler gauge still in place.

The remaining adjustments are made with the cvc wired to the machine. Put card between the cut-out points and disconnect lead from A terminal. Insert voltmeter between D and E and run dynamo at about 3000 rpm. At 20°C the reading should be 8.0 – 8.4 volts and can be adjusted with the screw at the rear. If the temperature rises deduct 0.2 volts for every 10°C and if it falls add it. Then run the dynamo at about 4500 rpm when the reading should not exceed 8.9 volts. Do all this quickly or errors will occur so if in doubt do it in steps.

Cut-out setting

For the MCR2 the armature to frame air gap should be 0.014 in. and to the bobbin core 0.011 to 0.015 in. With these two gaps held correct by gauges, press the armature down on them and check that the gap between armature and stop plate arm is 0.030 to 0.034 in. Bend the arm to adjust. Then place a 0.025 in

gauge between armature shim and core face and check that the contact gap is between 0.002 to 0.006 in. Bend the fixed contact bracket to adjust.

The RB107 is set by pressing the armature down to the core face and checking the gap between its stop arm and its tongue which should be 0.025 to 0.040 in. Bend the stop arm to adjust. Then adjust the fixed contact blade to give a blade deflection of 0.010 to 0.020 in. when the armature is pressed firmly down on the core face.

Cut-out checking

This is done on the machine and a full test covers both cut-in and -out. For the first connect an ammeter in the lead from dynamo D to cvc D and a voltmeter between there and E. Gradually bring the engine speed up and watch for the voltmeter pointer to flick back as the points close. This should occur at 6.3–6.7 volts and is adjusted by the screw which increases the setting when turned clockwise. The ammeter should show a charge when the points close. When the engine stops the ammeter discharge reading is taken and should be between three and five amps when the contacts open.

The cut-out check is done by detaching lead A from the cvc and connecting a voltmeter between terminal A and E. Run the dynamo up to 3000 rpm and then let its speed die slowly away. The voltage should be between 4.8–5.5 volts when the contacts open and the reading drops to zero.

Regulator oddments

The resistance used in the cvc which is placed in the field circuit can be measured if you have a good meter. The value for a carbon one is 36 – 45 ohms while the wire wound type is 27–33 ohms.

If your machine has the short E3 dynamo fitted it would normally have a MCR1 cvc. If this is not available the MCR2 listed under part number 37144A should be used.

You can use the machine without battery as long as the cvc is working correctly. This may not be fully legal in some way but can be useful in an emergency. However, if the battery is in circuit it must be topped up or the control is fooled into providing excess current which can ruin battery, dynamo and cvc.

The contact points do get dirty and may need cleaning. If they do they will need re-setting for sure.

Should the dynamo polarity have reversed itself, which does happen, just hold the cut out points together for a second or two and then pull them apart.

Do make sure that dynamo D is connected to cvc D and F to F. Although the dynamo leads are held by a kidney shaped plate and the cvc one is non-reversible they could have been switched at some time. Detach and check by meter as they often run out of sight on the machine.

Modern regulators

By using modern electronic components the problems of the electro-mechanical cvc can be removed with solid state devices. This is electronic engineering quite outside most people's knowledge but specialist suppliers make it easy for the rest of us.

A unit is available to replace the cvc and is one waterproof box which does the same job and enables the machine to convert to 12 volts. Battery and bulbs also need changing but not the horn and the change boosts output so better lights can be fitted. The new assembly is small enough to tuck out of sight so the alteration is not at all obvious for owners who wish to keep up appearances.

While this change departs from total originality it is to be recommended for any machine used on a regular basis in modern traffic where good lights are essential. The move to 12 volts not only greatly improves the electrical efficiency of the system but also allows halogen lights to be used to give a further bonus.

Alternator

Triumph were among the first of the major firms to adopt the crankshaft mounted alternator on a large capacity, four stroke, road model. With it came the advantages of no touching parts to wear and other delights but these included control problems and boiled batteries so all was not quite as good as it might have been. In time the zener diode came along and with it arrived better control and 12-volt systems.

The first model to use an alternator was the 5T in 1953 which was fitted with the Lucas RM12 system. During the year three series, A B and C, were made and all used in turn although all B type were converted to C as far as was possible. The series A had four leads from the stator and a double rectifier while the B and C had a single bank rectifier. Of the last two the C also had a resistance and six leads from the stator. Both A and C stators were of overall hexagonal shape with five fixing screws.

In 1954 a change was made to the RM14 unit and this went onto the 6T as well as the 5T. It was similar in form to the RM12 but with three leads only and for 1955 the thin stator was fitted and this continued on to 1958. For 1959 a change was made to the circular RM15 which became standard for all pre-unit machines in 1960. In 1962 the RM19 replaced the RM15 with larger diameter rotor with straight sides and not recessed as on the RM13 and RM15. The RM12 and RM14 also had straight sided rotors but these were of a larger size than the RM19.

The smaller unit twins began with the RM13/15 which used the RM13 stator and longer RM15 rotor to boost the output a little. In 1962 the RM19 was adopted and it also went on the unit 650 the following year. In 1969 all models changed to the RM21 unit with encapsulated windings.

In addition to the standard systems there is the

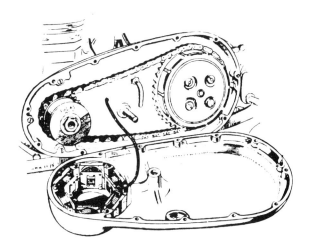

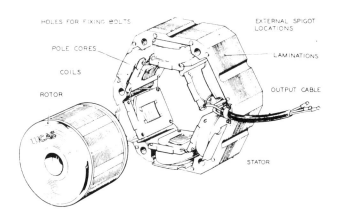

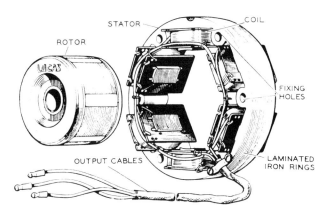

ABOVE *Lucas alternators with RM14 above RM15. Note changes to both rotor and stator shapes*

TOP *The Lucas RM12 as installed with the stator fitted to the outer chaincase and this dowelled to the inner*

aspect which may help a good deal when sorting out the connections to the rectifier.

Make sure the rotor is a good fit on the crankshaft. If it is not it is possible to machine it to locate on a made up spacer against the engine sprocket and with care and ingenuity to achieve a better design than the original. This will also allow a damaged crankshaft end to be overcome by using other means to hold the rotor true.

It is possible for the rotor centre to become loose within the assembly and this can give rise to a nasty knocking noise in the engine. A cure is to machine away the alloy side enough to allow the core to come out and then to refit it using a Loctite gap filler.

Rectifier

Early alternators had their output turned into direct current by massive selenium plate rectifiers. The

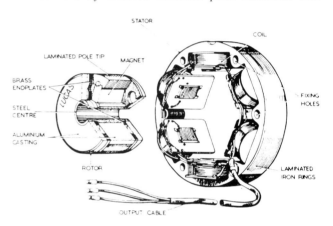

ABOVE *How the rotor is built up. A loose centre can be repaired with care*

RIGHT *The later RM18, a thinner version of the RM19 used by Triumph. The RM20/19 is thicker still and numbers of laminations are respectively 25, 32 and 45 in the rotor and 14, 16 and 26 in the stator*

original boxes soon became a smaller set of four plates on a single central bolt and in time this assembly was replaced by a similar silicon diode rectifier.

All the four plate types give full wave rectification and the centre stud is one of the direct current connections and must be treated as such. It connects to the earthed side of the battery. The three plate connections have the other direct current line in the middle flanked by the two alternating current ones. These last two may connect either way round as reversal at that point will not affect the rectifier operation at all.

The rectifier can be cleaned and its electrical function checked for the correct working of each diode. These must pass current one way but not the other and a meter or battery and bulb will act as a tester. Do not move the central clamping nut or the device will fail. The nut tension controls the efficiency of the unit and must be left alone. Care is therefore needed when fixing the device to the machine.

energy transfer set up used by the T100A for 1960–61 with five leads from the stator. This model may be run minus lights and battery and requires that the rotor is accurately timed to the engine so a dowel is used to locate it to the engine sprocket. The same arrangement was also used in 1966–67 under the guise of AC ignition to suit some US requirements for off road use.

Alternator checking

There is not a great deal that can be done other than cleaning and inspection. Check that the rotor has been running clear of the coil poles and look at the wiring for any damage. Use a meter to check continuity and insulation and establish which coils are connected together and how the wires attached to them. Compare this with your wiring diagram and keep notes on this

Alternator control

On the face of it the stator coils connect to the rectifier which connects to the battery to complete the circuit.

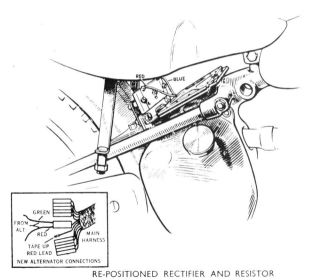

RE-POSITIONED RECTIFIER AND RESISTOR

Unfortunately there are complications. First the output needs to be controlled to suit the load and secondly it would be nice to be able to start even with a flat battery. To cope with these problems introduces complications in the switches and wiring and the result can be confusion.

The control is done for 6-volt systems by stator coil switching. The basic control is that two coils are permanently connected and with the lights off the remaining four are short circuited to reduce the output of the two in use. With the pilot light on the four are open circuit so they don't affect the two and with headlight on all six are connected. This means that the light switch has to be joined electrically to the charging circuit.

Problem two is overcome by switching four coils to supply the ignition circuit direct to leave two to assist the battery on an emergency basis.

Where a 12-volt system is in use a zener diode is used for control. At first this was in conjunction with the light switch so that either four or six coils were in circuit but this soon changed so that all six were permanently connected and the zener diode did the work. The same type of zener diode was fitted from 1964–72 and up to 1967 was mounted on a flat plate. From 1968 a finned heat sink was used to 1972 for the 500 but only to 1970 for the 650. For 1971–72 the zener used the coil mounting bracket as its heat sink.

If the connections are not as they should be or the switch contacts are dirty then all manner of charging problems will arise. The situation is further confused by variations that were available over the years and which may have been incorporated in a system. The mechanical components are generally interchangeable and on the electric side it is just a question of joining wires so anything is possible.

To add to the problems Lucas also changed the wire colours on the RM13/14/15 alternators as the originals

ABOVE *Twin 6 volt batteries installed on a 6T in 1964, the first year for a 12 volt system. By 1966 it applied to all models with a few still with the twin batteries for that year*

LEFT ABOVE *Early and massive rectifier installed under the dualseat. Modern components are minute in comparison*

BELOW *Zener diode installation on the 6T in 1964. The component may be small but it still must have a good sized heat sink*

tended to become indistinguishable. First they were light, mid and dark green. Then light green, green and yellow, dark green. Finally green and white, green and yellow, and green and black. If you don't have an original stator, rectifier and harness you could have variations.

Further complications arise in that where the machine has magneto ignition the above applies with two coils always in circuit. For models with coil ignition it was common to have four in use and the mid and dark green connections reversed. Another version had them all joined together to put all six coils in circuit all the time. The lead from rectifier to light switch, usually light green, may be simply disconnected and taped up as this has a further trimming effect on the output.

To sort out what you have and how to connect it you need to work out the alternator leads and circuit, the rectifier leads and the switch circuits. Then use the wiring diagram for the model and trace out what happens in each switch position. Not easy, I know, as the diagrams don't normally give the switch circuits and without those it is hard hence the need to check the switch itself with a meter and write it all down.

Alternator voltage conversion

This is a popular way of getting more out of the system and can easily be carried out. It simplifies the wiring as all six alternator coils are permanently connected to the rectifier which has the zener diode fitted between its supply terminal and earth. The actual details vary according to the machine circuit but can be sorted out using the wiring diagram and the information already established for the switches.

When first introduced the then available zeners could not cope with controlling the full output when there was no headlight load so the switched connection was still needed. This had two coils permanently on for machines fitted with a magneto and four where coil ignition was used. Modern zeners can cope.

Battery, ignition coils, bulbs, possibly rectifier and maybe ignition condenser will need changing. The horn is not essential and any ancillaries need to be remembered.

Coil ignition

This was first used on the 5T in 1953, the 6T the year after and the 3TA in 1957. In time all models changed over to it. All pre-unit and unit engines to 1962 have a distributor with one set of points but from then on the points moved into the timing chest and two sets were provided to fire the coils.

Distributor and timing cover points

Essentially you clean and inspect. Replace the points, oil the advance mechanism and make sure there are no cracks in the cap or the rotor arm. See if the bearings

The zener diode itself with push on connection on the 1964 Thunderbird

Checking the points gap on a 1966 T120. An easy job with them in the timing cover and the cam on the end of the camshaft

are in good order and that the spindle turns freely. Attend to anything in trouble and rebuild.

Do make sure the points wire connection is the correct side of its insulation washers and check it with the meter.

Inspect the small pivot points in the advance mechanism and repair or replace as necessary. Replace the advance springs if these are tired.

Distributor types
The 5T began with a unit giving it a 15 degree advance at the cam, and thus 30 degrees on the crankshaft, and this remained in use for all years of that model. The unit fitted in 1954 had a revised spring set and was used on the 6T as well but while this continued on the 5T to 1958 the 6T changed for 1955. Its new unit had the advance reduced to $12\frac{1}{2}$ degrees and remained in use to 1959. For 1960 the old DKX2A was replaced by type 18D2 which continued in use to 1962.

Timing chest points
Two types were used, these being the 4CA up to 1967 and the 6CA from 1968. The correct advance unit should be used and attention is on the same lines as for the distributor system.

Energy transfer and AC ignition
In these designs some of the alternator windings are connected directly to a special ignition coil. This allows the machine to run without battery on the lines of one fitted with a magneto, but the ignition timing is critical. Points cam and advance unit are specially designed for the job and must be used for it to operate effectively. The distributor range is limited to five degrees and essential to the workings. Otherwise it is checked over as the others.

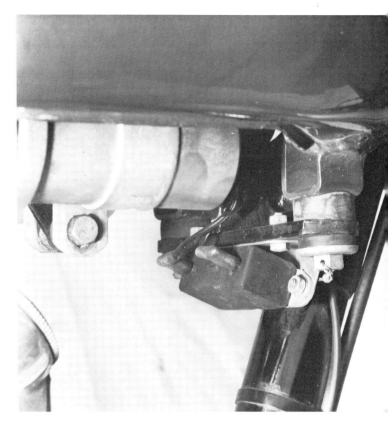

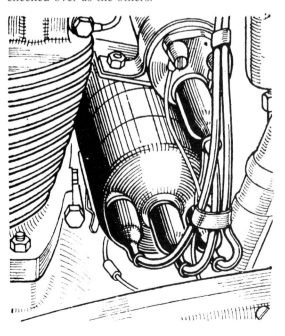

ABOVE *Access cover introduced in 1968 to enable a strobe to be used to check the ignition timing*

TOP *Location of the ignition condensers up under the tank and close to the coils rather than the points. Works just as well and shown on a 1968 T100T*

LEFT *Distributor in old magneto position with coil above as adopted for the Speed Twin in 1953. Hardly very accessible*

Ignition timing

This is often a source of great concern to owners and in one sense this is important. On the other hand the actual figure used may be less so. What is often forgotten is that the engine may be 20 or more years old, worn in various ways and running on a different blend of fuel to that available to it when new.

So while the original figure makes a good starting point it is not sacrosanct. The old-fashioned technique of advancing the setting until the engine pinks on a rising road and then backing it off a little, still works well even if it is awkward to carry out on some models.

Check the timing you decide to use on full advance and on both cylinders. The retard figure is much less important so may be ignored although the particular will check it also to be sure. It is not uncommon for a variation to arise between the cylinders and this should be removed if possible as the engine will run much better. Beware of slack in the drive when checking and for slack in distributor bearings which can give a false reading. Recheck if in any doubt.

Electronic ignition

A worthwhile modification for late type machines and available in various forms to replace magneto or coil ignition. It is also possible to adapt them to existing parts to retain the original drive system.

The installation instructions supplied with the kit should be carefully followed especially regarding the timing. Electronic advance is normal so the mechanical device must be discarded or locked up and the timing will have to be checked with a strobe. Therefore a timing mark will be needed and this must be checked with a timing disc before the ignition is set up.

In addition to the electronic ignition kits a further option is open in the form of capacitor ignition using the alternator as a power source, a 12-volt zener diode control, a storage capacitor and the original points and advance mechanism. Effectively a variation of the earlier energy transfer system but much better in use.

Spark plug, cap and lead

The plugs should be replaced by a modern equivalent although many owners do like to keep the originals if they are to hand. Some refit them for a concours but for normal use a new pair of plugs should be fitted. Grades are listed in an appendix.

The caps should be the type that contains a suppressor and the leads must be in good condition. Make sure the ends are clean and make a good connection or an odd misfire may appear.

Lighting

Renovation of the lights is mainly by replacement as most of the parts are fragile and are either complete and working or in pieces. The bulb containers may need repair work carried out and finishing which should be done in the same way as any other item.

For any machine being used on the road the current legal requirements need to be considered as some of the earlier fittings do not comply with them. In particular rear lamps have increased in size and needed to for modern traffic.

Triumph used a variety of lighting systems over the years but essentially most changes were brought about by alterations to the electrical system or by styling. Early models had an instrument panel set in the fuel tank, then came the nacelle and then separate headlamp shells for the more sporting models. To suit these changes the switches also moved about.

Headlamp and switch types

The Speed Twin was first built with a large headlamp controlled by a switch on the tank top instrument panel. Included in this was an ammeter, oil gauge and panel lamp. This arrangement was also used by the T100 and 3T until the nacelle came in 1949. With its appearance the switch and ammeter moved into its top surface with the speedometer and were joined by a cut-out button. The oil gauge was no longer fitted. This arrangement was used by the 3T to 1951, 5T to 1952, 6T to 1953, T100 to 1959, T110 to 1959 and for the T120 for 1959 only.

The TR5 came in 1949 with a separate headlamp shell with a small panel set in this in which were mounted the ammeter and light switch. This arrangement went onto the TR6 in 1956 and continued up to 1959.

During this time the lamps themselves changed. All the early models had the pilot bulb set in the main reflector and prewar and in 1946 the headlamp glass was flat. For 1947 it became domed and continued in the same form when the nacelle appeared, to which it was fixed by an adaptor ring.

In 1952 two changes were made on the road models although the TR5 continued as it was with its quickly detachable shell with plug and socket in the wiring harness. The light unit for the others became a pre-focus type with the bulb dropped in from the rear and this greatly improved the light output. Less popular was the pilot lamp which had to become separate. It was fitted below the main lamp with a rectangular lens nearly invisible on the road.

By 1956 the technical problem of mounting the pilot bulb in the prefocus light unit was solved so the underslung pilot went. At the same time the TR5 and

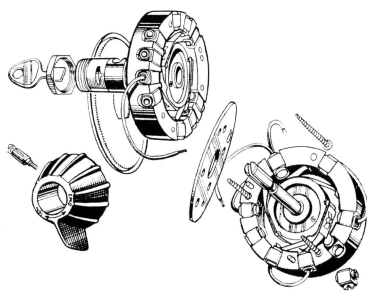

General construction of the combined lights and ignition switches. Can be renovated with some care but rather delicate

LEFT BELOW *Plug and socket connection to the headlight on a TR6 in 1961*

BELOW *The finned zener diode heat sink adopted for 1968 and shown installed of a T120 from the following year*

TR6 adopted prefocus light units and from then on that form was fitted to all models.

With the introduction of the alternator on the 5T in 1953 the controls were modified to light switch, ignition switch and ammeter in the nacelle. For 1954 the two switches were amalgamated into one unit for both 5T and 6T and continued in this style to 1958 and 1962 respectively. It also went onto the 3TA in 1957 and the 5TA in 1959, continuing on both models to 1963.

In 1960 a new style appeared for the T120 and TR6 with a separate headlamp with ammeter and the light switch mounted on a small panel under the right side of the seat nose. This was used to 1962 and also on the T100SS for 1961–62 although for that model a combined lights and ignition switch was fitted on the left skirt beneath the seat nose. The T100A which preceded it retained the nacelle and used the early arrangement of light switch, ammeter and cut-out for 1960–61.

For 1963 the 6T kept its nacelle but changed to separate lights and ignition switches plus an ammeter mounted in it. The T90, T100, T120 and TR6 all had separate headlamp shells with ammeter and separate lights and ignition switches mounted on the left panel just below the seat nose.

In 1964 the 3TA and 5TA adopted the same system as the 6T and they and the others continued as they were to 1966 and the end of the nacelle. For some export machines direct lighting was offered and this meant a smaller headlamp and revised switches to suit the electrics.

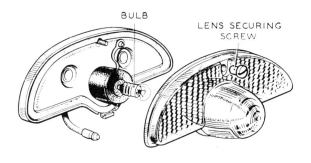

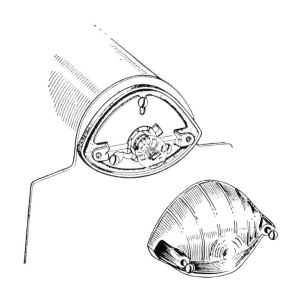

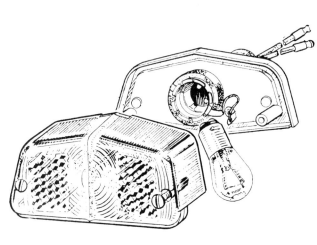

Various Lucas rear lights. Top is the 590, centre the 529 and bottom the 564 rectangular unit used by many machines

In 1967 there were changes with the separate headlamp shell continuing with its ammeter which was joined by the light switch and red and green warning lamps. The ignition switch stayed on the left panel for that year but for 1968 moved to the left headlamp shell support or fork shroud. This was unchanged until 1971 when all models lost the ammeter but gained one more warning lamp in amber. The light switch stayed in the shell and the ignition one moved to the right side panel on the 650s only.

Bulb types and ratings should be to the parts list if a standard build is sought but for those riders seeking an improvement there are replacement light units available. If you have a 12-volt system a halogen lamp can be used and this is well worth fitting if you seek the best in lighting.

Stop and tail lamp

Prewar, and for early postwar models, the standard fitment was a Lucas MT110 tail lamp with round ruby glass. Also available in 1938 was a combined stop and tail lamp offered as an extra. It was not listed postwar until 1950 and the single tail continued to be available to 1952.

For 1951 the lamp body form changed from parallel cylinder to tapered which increased its rear area a little and for 1953 just one stop and tail lamp was listed with a new rectangular form and a moulded red plastic lens. This was the Lucas Diacon 525 which became the type 564 in 1955 with the addition of an integral rear reflector. This replaced the twin reflector bolts which held the base of the rear number plate for 1953–54 to provide this function.

The type 564 was used on all models to 1968, missed 1969 on the 650s only, and was fitted to all for 1970. The type 679 was used for machines with AC ignition in 1966–67, for the 650s in 1969 and on all models in 1971–72. It was also fitted to the high performance 500s from 1966–69.

All bulbs as per the list.

Horn

For most riders trouble with the horn comes in two forms. First it does not work which turns out to be a fault in the horn button or wiring and second is locating it on a basket job.

The first problem should be bypassed by checking with direct wiring between horn and battery. The second is dealt with below. If current is reaching the horn and nothing is happening then it may need adjustment. This may be by a screw in the back or a nut under a cover or there may be no adjustment at all. Where provided it should be moved not more than one or two notches at a time. On a scale of 24 notches equals one full turn of the screw. Six notches from just not sounding should be about right but the current flow should also be monitored and anything over five amps indicates a need for specialist attention.

Rear light unit with side reflectors as fitted by a T100C in 1968

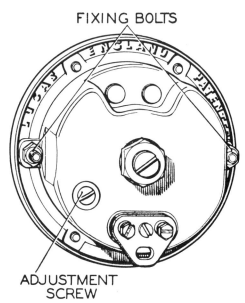

FIXING BOLTS

ADJUSTMENT SCREW

Rear of Lucas horn HF1234 showing adjusting screw and wiring clamp

Don't move the centre screw as this controls the basic points setting and needs special equipment to set. Given this and care the horn may be stripped and the case renovated in the same way as any other part.

Horn types and position

The prewar machines were fitted with a Lucas Altette horn type HF934 which went on a bracket hung from the left saddle fixing, fitting to the underside of the lug. For 1946 the horn had become the HF1234 but it stayed in the same place to 1948. In 1949 the type changed to the HF1235 and it moved into the nacelle other than on the TR5 where the horn type was the HF1441 and the location the left saddle lug.

The HF1441 went onto the road models in 1950 and stayed there until 1960 either in the nacelle or under the left side panel on the TR models. The same horn went onto the 3TA in 1957 and also the 5TA and T100A. A type 8H horn was fitted to the T100SS in 1961 and all the other models in 1962. The location continued to be in the nacelle where this was fitted but varied on the others. The headstock was the area used but the horn was either up under the tank or just below the tank nose.

For 1967 there was a change to a type 6H horn and this remained on the 650 models to 1972. For the smaller twins a further change was made in 1968 to a Clearhooter model. The same maker also supplied the AC horn for some 1966–67 models and the one other variation came on the T120 in 1969. For that year twin Windtone horns operated by a relay were fitted and for 1970 they were changed for a louder pair.

Twin windtone horns installed on a T120 in 1969. This also shows the early type of exhaust balance pipe changed during the year

Battery

The problem on some models is appearance as while the battery lived outside enclosing panels its looks were an important aspect of the left side of the machine. It is possible to obtain facsimiles of the early black bodied 6-volt battery which is one solution. Another is to adapt an old battery by cutting out the interior and fitting a modern one inside it.

For the rest, keep it clean, check the specific gravity and smear protective jelly on the terminals to keep corrosion at bay. Keep the battery working so if off the machine run it down with a three-watt bulb and then recharge it. This will prevent it from collapsing when asked to do some real work.

Up to 1963 all models had a 6-volt system. For 1964 the 6T was fitted with twin batteries and from 1966 all models either had a single 12-volt battery or, in a few cases, two 6-volt ones for that year alone.

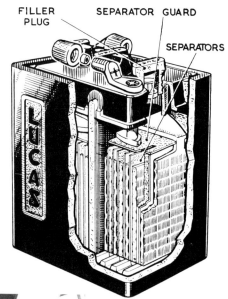

ABOVE *Lucas 6 volt battery type PU7E/11 with screw on connectors*

LEFT *Battery, fuse and some wiring under the seat of a 1968 T120*

LEFT *Same parts and area of a T100S of the same year. Note rectifier and its angled connectors*

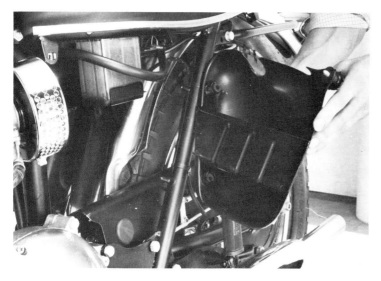

LEFT *Side cover cum toolbox as used by the 650s in 1968 to keep the battery and wiring out of sight*

BELOW *Fitting a Lucar push on connector to a wire. All makes and types reward care in the operation by being reliable*

Ammeter

There is not much one can do to repair one of these so either you have one working or it just acts as a dummy to keep the original appearance. In this case one terminal can be used as a junction point but if the insulation of the case is in any doubt it is best to keep the wiring away from it altogether.

Various ammeter types were used over the years with the 1938 one changing for 1939 and postwar to 1948 to part 36000. From 1949 the dynamo models used part 36129 up to 1959 while the 5T fitted 36168 for 1953 and 36189 for 1954 and on the 6T up to 1962. The TR5 steered its own course with 36084 from 1954.

The 3TA began with the 36189 and for the sporting smaller unit twins from 1961 and the 650s from 1962 the fitment was 36296. For 1968 this was changed to 36403 which was used up to 1970 after which they were not fitted.

Wiring

The prime source of electrical troubles with poor connections, poor earths and intermittent leaks to earth the major problems. Switches can also cause many headaches if the contacts are not clean and making good connections.

If you intend to use the existing harness it must be checked over carefully for any signs of damage or chafing. These must be repaired. All wires must be checked for continuity and for this a wiring diagram is most useful. Most given in manuals are really circuits and very hard to use in practice so it is well worth drawing your own. While doing this you can lay it out as on the machine and add the switch internal connections so it becomes easy to see where the current is supposed to flow.

You will find that one section is to do with charging the battery and connects generator and control. The other is the consumption side and all flows from one point. The item using the current may be directly

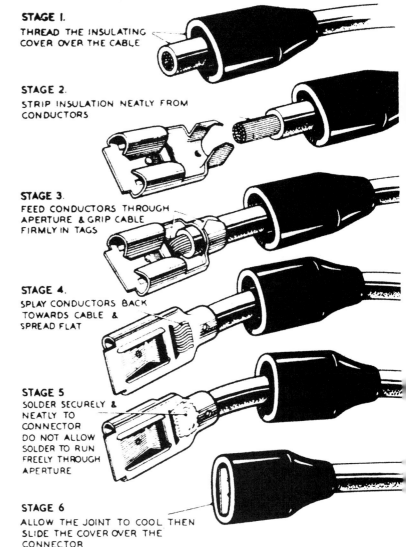

STAGE 1.
THREAD THE INSULATING COVER OVER THE CABLE

STAGE 2.
STRIP INSULATION NEATLY FROM CONDUCTORS

STAGE 3.
FEED CONDUCTORS THROUGH APERTURE & GRIP CABLE FIRMLY IN TAGS

STAGE 4.
SPLAY CONDUCTORS BACK TOWARDS CABLE & SPREAD FLAT

STAGE 5
SOLDER SECURELY & NEATLY TO CONNECTOR DO NOT ALLOW SOLDER TO RUN FREELY THROUGH APERTURE

STAGE 6
ALLOW THE JOINT TO COOL THEN SLIDE THE COVER OVER THE CONNECTOR

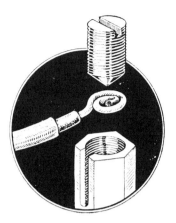

LEFT *Older switch terminal post and the wire form it will best retain*

BELOW *Under the seat of a T120 in 1972 showing battery, coils, wiring and tools all rather confined*

connected as is the horn, via the ignition switch to the coil or via the lights switch. Total isolation of battery from system did not come until later. The horn current is not taken through the ammeter so the lead to this comes before the instrument and the same applies to some stop lamps.

If you have to rewire first sort out the wiring diagram and then decide on the wire type and gauge you will use. Early models usually had black rubber covered wire, possibly with a coloured or numbered sleeve at the end. This form of insulation perishes so is no longer used and wires are colour coded to ensure correct connections. The gauge depends on the cur-

rent carried and it is as well to err on the fat side to keep voltage drop to a minimum.

A new harness is best built up on the machine as this will make sure it fits well. Tape it into place while doing this and then remove as one unit and bind the wires into one bundle to keep the weather at bay. Either tape or heat-shrink tubing can be used for this as long as the final job will accept the movement it must in the headstock area. Elsewhere it must be held firmly so it cannot fray away and is not trapped or pinched at any point.

Joints and connections need careful attention. Joins in the wires are best done with modern connectors

Hooking the battery strap into place on a 1968 T100T

with each wire crimped or soldered to its terminal. When doing this avoid nicking the wire when stripping the insulations, although this is hard to avoid, and don't use an excess of solder. In avionics, inspection count the strands to make sure none are missing, inspect each for a mark and expect to see each one just outlined by its solder shroud. Get halfway to that standard and you won't have any problems.

Crimp connectors normally call for special tools but a serviceable job can be made using pliers of one sort or another plus common sense. Make sure the wire is firmly held and not slightly loose. If the wires are soldered in place don't let the solder run back into the wire or its rigidity will cause it to fracture under vibration. On the same lines when dealing with older types of switches with terminal posts just roll the wire into a ball under the fixing screw. If you do use solder play safe by clamping the wire securely a short distance from the terminal. Electrical strapping will look neater than tape on the final assembly.

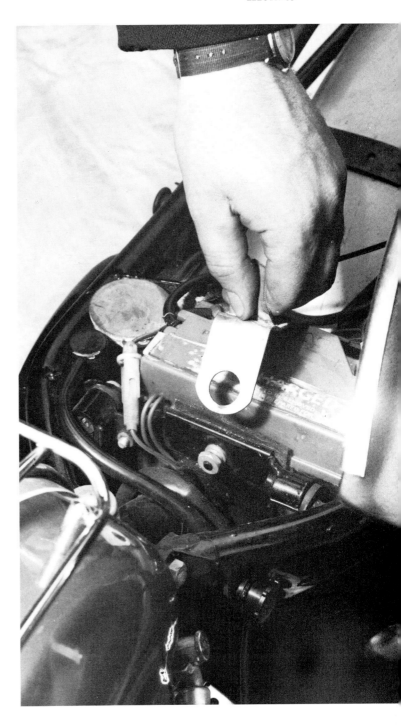

Switches

These must be checked using a meter for their correct operation. The older type can usually be taken apart for cleaning but watch for rollers with springs behind them that can fly out and roll all over the floor. Re-check the operation after assembly. Draw the connections on your wiring diagram so you can see how the components connect up in each switch position.

In addition to the more complex lights and ignition switches also check out the dipswitch, horn button, stoplight switch and cut-out for correct operation in the same way. As you connect them into the circuit check each in turn to ensure correct operation without any errant connections.

Earthing

All the older machines rely on the cycle parts to do this job which is why they often have problems. Having carefully restored the protective paintwork of frame, forks, mudguards and panels it is rather a shame to damage this finish to complete the earth return.

The answer is to run an earth wire from each item back to the battery or to a suitable junction point. The wires must be of a gauge able to carry the current from all the items they are collecting for and at one point are best earthed both to the frame and the engine. Don't forget that the ignition system must have a complete circuit for both high and low tension loops.

Fuse

These were not fitted to early machines but are a good insurance for all. At worst a single 35 amp fuse in the main battery line can save the day in the event of a short circuit while for more sophistication a modern fuse box with several fuses and spares can be wired into the circuit. Separate protection for the lights and ignition makes sense but this can be extended to one for each circuit.

8　The finish

This is the process that produces the final appearance whether that is polished, plated or painted and always the result depends on preparation. The final top coat is the easy stage, it is the work done to bring the surface for that coat to the required standard that takes time and effort.

The production finishes used by Triumph were to either polish castings or leave them as cast, to plate certain major items and the details with either chromium or cadmium and to paint the steel parts that made up the bulk of the cycle side and also certain cast iron items using the stove enamelling process.

Petrol tanks and wheel rims were both chrome plated and painted on the earlier models while the plastic and rubber items were as moulded. Transfers were added as a final touch at certain points.

Cleaning the parts
Right at the start you will have removed the outer dirt from the machine but now each part needs attention. The process used depends on the part, its job, its material and the required finish. For internal items the cleaning process is most likely all that is needed but the visible ones take more.

Cleaning can be done mechanically or chemically depending on the surface smoothness desired and the shape and area in question. Some of the chemicals are not readily available in the small quantities needed by the amateur and all must be treated with caution and only used when protective clothing is worn. Read the instructions carefully including the warning notes and what to do if you splash yourself.

Detergents
Straight from the kitchen a household washing powder is most useful for cleaning castings. They are best done in a heated saucepan and before immersion all steel items must be removed. Don't leave the parts in for longer than is necessary as many of these products are acidic in nature and will attack the castings. When the cleaning process is complete wash all the detergent away with hot water and then dry the casting.

Often this is all that will be needed to restore an engine or gearbox casting that is simply dirty with ingrained oil but do make sure all the detergent is removed.

Mechanical
At its simplest this involves scraping the finish, usually paint, away with a knife or some similar tool. This is slow, tiring and tedious but will get you down to the bare metal in time. It can also damage the surface if you are not careful enough to prevent the knife digging in.

More usually it means some form of blasting process where small particles are blown at the item to be cleaned so they knock the finish off. The speed, severity, substrate damage and visual finish depend on the abrasive material used.

For removing rust, paint and corrosion aluminous oxide grit blasting is suitable for motorcycle parts. Iron grit or shot are not and would badly damage castings and blow holes in sheet metal so avoid them. A less common and more delicate process is vapour blasting which carries the abrasive medium in water but the most popular method for smaller items is bead blasting.

This uses glass beads so does not take material away. It is also used on castings that have been grit blasted as that process tends to open the metal pores. The beads close them up again, flattens the surface out and gives it a polish that can range from matt to gloss.

All parts should be thoroughly cleaned and oil, grease and loose rust removed before they are taken for the blasting process. Threads, cylinder bores, tight tolerance holes, headstock bearings, oilways and tapped holes will all need protecting, not so much from damage as to make sure nothing is trapped which could cause damage later. It is only too easy to block an essential oilway with beads and a wrecked engine will result in minutes.

Blanking off can be done using nuts, bolts, pieces of tube, several layers of masking tape or even Blu-tack. This last is excellent in recesses as it just absorbs the beads which come away with it afterwards. Items such as headstocks in frames can be sealed using a length of studding, two metal discs and rubber discs cut from an old inner tube. Don't forget a screw for the grease nipple hole or your work will have been wasted.

The alternative to blasting is to remove paint, rust and, inevitably, some metal using emery. The manual method involves cloth strips which can be useful on frame tubes but for most items mechanization is essential. This takes the form of an electric drill and an emery flap wheel and is used more to remove deep scratches from the metal and to blend the damaged area into the rest. As with the blasters you should let the tool do the work without forcing it for the best results. Don't use a sanding disc as it will take off too much and most likely score the surface.

The extension of this type of work is to finer and finer grades of abrasive so that you finish up with a polished surface. This was normally applied to the timing cover, gearbox end cover and outer primary chaincase but is often extended by owners to many more of the light alloy castings. This will reduce the metal's heat dissipation and may not be as original but many owners like to have more polish than normal and that is their right and decision for their machine.

Polishing can be done by hand, with mops or by a combination of the two. Industrial polishers use large mops driven at speed by a good sized electric motor for they take a lot of power. They can also round off edges and draw out drilled holes in a very short time so if you do have access to such equipment practice on something that is scrap before beginning on your Triumph parts.

Small mops can be used in an electric drill and must be kept charged with mop soap. Again proceed with care, especially where there are sharp edges you wish to keep. Before mopping the easy areas you should deal with the awkward crevices. Very tempting to do it the other way round but not advised.

The manual way of polishing involves wet-and-dry emery cloth in paraffin. You need medium and then two grades of fine and it is a tedious and dirty job. The recesses can be done with an emery stick and this may be driven by a drill. The major areas can be done using a Loyblox which is a block of rubber impregnated with emery grit which can be used wet or dry.

The final touch is a polish with Solvol Autosol applied with a soft cloth.

Chemical

There are chemical cleaners available for light alloy parts and as with the detergent mentioned above they must be well washed away after use. Most are acidic in nature so care is necessary when using them and the instructions must be followed.

More usually chemical cleaning means a paint stripper and this is another messy operation but one that is quick and effective. Wear protective clothing and avoid contact by wearing gloves and eyeshields. It is a nasty substance.

Spread plenty of newspaper out, put out the parts for stripping and paint the liquid on. After a while the paint will start to bubble up and often comes away in sheets. A scraper may be needed to help it along and all the old paint must come away. Then get rid of the old paint and paper remembering that it is now an industrial hazard. Burning is a good method if possible but will smell and must be done out-of-doors.

The parts will need to be cleaned with water if the stripper was so based or thinners and wire wool. You *must* make sure that all the old paint and stripper is removed or the new coat will lift within days of application.

At this point you may find that under the paint there were patches of filler from some long distant repair. These will all have to come away so you can get down to bare metal and can check on the exact damage. Don't be tempted to leave it as having been disturbed by what you have done so far it will be close to falling away anyway.

Rust

You now have the steel parts in an ideal state for them to rust. However they have been cleaned they will immediately begin to oxidize and any handling only makes matters worse due to the acids of the skin.

So proceed to the next stage quickly.

If there is a delay and surface rust forms then it will have to be removed again before the finishing process is continued. There are a number of products available to do this and most have a phosphoric acid base. Many will also act as a primer for painting but if the part has to be plated, wax or oil would be a better protection as they can be removed by degreasing.

Parts that are due to be painted should be given one coat of etch primer as soon as possible after the blasting or stripping process. This will keep the rust at bay while you draw breath.

Restoring the surface

If the part is to be plated then a metallic surface is essential and defects cannot be resin filled as they can for painted items. Thus it may be necessary to weld or braze, depending on the material, in order to obtain the required surface in the right substance.

This technique will work for castings and the heavier steel parts but sheet steel components in general and the petrol tank in particular need sheet metal skills. If you have these you will have the hammers and dollies to do the work and if you don't then you had best farm all but the simplest tasks out.

Even professional restorers often send petrol tanks to a specialist as a repair usually entails cutting the bottom out to give access for the panel beating and then welding it back in again. A skilled job and not one to be attempted unless you really know what you are doing. Round off all sharp edges as this lessens the chance of paint chipping.

Filling

Steel or iron parts which have been left for years are likely to have a pitted surface and it is not practical to fill these with braze or clean the surface down to remove them. The first would take forever and the second weaken the part far too much.

One answer is a resin filler which may come as a brushed on liquid or a two part resin and hardener kit. Several coats will be needed to give body to the surface and ensure all traces of pitting have gone. Once this is done the part will need to be left for several days to harden fully.

An alternative is lead filling as used for cars. The area to be treated has to be tinned first and this is done using a flux with powered lead in it. This is brushed on and warmed with a blowlamp. Do not use a welding torch as the heat will be too hot and too local.

Then continue with the lead which comes as an alloy of lead and tin in sticks. The blowlamp will allow the lead to be kept movable without running about and a hardwood spatula will let you push it about. Wear a mask, try not to put too much on, remember you can always add more if needed, and finally dress down with file and flattening paper.

The surface then has to be rubbed down and this is done using 320 grade wet-and-dry emery used wet. It is a tedious job as the aim is a smooth, even surface that blends in with the rest of the part without bumps or hollows. This is not easy to get completely right first time but hollows can always be given another coat of filler so you have another chance.

Pinholes in the surface are dealt with using stopper in a similar way.

Once you are quite certain the whole surface of the part is just right you can move on but don't delude yourself. Any mark, any imperfection will shine through no matter how many coats of paint you put on.

Painting

The traditional method of applying paint is by brush with a number of coats and the surface rubbed down between each. This was far too slow for mass produced machines so the job was speeded up using spray or dip techniques and stove enamelling paint. This gave a hard finish with deep gloss that stood up to knocks well.

In contrast a brush finish either took a great deal of time to apply or looked poor and was easily damaged. Fortunately not any longer although time and care is needed if a really good finish is wanted. What is now easy to obtain is good coverage, a deep gloss and a hard surface that won't chip easily and even if it does can be touched in without much trouble.

Most restorers therefore use a synthetic enamel and the most common make is Tekaloid which is favoured by many professional men. Others simply shop at a high street store and produce very good results using either the enamel as it comes or as a two part product. The second item acts as a hardener so the drying time is reduced and it is also possible to low temperature bake the finish.

A short drying time is characteristic of cellulose which is normally used for spraying. It has to be mixed with thinners, is volatile and flammable, and must be handled with care as it can be medically dangerous.

A fast drying time is desirable as it helps to combat the home restorer's greatest enemies when painting which are dust and midges. For this reason some do use a cellulose but in the end the finish depends far more on the preparation, clean atmosphere and operator care than the paint type.

To get this there are certain guide lines to follow. Paint after rain has washed dust from the atmosphere. Choose a warm still day and damp down the working area. Wear clothes that do not harbour dust so avoid wool. Work in an area free from draughts and don't open the door once you have begun. But don't forget you do need air to breathe with. Don't breathe on the work and hang it from wire, not string, with the least important face pointing upwards. Use a tack rag on the surface immediately before you start and leave the working area as soon as the painting is finished.

The paint is applied by a brush and the name Hamilton is the one that comes up most often. 1 in. wide will cover most items but a $\frac{1}{2}$ in. may be needed for details and a 2 in. for mudguards or the bathtub. Run the brushes in on something unimportant and wash out dirt with clean paraffin in several stages until it really is clean. Tap the handle against a piece of wood to shake the surplus out, do not finger the bristles or wipe them with a rag. After use clean in paraffin, wash in warm, soapy water, then clear water and leave to dry.

To do the actual painting pour some paint into a clean cup and load the brush from that. Do not put the brush in the paint tin. Apply with long flowing strokes with the brush running down the part under its own weight to avoid brush marks. A light touch will give a lovely finish.

Two or three coats are usual and between each the surface has to be rubbed down using 500 grade wet-and-dry, used wet. This gives a smooth surface and allows you to see where the next coat has to go, not always easy on a dark, glossy surface.

There are two areas where the above will not work so well. One is where there is heat so brake drums and cylinder barrels are better stove enamelled which means masking off and filling using materials which will cope with the baking temperature. The other is the petrol tank where the problem is resistance to petrol and staining. Fine if you never spill anything when refuelling and the cap seal does its job but otherwise consider going to an expert.

Some restorers give the tank a coat of polyurethane

lacquer but this is not advised as it will react with any spilt petrol and act as a paint stripper.

Paint colour

Black is black for most of us but amaranth red seems to come in so many shades and to suffer from fading. To some degree it is the same for all colours and this leads to matching problems.

Also remember that all paints are not the same and while you can spray synthetic onto cellulose it won't work the other way round. Using a sealer or isolator may work but don't expect too much. Better to get back to the basic surface.

For the paint you should keep to one type for all stages and colours including any lining you do.

Paint colours are given in an appendix and to more detail than in *Triumph Twins & Triples* so should therefore take precedence over that volume with regard to the information given. Matching is another matter and an area of original paint that has been shielded from the light will act as the best guide. The inside of the toolside or the underside of a clip are possible places but of course if your machine has been fully re-painted at some time then this matching is lost.

It may be possible to judge what you are after from a brochure or a contemporary magazine advertisement but otherwise you will have to find a machine to study. Museums, shows and meetings are all possible sources. Or you may be able, or lucky, to find a part in its wrapper in the right colour. Worth buying whether you need it or not just for the match.

Once you know what colour you need you then have to get the paint shop to mix it for you. Start from the British Standard Colour Chart as this should get you near and expect to have to experiment a little. Persevere on odd parts until you are satisfied you have it correct or to the shade you want it to be.

Spraying

This takes more cash to get the equipment and tends to be expensive in paint as much goes past the work onto the walls. The technique has been much described but as with the brush, practice, preparation and no dust are the keys to success.

Investigate paint types as some give off a lethal vapour and are not for the amateur at all. Learn how to operate the spray gun, the effects of your techniques and changes to them and practice first.

Observe all safety precautions which are more stringent for spraying due to the fire risk and the fumes. Keep a fire extinguisher of the correct type to hand. Make sure ventilation is good, don't have naked flames, gas heaters or open radiant fires and check on your electrics in case anything can spark. Wear a mask when working.

Coatings

An alternative to painting is plastic coating or powder coating. These will not give the gloss required by the perfectionist but the coats are tough. There are limitations on colour choice, filler cannot be used as it won't stand the process temperature and plastic coating can strip off if rust gets under the surface at any point.

So, again, preparation is important and will reflect in the final appearance. Dip coating can be done at home on items such as stands as the main requirements are means to heat the part up to around 300 degrees C and a container for the power the part is dipped into. An old, cleaned, oil can is a good starter.

Plating

Plating, like painting, depends on preparation for a good result. This means cleaning the surface and polishing it without damaging it. So once more the files, the emery and elbow grease are needed and with some of the small parts the biggest problem is holding them.

You can pay the plater to do this but it is a labour intensive job so costly and the more you can do yourself the better. Some parts you cannot replate as no-one will touch them or allow them in their chroming bath. The two common ones are silencers and wheel rims as they would contaminate the bath.

After preparation the trick is to find a good plater who is interested in your motorcycle work and for this recommendations should be sought. Whether you are aiming for a concours job or not expect to pay for good workmanship which is always less expensive in the long run than a cheap job.

The major plated parts are finished with chromium but other plating processes are needed as well. Nuts and bolts that are not chromed are normally either cadmium or zinc plated. Bright nickle may be found on the spoke nipples.

Aluminium castings may be plated, although this does nothing for heat dispersion, or they can be anodized. This improves their corrosion resistance and the film formed on the surface can be dyed in a range of colours with matt black helping the heat and looking very smart. Note that the process acts as an insulator so don't forget that your electrics need a path for the current.

Lining and transfers

Signwriters do this freehand and this is one solution used by many restorers – they farm the job out. Alternatives are plastic tapes which are simply laid on and either left at that or varnished. Or masking using pvc tape to give the outline required. An alternative for the straighter parts is car lining tape which has a centre strip which is removed to leave two outers spaced parallel to each other. Tricky but not as much as trying to do it freehand. Don't forget that the lining paint must be the same type as that it is being applied to or you will have trouble. Remove the tape before the paint is fully dry so it can flow smooth. Gold lining will then need a clear coat to protect it and yacht varnish is often favoured.

Transfers are the final touch to a machine and should be applied with care according to their directions. Make sure they go in the correct place and when dry protect with a thin coat of clear varnish.

Stainless steel

An alternative for many steel parts that are normally chrome plated is stainless. Many owners refuse to use parts made in it but in the right application and the correct grade it can say goodbye to a corrosion problem forever.

There are a good number of stainless steels, some magnetic and able to be hardened, some not fully corrosion resistant and so on as with other metals. With the correct specification all will be well as long as the part is correctly machined. And not if not.

9 Frame and stands

With these items you have something solid to work on so most minor repairs are easy to do. Bent brackets can be heated and returned to their correct position and cracks around them welded. Holes may need welding and re-drilling if elongated or tapping out if their threads are damaged at all.

All this is easy to do but the real work on the frame is to check its alignment. This can be done with string and straight edges but does take a good eye to spot areas where there is a problem. A straightforward bend due to a crash is easy to see but the twist that five years of sidecar work may induce is more subtle.

Getting the frame straight again is a specialized job and should be farmed out. Before this is done check it over for cracks which will need welding, for the fit of the head races in the headstock and the rear fork pivot as attention to these areas will involve heat which could cause distortion. Best to get all the minor work out of the way so that once straight the frame can be painted.

Parts list drawing of the 1946 5T and T100 rigid frame. The 3T used a different frame

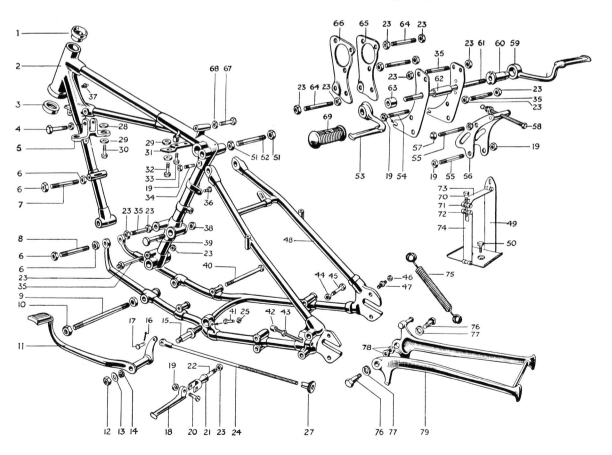

125

The stands need similar attention and are often distorted due to misuse. Expect to find damaged pivot holes needing attention and check that the spring attachment point is in good order and will hold the spring as the stand moves. Inspect the stand feet as these do wear and may need to be built up again to ensure the machine stands correctly when parked.

Rigid frames

These were used for all models from 1938 up to 1953 for the T100 and 1954 for the others. The frame came in two major sections which were bolted together along with the engine, gearbox and engine plates to form a rigid structure.

The front frame for the 5T and T100 was altered postwar to accommodate the front mounted dynamo. It had the top seat tube clip reversed to the right in 1949 and was used by the 6T in 1950. In 1951 the T100 reverted to the 1946 design and in 1952 all had the seat tube changed to accommodate a lug with large hole through it for the air filter hose. In all cases these frames had both front and rear petrol tank supports bolted into place. The front was common from 1939–54 while the rear was modified in 1950 and 1953 to accommodate changes in bolt sizes.

The 3T frame had the tank supports formed as part of the frame and was unchanged during its life. That of the TR5 differed from the others in that the downtube was shorter and finished above the dynamo. In place of the usual lug at its lower end went two cross tubes welded into place to pick up with the engine plates. The TR5 frame had no front tank support as this job was done with a cross-bolt while the rear support was formed as part of the frame. For 1952 the TR5 frame was altered to change the steering head angle and increase the trail.

The rear frame of the 5T and T100 was the same from 1938–47 but from frame TF17790 was altered to add two more lugs to the upper cross-stay to support a revised rear mudguard. The 3T had its own frame and this had this change in 1949 when it and the others had the air lever moved onto the left seat stay just below the saddle. In 1950 they were given a prop stand lug and the T100 only had further lugs added in 1951 to suit the rear mounted footrests of the race kit. The 6T used the 5T frame and the TR5 had its own which was modified for 1952.

Rear and prop stands (rigid frame)

No changes were made to the rear stand used by the road models but the TR5 had the frame stop shape modified for 1953. Prop stands were listed from 1947–49 as fitting to a separate lug but from 1950 pivoted from a built-in frame lug.

Swinging fork frames

This type was introduced in 1954 for the Tiger 100 and then new Tiger 110 and went onto all models from

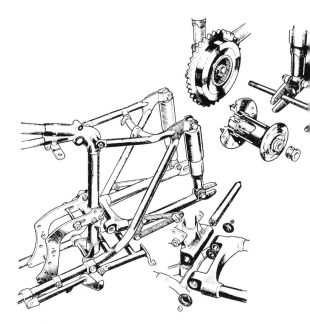

The first swinging fork frame for the Tiger models of 1954 and the quickly detachable rear wheel that was an option for it

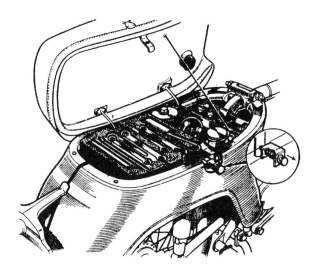

The underseat toolpad introduced for the 3TA in 1957 and fitted up to 1960 on the smaller unit construction models

1955 onwards. Attention is as for the rigid models plus the pivot bushes and these can present a real problem. All pre-unit and all smaller unit models have a design with the fork arms bushed at their forward ends. These bushes pivot on a spindle pressed into a frame lug between them with side play curtailed with shims

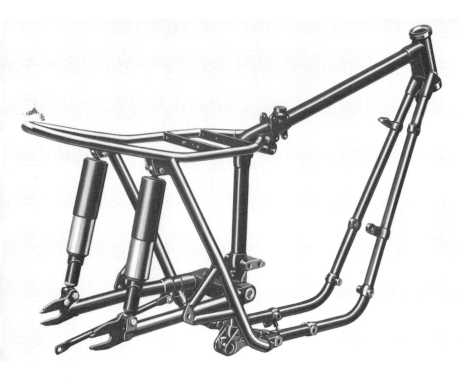

LEFT *The first duplex frame introduced for the 650s in 1960 . . .*

BELOW *. . . which quickly gained an extra top tube early in the year*

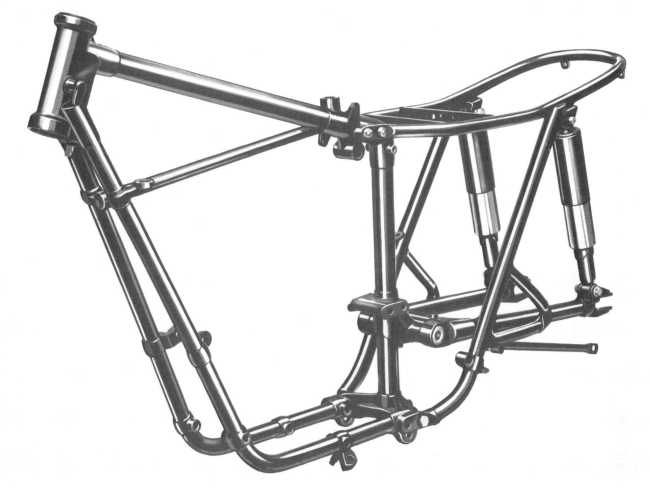

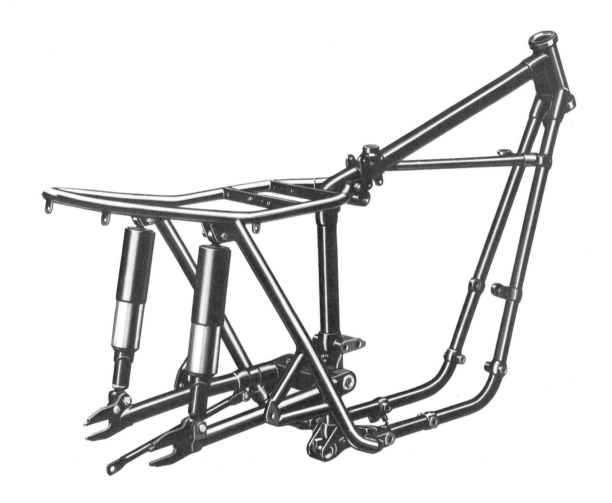

*A further picture of the 1960 duplex frame for 6T, T110,
TR6 and T120*

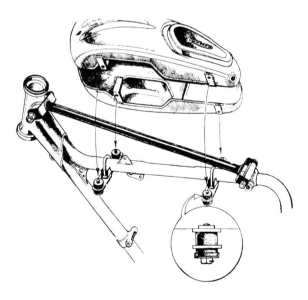

*The bolted in frame strut and revised tank mountings
adopted by the smaller unit models for 1965*

on the right side. These come in 0.003 and 0.005 in.
thicknesses and the end float should be set at
0.005–0.0065 in. It can then be allowed to wear to
0.020 in. when it should be corrected. Paint must be
kept from the working faces or the end float will not
be set correctly and thorough greasing with high
pressure equipment will help the parts to stay in good
order.

Sadly the lubrication is often neglected and this
produces very real problems. The bushes and spindle
wear badly, or worse, seize so the spindle turns in the
frame. Normally it is a drive fit and either way hard to
remove. In theory it should drift out but in practice it
is usually necessary to strip the frame and use a
hydraulic press to remove the spindle. On occasion
this is not enough and heat will have to be applied to
get the parts to move. In extreme cases the spindle will

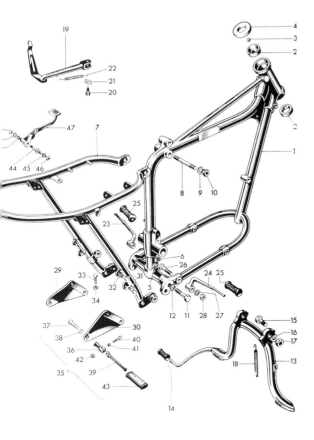

ABOVE *The T120 for 1970 when it gained small front engine plates bolted instead of welded in place*

TOP *The 1966 frame for the smaller unit models with the top strut welded into place. For 1967 the larger tube went on top to reverse the layout*

have to be cut in order to remove it. If the frame hole is worn it will need to be machined and an oversize spindle fitted.

All in all this is a swine of a job and a poor design. Owners of 650s from 1963 on benefit from an improvement with the fork pivot fitting between the frame lugs with separate bushes and spindles on a pivot bolt. This last may need driving out but at least this then lets the fork out for attention.

It is well worth keeping the repaired bushes well greased.

Frame types

The 1954 frame front half was modified for 1955 with the addition of sidecar lugs and joined by a TR5 frame. This went in 1956 when all models used the same frame with a new headstock lug. It was changed again for 1958 with the addition of a steering head lock in the right side of the headstock.

In 1960 the frame front, now used by 650 cc models only, gained duplex downtubes and became a complete loop. Within a short time the single top tube was joined by a lower tank rail beneath it. In 1962 the head angle was changed and for 1963 the unit engines were fitted into a loop frame front with single downtube and revised rear fork pivot lug. 1965 brought a change to the prop stand angle and 1966 another headstock angle plus built-in fairing mountings. In 1967 threaded steering stops were fitted along with a plate at the top of the headstock drilled to take the pin of the steering lock in the top crown.

1968 brought steering lock changes and for 1970 the welded on front engine plates were replaced by separate items bolted to two cross tubes set in the downtube. In 1971 came the oil in frame design which was revised and lowered for 1972.

The smaller unit models had a frame front half change for 1961 with the addition of steering stops for the 3TA and 5TA. In 1964 a coil bracket appeared on the top tube and for 1965 a strut was bolted between headstock and seat nose to brace the frame and take that load and duty away from the fuel tank. In 1966 the strut was welded in place and for 1967 the layout was reversed to put the main top tube on top of the lower tank rail. In 1969 there were changes to the frame front threads.

The rear half of each frame changed less with the 1954 part not altering until 1960 when it gained welded on tubular loops to support the pillion rests with variations for the 6T and T110 with bathtubs and the TR6 and T120 without. The unit engine 650 rear frame had a pivot bolt fit change for 1965 and in 1966 the two lugs on the top left tube that supported the cross straps were changes for pegs. In 1967 came Unified threads and in 1968 lugs for the side panels.

The smaller unit models did not change until 1964 when a new centre stand was fitted plus pump brackets to locate that item along the right subframe

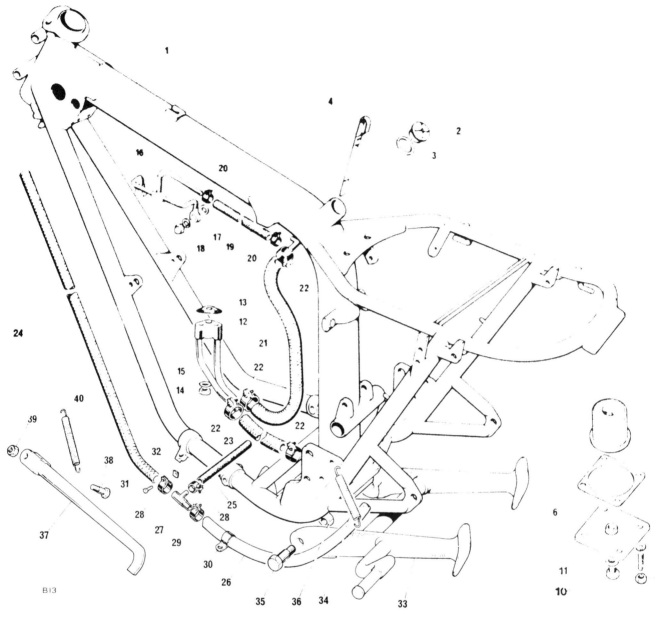

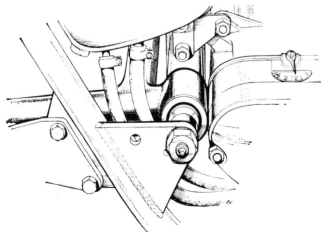

ABOVE *Oil-in-frame 1971 parts list drawings showing filter unit that acts as oil tank base*

LEFT *Frame support for rear fork pivot on the smaller unit twins of 1967*

RIGHT *Rear fork support on the T120 in 1972 using the joggled rear engine unit plates*

tube. In 1966 the welded in cross stays went and pegs appeared on the left as on the 650s while in 1967 the brackets on the right became longer. 1968 saw a change to side panel lugs as for the larger models.

Rear fork

Work on this item is much as for the main frame plus replacement of the bushes if necessary. They will need reaming to size after they have been pressed in.

The original rear fork was altered for 1955 by the addition of a torque stay lug and modified again in 1957. On the unit 650 changes can in 1966, 1968 and 1969, the last two to strengthen the part which was revised in 1971 to suit the oil-in-frame design.

The smaller unit models did not change their rear fork until 1966 and then changed again for 1967–72.

Head races

Expect to renew these on a restoration unless they are in perfect condition. Even if they are change the ball bearings. All Triumph twins fitted cup and cone bearings with loose balls except on the 650s in 1971–72. These models had taper roller races and kits to fit this type to other machines are available and well worth using. Follow the adjustment instructions.

The only prewar parts that were still used in 1946 were the lower head cup and the balls with 22 off $\frac{3}{16}$ in. diameter at the top and 20 off $\frac{1}{4}$ in. diameter at the bottom. The 3T choose to be different with 22 of the smaller size top and bottom plus its own cups and cones. Both cups were the same but not the cones.

On the 500 went one of each part up to 1955 but from 1956 the lower cup, as used since 1938, became common and a new top cone was introduced. At the same time the top balls were changed to match the lower ones so in total 40 of $\frac{1}{4}$ in. diameter were fitted and this continued on to 1962.

The unit 650s continued with the 1938 cups, the $\frac{1}{4}$ in. balls and the 1956 top cone to 1970. The lower cone was that used from 1946 but for 1971–72 all this was replaced by taper rollers.

The smaller unit models had their own design from 1957–66 with common cups, dissimilar cones and 48 ball bearings of $\frac{3}{16}$ in. diameter. From 1967 they fitted a pair of the 1938 cups, cones as on the unit 650 and used 40 balls of $\frac{1}{4}$ in. diameter so were just as the larger models.

Centre stand

A centre stand was first fitted on the Tiger 100 and Tiger 110 in 1954 and went on the other models in the following year. In 1957 the operating foot peg was made longer and for 1958 it was fitted with a small rubber. This stand continued for the 6T and T110 in 1960 with a new spring and connecting link which also went on the TR6 and T120 with a modified stand.

The unit 650s had two stands listed in 1963 to suit either a 3.50 in. rear tyre or one of 4.00 in. section. Both were changed on the attachment of the operating peg for 1964 but only the one for the wider tyre continued after that. It was modified for 1969, and its rubber changed, and further altered for 1970. In 1971 a new stand to suit the oil-in-frame model was used.

The smaller unit models had the same stand for the 3TA, 5TA and T100A between the years 1957–63. In 1961 a new type was introduced for the T100SS and this went onto the T90 in 1963. 1964 saw a new stand for the tourers but in 1966 all models were fitted with the T100SS type stand except the T100R which had its own style. In 1967 bott forms changed with the T100R still having its own stand until 1970 when all models had the common 1967 type. For 1971 they all changed to the 1967 T100R type and kept this for 1972. The pedal rubber was changed for 1969 and the earlier one was as used for the unit 650 and pre-unit models. It was the same rubber used for the gear lever from 1938 to 1967.

Prop stand

This continued to be offered for the swinging fork frames and for 1954 the 1953 parts were used with the TR5 using the 3T leg. In 1955 a new part became common to all models and continued on the TR6 and T120 when the duplex frame was introduced for 1960. A different part was used for the 6T and T110 that year and up to 1962. It continued in use on the unit 650 with a 4.00 in. rear tyre up to 1965 and an alternative was listed for use with the 3.50 in. tyre up to 1966. The 4.00 in. one was altered for 1966 and both had a new pivot bolt for 1967. Only one was listed for 1968 and this had the pressing on the end of the stand leg removed and the leg just extended further in a curve. For 1970 this was further altered to add an adjustable stop to the stand.

The smaller unit twins had a common stand from 1957–65 with a revised version for the T100SS and T90 from 1964. In 1966 this went onto all models except the T100C and T100R which had their own pattern. 1967 saw both with new pivot bolts and in 1969 the 650 leg and its spring was fitted to the smaller machines. For 1970 the leg with adjustable stop was used so all models continued with the same parts to 1972.

Steering lock and horn location for the smaller unit models in 1967

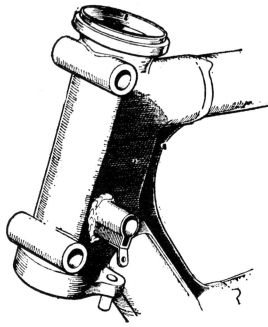

Fairing mounting lugs introduced for the twins in 1966 plus the steering lock barrel

10 Suspension

Front suspension was by girder fork prewar and telescopic fork postwar. The appearance of the initial design was changed with the introduction of the nacelle in 1949 but in time this was phased out for a more sporting appearance. This brought back a separate headlamp and introduced fork gaiters but in the end the latter went in the name of styling.

At the rear of the machine there was no suspension until 1947 when the unique sprung hub was introduced. Despite some limitations this did provide wheel movement with minimum unsprung weight and it did bolt straight into the rigid frame. In 1950 a 'mark 2' version was built and continued to be available up to 1954. That year the Tiger models went into a new swinging fork frame which became standard for all models from 1955 onwards.

Girder forks
These are easy enough to dismantle and assemble but more tricky to repair and adjust. The main girder needs to be checked for alignment and damage just like the frame itself and repairs are carried out in the same way. The side links also need checking for straightness and the condition of the holes and threads.

The usual job needed for most forks not bent or damaged is new spindles and bushes. This is a machining job and the amount of work will depend on the wear in the bush and whether it has been bodged at some time. Normally the bushes can be driven out and new parts pressed in and line-reamed to suit new spindles.

In practice the bush may have seized on the spindle so it turned in the fork, the spindle may have worn through the bush and into the housing or it may all be solid. To deal with this may mean boring the housing out and making bushes to suit.

While the forks are apart fit a new set of ball bearings at least and check the cups and cones carefully. Check all the other details and re-furbish accordingly.

Adjustment begins by assembling the parts loosely and during this stage the steering and fork dampers can be left off. The four spindles and the head race then need to be brought in to their correct positions in stages. When close each spindle can be dealt with in turn but must only be tightened to the point where the knurled thrust washers are just free to turn.

When checking the movement all spindle nuts must be tight but to adjust you must slacken both, turn the spindle and then re-tighten the nuts. Care will be rewarded by better steering.

Telescopic forks
Most of these are similar in nature and restoration follows common lines. Strip the forks following the

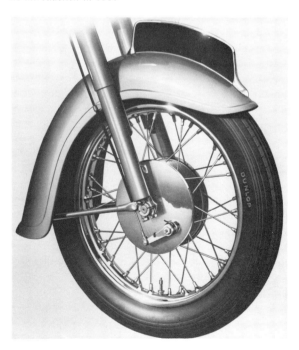

Front forks and wheel with full width hub for the 3TA on its introduction in 1957

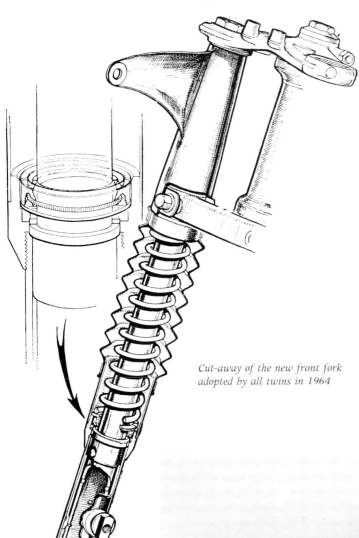

Cut-away of the new front fork adopted by all twins in 1964

procedure given in the manual and examine the parts for wear. Check each leg for worn bushes or sliders which may call for repair or replacement.

It is common for fork legs to be bent and rolling them on a flat surface will reveal this. Wear can be overcome by hard chroming and grinding to size if new parts are not to be found. This will also deal with any pitting of the surface but where this is minor it can be filled with epoxy resin which is rubbed down when hard.

Expect to renew fork bushes and seals but most of the other internal parts operate in oil and seldom wear. Check the springs for tiredness and shortening. If this has happened try to find new springs of the correct rate. Packing can be, and is, done but will affect the rate and may restrict fork movement. It can also give rise to clashing sounds if things have worked out against you.

All threads need to be carefully checked and repaired as required. As they hold the forks together or the front wheel in they do have a bearing on your well-being. Check the lower legs especially for any signs of damage.

If the fork tubes have been bent then it is most likely that the crowns will also be bent or distorted. Sometimes this manifests itself in the head races going tight at one point but slack at another. The crowns must be true to the forks and the frame and their threads checked.

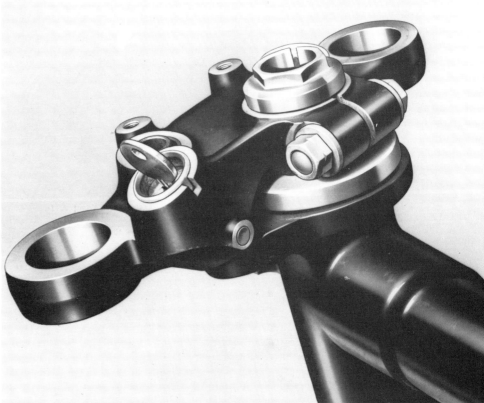

RIGHT *Top crown with steering head lock and handlebar mounting bushes as on the 650s in 1967*

Assemble to the book, make sure the head races are correctly adjusted and that the fork legs are parallel so they can move freely without binding. Fill with the correct grade of oil and try to get the same amount in each leg.

Telescopic fork types

The first forks were used for a decade with just one change. In 1949 the stanchions were drilled and tapped near the top so that oil could be injected into them that way. This arose due to the nacelle which made the original method of removing the top nuts difficult. It was a feature of all the nacelle models to the end and the stanchions should be positioned so that the screw faces the front. It is thus accessible once the headlight unit is removed.

The TR5 did not need this feature so the 1946 fork legs were used. In 1956 the bump stop in all fork legs was modified to prevent fork bottoming under heavy braking and in 1957 the legs changed to split ends to clamp onto the wheel spindle. Up to then the right leg was threaded and the left split to clamp on the spindle once it was tight.

This same arrangement was used for the 3TA when introduced in 1957 but internally this fork was changed to provide two way damping. In 1958 the pre-unit machines had the fork legs changed again as only one mudguard stay was then fitted, to the rear, in place of the two used up to then. At the same time a boss on the inside of the leg replaced the clip to support the mudguard bridge. The TR models also changed but used their own external parts.

In 1960 the pre-unit models adopted the 3TA fork with gaiters for the TR6 and T120 and from then on a basically common assembly was used although there were detail differences from model to model. The T100SS in 1961 and T90 in 1963 both used the gaitered fork and in 1964 all models changed to a new design with exteria spring.

For 1965 this altered with longer stanchions, longer and lower rate springs and a new method of fork leg construction. This supported a single mudguard stay on the more sporting TR and Tiger models but went back to twin stays for the tourers. This continued for 1966 but all models just had the one stay in 1967. For that year steering locks went into the top crown and a revised damping system was fitted to the T100C, T100R, TR6C and T120TT models offered for the USA.

For 1968 there was a damper change and a move to Unified threads and in 1969 the fork crowns were altered to spread the legs out to accommodate wider tyres. In 1970 two extra holes appeared near the lower end of the stanchions and the fork legs changed in two areas. First the brake anchor became larger and longer and second the tapped hole for the mudguard bridge was replaced by a welded on lug which carried a separate square nut.

On the 500 cc models the crowns and shrouds

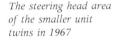

The steering head area of the smaller unit twins in 1967

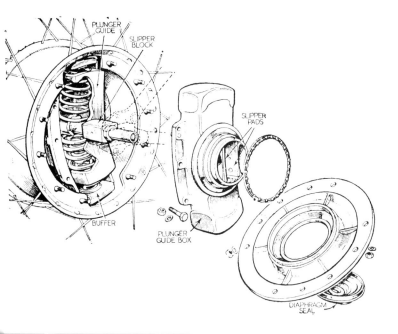

changed for 1971 but internally the forks were unaltered. For the 650s there were all new forks with internal springs, no gaiters, new damping and wheel spindle caps held by four studs. For 1972 the top nuts, fork legs and lower crown were all modified.

Steering crown types

Also known as fork yokes or, by Triumph, as the top lug and the middle and stem lug, these are checked over as above. Prewar they were to suit the girder forks but for 1946 were revised with the introduction of telescopic forks. In their early form the handlebars were held to the top crown by caps but for 1949 the design was changed for the road models.

To suit the nacelle the bars were held by U-bolts so new crowns were fitted. The new TR5 continued to use bar caps but with its own style of crown. This was revised in its geometry for 1952 and for 1955 the TR5 top crown became that used in 1946 for the road models. The top crown for the road models continued as it was but the lower one was modified for 1955 with

LEFT TOP *The Triumph sprung hub in its original form with ball bearings and slipper blocks*

LEFT CENTRE *The hub in the metal on a Tiger 100 in 1947. Handle with care*

BELOW *The Mark II sprung hub with ball races and slipper roller as introduced during 1950*

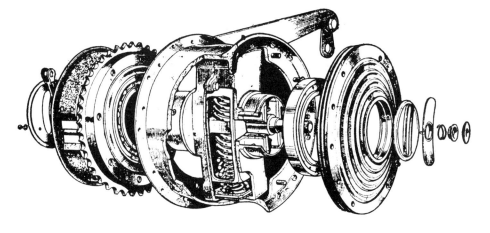

$\frac{3}{8}$ in. clamp bolts in place of $\frac{5}{16}$ in. In 1958 it was altered again with a steering lock slot added to the stem.

For 1960 two top crowns were used with the 6T and T110 continuing with the U-bolt bar clamp on a new crown with revised sleeve nut while the TR6 and T120 had bar caps on their new top crown. A single new bottom crown went with either.

The 3TA was introduced with its own crowns which remained common to the nacelle models to 1966 for the top one and to 1963 for the lower. U-bolts held the bars on all nacelle models. This type was joined by an alternative in 1961 for the T100SS and used the 650 top crown with bar caps with its own lower. This continued to 1966 for that model and the T90 but the tourers changed with new forks for 1964 and then used the sports lower crown for 1966.

The unit 650 began with new crowns in 1963 and these had the bars mounted in eyebolts which were carried in bonded rubber bushes pressed into the top crown. For 1967 a new top crown was introduced with a steering lock set in its left side so the lock slot in the

ABOVE *Rear suspension of the 3TA in 1957 showing the Girling unit with its three load positions*

LEFT *Cut-away of a Girling hydraulically damped spring unit of the late fifties*

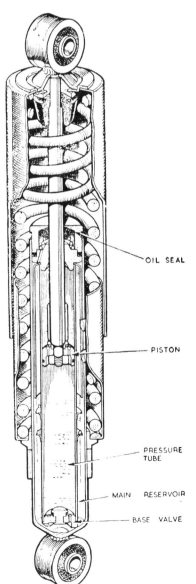

OIL SEAL

PISTON

PRESSURE TUBE

MAIN RESERVOIR

BASE VALVE

steering stem was deleted. The crowns became common for all models and a rigid bar mounting was introduced as an option for use when a windscreen was fitted to the bars. For 1968 the lower crown was Unified and for 1969 the top one was and both were widened to increase the space between the fork legs.

For 1971 the 650s were fitted with new crowns to suit the new forks and the top one had a central lock position and the lower one revised headlamp mountings made from bent wire. For 1972 the stem thread was made finer which made it easier to adjust the head races but the top crown was unchanged. For the 500s for 1971–72 the crowns were revised and the top one fitted with caps to hold the handlebars.

Handlebar fixings

Only two types of bar cap were ever used by Triumph. The first went on all models 1946–48, sports ones 1955–62 and sports small unit twins 1961–66. The other caps appeared on the TR5 1949–54, sports 500s for the USA 1967–70 and on the T100 models in 1971–72.

Where the nacelle was fitted the bars were held by a

U bolt and just one item served machines from 1949–66 but not the 6T from 1963 on. For all unit 650s and the smaller models from 1967–70 the bars were held in eyebolts. These came in two types, the first used up to 1968 and the second, with Unified threads, from then on.

Steering damper

This only needs checking as to the condition of screw threads and the friction disc plus its general good order. Dampers were fitted prewar and were included on the 1946 range. The damper knob was changed for 1947 and a special version produced for the TR5 up to 1954. In 1960 a new knob and new damper plate which located to the frame without a bolt were fitted.

The 3TA shared parts with the other models but had its own style of anchor plate. On the unit 650s the pre-1960 plate was used up to 1965 but then changed to one that located on a fixed pin. In 1964 a rubber sleeve was added to the damper rod on all models to stop it unwinding when not under any load. The rods received detail changes in 1968 when they became optional for most models and again in 1970 but for the 650s only as the damper was no longer offered for the 500. It was revised in 1971 to suit the new forks.

Sprung rear hub

There are two types of these, the 'mark 1' supplied from 1947–49 and the 'mark 2' fitted from frame 7439 in 1950 to 1954 after which the swinging fork took over. In both the plunger spring boxes must *not* be dismantled without the correct jig. The castings carry a warning to be heeded for the springs inside are under considerable compression and if allowed out without restraint have been known to punch a hole through the workshop roof. Could be lethal if not correctly handled.

Early mark 1 hubs had rubber oil seals but as they tended to deteriorate they were changed for a metal type. The brake drum and sprocket were changed for 1949. All mark 1 hubs turn on ball bearings and have square section slipper blocks. The mark 2 has large bore ball races and hardened rollers in place of the blocks. It is lubricated on assembly so has no grease nipple unlike the mark 1.

Dismantling should be by the book and the hub itself needs to be treated as any other in the matter of bearings, spokes, refurbishing and painting. The rear brake drum and shoes will require attention as detailed later for wheels in general.

The same care is needed in assembling the plunger spring box to make sure the springs don't escape.

ABOVE *Rear end of a T100T in 1970*

LEFT *And that of a Bonneville in 1969. Both pictures show details of the area as well as the spring unit and swinging fork*

Rear suspension units

Triumph fitted Girling rear units on their machines and these offer limited scope to the restorer. In all cases the outer covers and springs can be removed but the actual damper unit is sealed. The rubber mounting bushes can be renewed but repair of the unit requires that it is dismantled which for most is not possible.

Given machining equipment it is feasible to strip, repair and rebuild units but it is a specialized business. If replacement Girling units cannot be found then an alternative make will have to be fitted. These are available and from the suppliers lists it should be possible to find one with similar closed and open lengths, end fixings and spring. In many cases these new units have improved, and sometimes adjustable damping and can be stripped for repair when this is needed.

In all cases check that the eyes at the ends of the unit and the frame attachments are in good order and will carry the loads they are called upon to support.

11 Painted parts and plated details

This title covers the mass of major parts and minor fittings which are mostly steel pressings and nearly all painted. A few are forged or diecast and some plated with either chrome or cadmium.

The steel pressings need to be checked over for repair. This may entail a simple bending job to straighten a bracket or a complex panel beating job for such items as bathtub or mudguard. Often the parts will need to be welded either to mend cracks or to rejoin things that have come apart. Excess holes will need to be filled and the external signs of all this work removed before the finish is applied.

The problems in this area arise not so much with the repairs which are usually straightforward but in collecting all the parts and ensuring that what you have gathered up is correct for your model. In all too many cases changes did not affect fit or if they did could be modified to suit. Thus, machines built up from parts can often have cycle details from many models included and worst of all can be the basket jobs.

These last need very careful checking over from the first. It is easy to see that you have a pair of mudguards, although less so to be sure they are the correct pair, but much more difficult to be sure you have a full set of engine plates or torque stays. The following sections are thus not concerned with the repair of the parts which follows stock lines but with their correct identification.

Knowledge, part numbers and changes will all help to ensure that the cycle spares bought from dealer or autojumble will be correct for your project.

Engine and gearbox plates

For the pre-unit engines there were four of these in two pairs in front and rear of the power unit. The 1938 engine had no front mounted dynamo so the front plates had two holes for bolting to the frame and three for the engine. The rear one had the same arrangement in a different shape of plate with the lowest engine hole taken out as a slot. All four plates differed in some detail although each pair had a similar outline. A cover plate was fitted on top of the front plates to box them in.

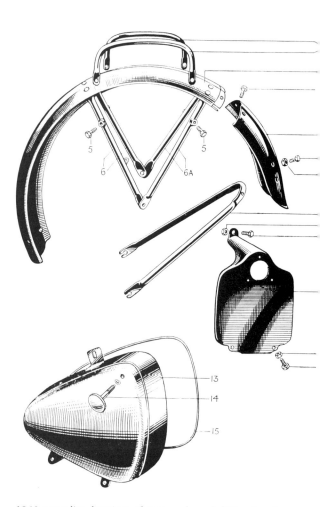

1946 parts list drawings of rear mudguard, lifting handles, number plate and toolbox

This design continued for 1939 but in 1946 the front dynamo called for new front plates with a suitable hole in them. The fixings stayed the same and the plates were handed by the area around the lower front hole which was pressed outwards to left and right respectively. The rear plates became nearly common with the right, the prewar part, as the left plus two footrest location pins.

The gearbox plates were bolted to the top and front of the shell and of curved form with a slot in them. They were bridged by a cross trunion which had a long bolt threaded across its centre and this acted as a jack against a frame lug to move the box. The plates were changed in 1946 from their prewar style but otherwise the system was common to all models and was unaltered until it was discontinued after 1954.

The 3T was fitted with its own engine plates and front cover plate and as the front ones were flat they were common although the rears varied due to the footrest pins.

These arrangements were joined by the TR5 in 1949 and this model had the two front plates formed in one with a forward bridge plate. Its side profile was different as although the three engine fixings and dynamo hole remained, the lower front hole was higher and the single top one replaced by two to suit the special frame. The rear plates also differed although the number of fixings was unchanged but the gearbox plates were common.

In 1953 the 5T was fitted with new front plates without dynamo hole and these went onto the 6T in 1954 and continued for these models to 1959. The other machines stayed with the 1946 front plates and these went onto the TR5 from 1955 and also the TR6, T110 and T120. The cover plate was fitted to all these models and was not changed from 1946.

The introduction of the swinging fork frame brought in new rear plates which extended back over the gearbox. They came in as a pair with a top cover plate on the T100 and T110 and for 1955 the design went on all models with one of the 1954 plates on the right and a new one on the left. These parts continued unchanged to 1962 but at the front the advent of the duplex frame in 1960 brought new parts. The plates became simple triangles with three holes and were formed in one with the top cover. To them went an engine plate cover to fill in the gap between the downtubes.

The smaller unit twins had four engine plates with the front pair flanged to give a boxed in appearance. The rear plates were smaller flat triangles and were unchanged from 1957–72 while the front pair were altered in detail only for 1967. The unit 650s had rear plates only except for 1970 when the front of the engine was held by two small triangular plates instead of a welded on bracket. At the rear the plates were modified for 1964 and for 1965 the left one had a short tube welded to its outer face. This pair continued to

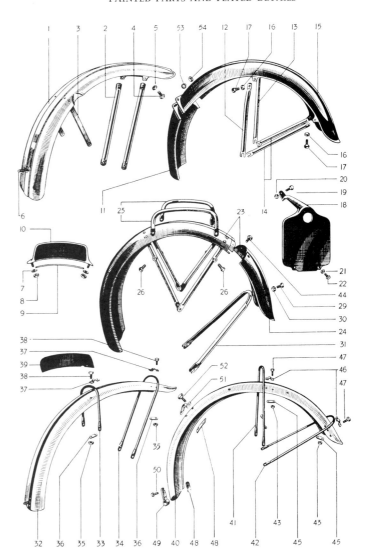

By 1951 there were three types of rear mudguard and two front to be listed as well as the number plate. Bottom pair are for TR5

1970 but for 1971–72 and the new frame there were new plates.

Engine torque stays

These link the top of the engine to the frame and need to fit properly if they are to do their job. The 500 and 650 cc pre-unit machines used a pair of stays from the front rocker box main bolts to a frame clip to 1954. The 3T had a bracket attached to the top of its integral rocker box while the TR5 used half clips to 1954.

The new frame for that year brought a revised bracket which became common to 1959. A further change occurred to suit the duplex frame used 1960–62. From 1963 the unit 650 had four stays with

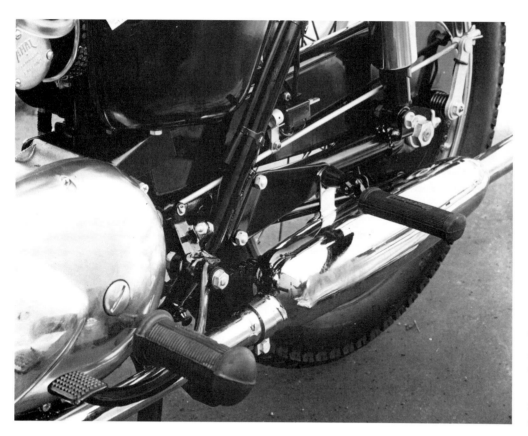

LEFT *Silencer bracket, pillion rest, brake pedal, brake rod and chainguard are just some of the details to be seen on this 1965 Tiger 90*

RIGHT *This is a similar area of a 1966 Tiger 100*

one attached to each major rocker box bolt, and this continued to 1970. With the advent of the new frame in 1971 a single bracket was fitted to link the engine to it.

The smaller unit engines had twin stays running forward to a clip on the top tube. At first these were matching left and right hands but from 1964 two of the 650s' stays were used and this continued to 1972.

Exhaust pipe and silencer brackets
These also support the pillion footrests on the swinging fork models but in early days the parts simply located to frame lugs. A pair of exhaust pipe brackets were introduced for the T100 in 1952, went on the T110 in 1954, 5T and 6T in 1955 and T120 in 1959. In 1960 they adopted a new form. From 1955 the silencer clip was linked to the frame by a simple strip stay on each side. Changes occurred in 1955 from frame 64324, in 1957 and 1960.

The combined silencer and pillion rest support plates appeared in 1954, were changed at frame 51200 for the left side only and fitted to the other models for 1955. In 1960 they were deleted as the support was changed to a welded on tubular member.

On the smaller unit machines the pipes were held to the frame by small brackets which began as a pair but had the left change in 1960 while the right continued unaltered. From 1968 the brackets became larger with a slot in the longer leg. The rear silencer support was

of T shape at first, was modified for 1961 and changed to a triangular form for 1964 on.

The unit 650s had a stay joining the pipes from 1965 which was changed to a pair of brackets in 1967. The silencer clips were also linked from 1965 but only up to 1970. The rear support brackets were handed for the TR6 in 1963 only when it had a single silencer but from 1964 a pair were fitted. For 1971 a triangular bracket replaced the earlier plate.

Undershields
This first appeared on the TR5 in 1952 and continued on the TR series with a change in 1955 to suit the new frame and another in 1960 when the duplex one appeared. A shield continued on the unit TR6 in 1963 and was held by hook bolts at the front and welded on clips at the rear. For 1969 the rear mounting became a one piece channel bracket formed to give lugs to each side and for 1971 these changed to twin angle brackets with slots for the fixing studs.

The T100C of 1966 was fitted with a shield held by clips at the front and a bolted on strap at the rear which clamped it to the frame tubes. The form of the shield was changed for 1967–69 and it re-appeared for 1971–72 in the same style but a modified shape.

HT lead clip
This was fitted from 1946–58 and held the plug leads neatly to the inlet manifold. On the right up to 1953 and then on the left.

Nacelle top

This was introduced in 1949 and over the years to 1966, after which it was withdrawn, quite a number of versions were used. Most changed to suit the switches mounted in the nacelle but not all.

The 1949 top was pierced to accept the speedometer, an ammeter, the steering damper rod, the lights switch and a cut-out button. The two instruments were fitted to all nacelle tops and the damper rod to most. On the smaller unit machines from 1961 on, the rod hole remained but was filled with a blind grommet when no damper was specified.

The first alteration to the top came in 1952 when the light unit changed to the pre-focus type which meant a new housing was needed. This carried the same five items as before. In 1953 the 5T alone was altered due to the fitting of the alternator and in place of the switch and cut-out went two switches, one for lights and one for ignition. In 1954 this arrangement changed again to combine the two switches into one and was adopted by the 6T also.

The next change came in 1957 with the introduction of the 3TA when a small hole was added to each side of the top for the clutch and front brake cables. Previously these had passed through the handlebar grommets but now they had their own and this re-arrangement made for a better cable sweep. The top carried items as on the 5T and in 1958 the pre-unit machines all had a similar arrangement for their cables. Three types were listed with one for the Tiger models and one each for the 5T and 6T with the latter simply the 5T part plus a transfer.

In 1959 the T120 appeared with a top as on the T110 plus its own transfer but this was the only year the Bonneville was equipped with the nacelle.

The 3TA and 5TA continued as they were for 1960 but the 650s changed with the 6T using the same top as the 3TA and the T100 sharing one with the T100A. The latter models used a different light switch to the tourers and retained the cut-out button. During 1961 from engine H22431 the T100A changed to the form of the 5TA so adopted that models light switch and lost its cut-out button. At the same time the damper rod grommet appeared to fill the vacant hole.

The first unit 650 6T had separate lighting and ignition switches but for 1964 a common top was used for all models. This continued with the same two switches and for 1965 the control cables went back to passing through the handlebar grommets so the small holes were filled with blind grommets. 1966 was the last year for the nacelle.

Nacelle legs

There are two of these, each comprising the lower side of the nacelle and the fork leg shroud or cover. They are thus handed left and right and mate up with each other, the nacelle top and the headlamp. The first type had slots in the area beneath the lamp but this changed in 1952 when the pre-focus headlamp was fitted. At the same time the underslung pilot lamp appeared and the parts were pierced to suit this. When it went at the end of 1955 the nacelle legs were unchanged and a horn grill was fitted to the same fixing holes.

In 1957 a new pair of legs were introduced for the 3TA while the right leg of the pre-unit models was altered a little for 1958. The pre-units changed both legs for 1960 when a new fork type was adopted and this pair continued onto the first unit 6T in 1963.

For 1964 all models adopted a revised design with the legs separate from the nacelle sections. The lower parts were revised for 1965 but otherwise this arrangement continued to the end late in 1966.

Nacelle motif

These are the plated strips which cover the join in the nacelle sides and they are handed for left and right sides. The screws that hold the nacelle together also hold them in place.

One pair was used on the pre-unit models from 1949 to 1959 and changed for 1960 to those introduced for the 3TA in 1957. These remained common to 1966.

Horn grill

This part fitted in place of the underslung pilot lamp and was first offered in 1955. From 1956 it was fitted as standard to all models with the nacelle and the same item did duty for all years to 1966.

Fork shrouds

These are also known as fork covers and in nearly all cases support the headlamp shell on welded on ears. They extend down the fork to reach the lower leg and cover the spring. If they are not true they will scrape on the leg and damage the finish before continuing to wear themselves away. It is thus important to make sure they move freely over the leg when bolted into place with the headlamp.

They were used for all models in 1946 but on the TR5 only for 1949. In 1955 the leg section was shortened with the introduction of gaiters and this style went onto the TR6 in 1956, the T120 in 1960 and the T100SS in 1961. For 1964 a new type went onto the T90, T100SS, TR6 and T120 with the leg part cut off just below the lower crown. These were revised for the new forks fitted for 1965 and joined by a version without the headlamp supports in 1966 for use on certain US models.

For 1968 the left shroud was altered to add the ignition switch mounting and both had the headlamp holes extended into slots to allow the beam to be adjusted sideways as well as up and down. On the 650s the shrouds went after 1970 as the new 1971 forks had none and used a pair of heavy gauge wire brackets to support the headlamp shell. Two pairs in fact as the TR6C differed from the other models.

On the 500 cc models for 1971 a built up construction appeared. Each shroud had two tapped bosses pointing forward and a headlight bracket bolted to it. To combat vibration a rubber block went between the two parts and the bolts had rubber buffers to isolate them. The left shroud continued to carry the ignition switch and both could be replaced by the plain type which was still offered.

Headlamp shell

Most of these are very similar as they carry the same light unit but there are variations. The shell is none too easy to repair but ones from other models can often be used if necessary. Threads, general shape and condition need to be checked and the finish may be paint or chrome plate.

The prewar shell was a massive chromed affair but postwar it was smaller and in the machine colour. It was plain up to 1948 and from 1949 only fitted to the TR5 when it carried a small panel for the light switch and ammeter. This continued until 1960 when a shell with just an ammeter went onto the T120 and TR6. The same style went onto the T100SS in 1961 and T90 in 1963.

In 1966 this standard arrangement was joined by the smaller AC shell which just carried a light switch and a separate dip one. For 1967 the standard shell gained a rotary switch plus two warning lights while the AC type continued with its two switches plus one warning light.

For 1968 the standard shell carried an ammeter, a

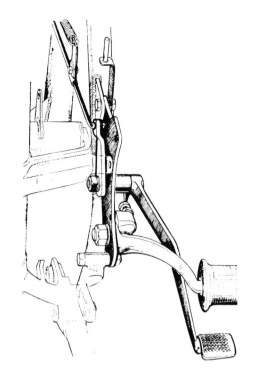

Brake linkage for the 650s in 1965 with the rod tucked away inside the frame tubes

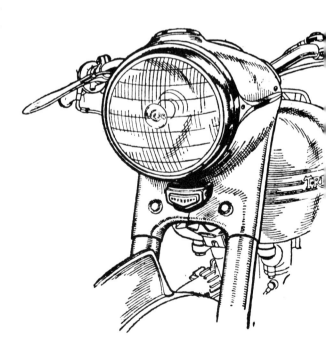

The nacelle with pre-focus headlamp unit and underslung pilot as fitted from 1952 to 1955

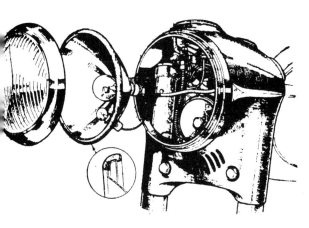

toggle light switch and two warning lights while the AC one had a toggle, push dip and the same two lights. This continued for 1969 and for 1970 just the standard shell was listed in the same form as 1968.

No model had an ammeter in 1971 but all except the TR6C had three warning lights, the exception had two. It and the 500s had a toggle light switch in the shell while the standard 650 had a turn switch. This continued for 1972.

Mudguards, stays, front stand and lifting handle

All these parts are associated together and as there were a good few changes over the years some care is needed to ensure that all the correct parts are to hand. If they are not then the mudguards may be fabricated from others or from stock parts. The stays and supports can also be made from strip or tube as called for. When flattening the ends of a tube for the mounting hole add a piece of flat stock inside the tube. This will give it more body and stop the walls from cracking.

Above all else do make sure the mudguards are properly secured and cannot revolve round the wheel. Check that they sit correctly with a good line to the tyres and that all the stays and supports line up and bolt down without strain. Only when you are fully satisfied with the mechanical aspects should you move on and complete the finishing.

Front mudguard

Prewar these were made to suit the girder forks and in addition to the standard type were also available with valances as an option. This was not continued for 1946 when the guard was revised to suit the telescopic forks.

For that year and into 1947 the guard was

LEFT TOP *The rubber mounting for the front mudguards adopted in 1971 and shown here on a 1972 T120*

LEFT CENTRE *The nacelle for 1949 with horn tucked in below the reflector*

LEFT *The nacelle top on a 1949 Tiger 100 showing the speedometer with rpm markings and other details*

145

supported at three points. At the front went a strip stay, bent to a U shape and riveted into place. Its ends bolted to lugs on the fork leg close to the wheel spindle. A strip bridge went between the legs attached to clips on them and was riveted to the guard. The third support was tubular and also acted as the front stand. It pivoted from a second pair of lugs on the lower ends of the fork legs and was held up by a nut to a fixed stud set in the guard.

During 1947 the design was revised to two separate front stays which were bolted to the guard. To assist this the guard edges were extended locally as small, drilled lugs. This style continued to 1957 for all the pre-unit road models and from 1954 a valanced front guard was also available for them. This last had the front stays formed in one and riveted to the guard in the 1946 style and was listed up to 1957.

The TR5 was fitted with more sporting guards and the front was supported by tubular stays. The front and bridge ones were both one piece items and ran over the blade to which they were held by clips and backing plates. At the rear went the front stand stay as usual. The same design went onto the TR6 in 1956.

The 3TA was introduced with its own style of well valanced front mudguard. It was joggled all round its edge for style and strength and held by a short riveted-on bridge and a tubular rear stay that continued to act as a front stand. The bridge bolted directly to the fork legs.

For 1958 the pre-unit road models adopted a similar format but with blades with a smaller valance. The tubular stand stay was retained and the bridge bolted to the fork legs. For the TR models the blade was altered and the two front loop stays both attached to the same lug just behind the fork leg near its top. The rear stay continued as before. Due to the changes the front stay ran back at a shallower angle than before and both it and the bridge had two lugs welded to them for direct bolting to the blade. The blade holes were thus re-arranged to suit.

There was a further change for 1960 when the 6T and T110 adopted the 3TA guard and the T120 took that of the TR6. For both the latter the stays were altered as their fork legs became common with the other 650s. This moved the bridge support boss down and onto the leg centre line. Thus in came new stays with a strip bridge and tubular front. The same mudguard went onto the T100SS in 1961 and the T90 in 1963.

For the first year of the unit 650 in 1963 there were three mudguards listed with the 6T and TR6 continuing with their 1960 fitment. For the T120 the form was the same but the bridge and rear stay were both different.

RIGHT *Middle area of a 3TA in 1964 when it had a skirt rather than a bathtub*

LEFT BELOW *Rear number plate for 1953 with its stop and tail light. In 1955 this gained a reflector in the lens but until then the two lower bolts had reflecting heads to do this job*

BELOW *Bathtub on the 1957 3TA with hidden flanges and rear number plate to suit*

All models had revised mudguards for 1964. The touring models had the bridge changed for two pieces of bent strip which were bolted to the guard and whose lower ends attached to a T shaped bracket. This in turn was bolted to the fork leg. The sports models had their tubular stay and strip bridge modified so both ran to a point just ahead of the fork leg. There they bolted to a small flat plate on each side and these in turn located on and were bolted to the fork leg.

In 1965 the tourers regained their bolted on front stays which attached to clips round the fork legs just above the wheel spindle. For 1966 the stays were extended and bent to run under the spindle caps where they were held by the two spindle cap bolts on each side. During these two years the sports models continued in their 1964 form.

1966 also brought variations for the US models in stainless steel and aluminium as well as the usual steel and one became the standard fitment in 1967. The stainless one was listed for certain models and a fixed rear stay was listed as well as the stand type. This

continued in 1968 for the smaller models which had a new blade but the 650s kept the stand stay for their new guard.

1969 brought a new part number for the painted front mudguard on the 500 and for the stainless steel one fitted to the T100C. For the 650 it was back to one of the 1966 US types and for all models a simple one bolt fixing for the rear stay. In 1970 a common guard was fitted to all models and the rear stay was attached to it by two bolts. This continued on the T100R for 1971–72 while a stainless steel version went on the T100C.

For the 1971 650 cc models a new design was produced with integral tubular stays running from front to rear. These located in rubber bushes clamped to each fork leg. They were modified to add a centre stay during the year and continued in this form for 1972.

Rear mudguard

For prewar models this was made in two parts so that

the tail with its stays could be easily removed to let the rear wheel roll out. The main part was supported by two stays on each side and to the frame chain stays. A lifting handle was bolted across the guard stays on each side and the same fixing points could be used for an optional rear carrier which could replace them. Valanced guards were also an option for both years.

In 1946 this design continued with the main stays riveted to the blade while the tail had its one piece stay bolted into place. The tail fitted onto side pins formed by the wire rolled into the blade edges and was held in place by two bolts. The 3T had its own blade, tail and stays but used the same lifting handles as the larger models.

This design continued for 1947 and on the 3T to the end of its production in 1951 but for the 500s was changed for 1948. Two blade sections remained but the front one was short and simply bridged the area between the frame chain stays. It ended in a plate with two studs and the rear part fitted to these and was supported by two bolted on stays on each side. Thus by removing this section the bulk of the wheel was exposed. The lifting handles went, except on the 3T, and the rear number plate bridge was formed to fulfill this duty.

Other than for a change to the front guard section on the T100 for 1952 this design continued unaltered to 1953 for all road models and 1954 for the tourers. They were joined in 1949 by the TR5 and this had a short one piece guard supported by two tubular stays run over the blade plus fixings to the main frame. For 1949 and 1950 an alternative blade was listed for use when the sprung hub was fitted but from then on just the one was called for up to 1954.

With the advent of the swinging fork frame for the Tiger models in 1954 a new one piece mudguard was introduced. This had a bridge attached which bolted to the rear unit top fixings and the same bolts also held the front end of the lifting handle. This was formed in one to run back from the fixings to a bridge under the mudguard that picked up on the top number plate bolt.

The same mudguard went onto the 5T and 6T in 1955 while the TR5 had its own, less valanced, blade. All models had a modified lifting handle on the same lines as the year before. The TR5 blade went onto the TR6 for 1956 and an optional rubber mudflap was offered for all models and remained available to 1959. The manufacture of the road model guards was altered for 1958 to remove the valance join but otherwise the parts remained as they were.

For 1960 the 6T and T110 adopted the 3TA bathtub and the TR6 and T120 were fitted with a blade to suit the duplex frame introduced that year. A similar style of guard went on the T100SS in 1961 and the T90 in 1963 and in that year the unit 650s all shared the same blade. 1964 brought changes with the tourers having one blade and the sports models another but there was

little to distinguish them apart. At the same time the lifting handle was reformed so it ran straight back and round the outside of the blade. This continued for 1965 for all and 1966 for the sports models but the tourers changed and all took the sports blade which thus became the standard fitting.

In 1966 variations were introduced for the US models and this continued into 1967. For 1968 there was a revised standard guard and modified lifting handle plus alternatives for the T100R and T100C, the latter in stainless. The next change came in 1970 with just one listed blade for all models. At the same time the lifting handle was altered by the addition of a second tubular loop to act as a grab handle behind the seat.

For 1971 new blades were introduced for all models and the lifting handles differed between the 500 and 650 cc machines. Both versions had provision for mounting side reflectors at the junction of the main tube and the grab handle.

Bathtub

This comprised two matching pressings with a beading between their juncture and motifs on each side to indicate the model. The panels need to be treated as any other large steel pressing so careful dressing of the surface is to be preferred to large amounts of filler.

The design was first seen on the 3TA in 1957 and went onto the 5TA in 1959 and the T100A in 1960. The early types were very sleek for the flanges at the rear which bolted together were turned in to hide the bolts and leave a neat join. For 1960 this flange was turned out which made assembly easier but lessened the attractiveness of the appearance although the flange was kept as small as possible. A few machines up to number H13115 that year did keep the inward turned flanges.

That same year the bathtub was fitted to the 6T and T110 and while the same basic parts were used there were variations which changed the number. The 650s thus had the flanges turned out.

The bathtub was fitted to the 3TA and 5TA up to 1963 but only to 1962 for the 6T and to 1961 for the T100A and T110, the last production year for those two models.

Bathtub rear mudguard

As the top of the bathtub was open and carried the dualseat a guard was fitted to keep the worst of the road dirt off it. This was a simple blade and one type was fitted to the smaller unit models and another to the 650 cc pre-units. There were no changes.

Rear skirts

When the trend to enclosure reversed, the Triumph answer was to reduce the bathtub to an abbreviated form. This took the shape of panels which covered the area beneath the seat and ahead of the subframe to the air filter which left part of the rear wheel out in the elements again so hence the need for a normal style of rear mudguard.

The skirts first appeared on the T100SS in 1961 and for this model extended past their rear fixing, to the top unit, on and up under the seat. This style continued for 1962 and had the left panel pierced for a single switch under the seat nose. For 1963 the design was modified to accommodate separate lights and ignition switches mounted side by side and also went onto the T90 with the two switches and the 6T but without switches in that instance so the panel was left plain. At the same time the skirts were amended to cut the panels off just aft of the fixing. To them were bolted valances which ran round the base of the seat to tidy up this area.

The 6T panels were as those of the smaller models but without the switch piercing and continued to be

fitted up to 1965. Those on the smaller sports machines were only fitted to 1963 after which they went.

Up to then the touring 3TA and 5TA had had the bathtub but for 1964 and 1965 they went over to skirts before dropping all enclosure in their final year in 1966. Their panels were much as those of the 6T but with three holes in each for the motif in place of the two used for 'Thunderbird'. They were fitted with the same valances to match the dualseat.

Side panels

On the pre-unit models this enclosing job was done by the oil tank on the right and the battery box lid on the left. It was not until 1963 that a panel appeared and then only on the left, as the oil tank continued on the right, except for the oil-in-frame 650s of 1971–72.

The 1963 TR6 and T120 were both fitted with a panel on the left which carried two piercings for separate lights and ignition switches. It was secured by two lugs at the top, a bracket at the front and a rubber bushed spike below.

A similar panel, also with two switches, went on the T90 and T100SS in 1964 but lacked the lower spike hole. There were no changes for 1965 but for 1966 the top fixings changed from vertical lugs to horizontal

The under seat area of a 3TA in 1964, the 5TA would look the same except for the skirt script

ones. One panel carrying two switches went onto the T90, T100, TR6 and T120 while three blank panels were listed. One without holes for a motif was used for the TR6C and T120TT but the others were one for the 6T and another for both the 3TA and 5TA. The twin switch panel also went on the T100R, T120R and 6T for the USA.

For 1967 the T90 and T100 changed their panel piercing to a single switch while the T100C continued with the blank panel used by the 3TA the year before. The 650s followed suit with a one switch panel for the TR6 and T120 but this differed from that fitted to the smaller models as it had a welded on strip at the front rather than the bolted one used up to then. The TR6C and T120TT continued with their blank 1966 panel.

The panel design was changed for 1968 to one that fitted to two grommets on studs on the sub-frame and was held by a single screw at the top front corner under the seat nose. This one panel went on all models which were distinguished by transfers. This panel continued to 1970 for the 650s and 1971 for the 500s. For the latter it was modified for 1972.

In 1971 the 650s gained a new frame and large air cleaner bodies which went just ahead of the side covers fitted, in this instance, on both sides. The right cover carried the ignition switch and both were modified for 1972.

Front number plate

Although these are no longer a legal requirement in the UK many owners like to keep them and either display the registration number or the model type and year. This is especially apt for a Triumph as for many years the plate was a feature of the marque with its chromed surround that set it off from other makes.

This was not fitted in 1938 but came in the next year on both models. It continued in 1946 with a new surround but about 1948 was modified so that the plate, surround and fixing studs became one item with just the fixing nuts and a rubber support bead separate. It continued in this form for many years and was joined in 1949 by a plain plate for the TR5 alone. This was held by two clips and had a cut-out in its lower edge to clear a mudguard stay. It went onto the TR6 in 1956 and also the T120 in 1960 although that model had the surround for 1959.

The 1948 type also went on the 3TA in 1957 and continued in use up to 1964 on that model plus the 5TA, T100A, 6T or T110 while in production. The 1949 TR5 plate continued to 1964 on the TR6, T120 and also went on the T100SS and T90.

For 1965 it was all change with a new plain plate for the 3TA, 5TA and 6T and one with a stay cut-out for the four sports models. This continued to 1969 when a new plate with moved cut-out and slotted clip holes went on all models. It was listed for the UK models from then on but not for the US ones.

Rear number plate

Still required and governed by local regulations so that in the end the company just provided a mounting bracket below the rear light and left it to the local dealer to find and fit the necessary plate. Not so in earlier days when white numbers would be painted directly to the plate. Later came transfers, plastic self adhesive numbers, pressed aluminium plates and finally the modern reflective one in yellow.

From the start the Triumph twin had the rear light in the top centre of the plate and not in one corner as on older designs. It also had a make transfer at the base of the plate and while the 5T one was in gold and white the one for the T100 was in blue and white.

The prewar plate continued to 1947 for all and 1949 for the 3T. The change of mudguard for 1948 on the 500s brought in a new plate with its bridge raised a little to act as a lifting handle. This type also went on the TR5 for 1949 while 1950 brought a revised plate common to all models.

This changed again in 1953 to accommodate the rectangular rear lamp and this type stayed in use up to 1963. For the first two years the two lower fixings were bolts with small reflectors fixed to their heads but these went in 1955 when a rear lamp with integral reflector was fitted.

The appearance of the bathtub on the 3TA in 1957 called for a change to the number plate so its top fixing could fit between the two tub halves. This changed in 1960 to suit the alteration to the bathtub flanges and the new plate was also fitted to the 6T and T110. For 1963 the 650s went back to the 1953 plate and this also went on the T100SS and T90 as they were introduced while the small tourers continued with the one to suit their rear enclosure.

For 1964 one common plate was used for all models extended in depth to accommodate the then new registration suffix letter while from 1966 plate brackets were specified for the US models. There was a further change in 1968 to the standard plate whose shape was altered and rear light fixing changed to three holes. It was amended again for 1970 but from then on only plate brackets were listed and a plain plate called up for the UK models.

Battery carrier

This was only fitted up to 1954 on rigid and sprung hub models and it is often one of the most corroded parts of the machine. Fortunately the main support and the two hinged straps are easy to remake if necessary but to do this the pins will need to be removed and the assembly dismantled.

One type was fitted from 1938 until 1949 when the base and back assembly changed. This entailed extending the back so it could run in and then up to its fixing instead of just up as before. The TR5 used the new back with this feature and the old base up to 1952 but then went over to the 1938 pattern which had returned to the other models for 1952. It continued in use for the 5T, 6T and TR5 in 1954.

Toolbox
As with the battery carrier this was fitted up to 1954 on rigid frames only. It went on the right side and for most models fitted between the two chainstays by the rear wheel. For the T100 from 1951–53 and the T100c in 1953 it was fitted above the upper stay in the quadrant between that and the vertical mudguard stay.

The original toolbox was fitted from 1938 to 1948 and was modified in respect of its lid screw fastener for 1949. It continued in this form to 1954 with a special clip for the T100 from 1951 on.

Battery and toolbox
The introduction of the sprung frame for the Tiger models in 1954 allowed these two items to be combined into one unit to match the oil tank. The air filter went between them so that all these functions became a single neat assembly.

The left box was divided into two sections with the battery in the forward one secured by hinged straps as before and the toolkit at the rear. A single cover enclosed both and was retained by a single central screw.

The lid and screw were changed for 1955 when the assembly went onto all models and continued unchanged to 1959. For that year another version appeared for the T120 which had no air cleaner but wore a 'Bonneville 120' transfer. Inside it carried all the standard fittings.

1960 brought changes as the 6T and T110 put on the bathtub so were fitted with a simple battery carrier and carried their tools in a roll under the seat. The carrier was a simple U bracket suspended from the frame for the battery to drop into. For the TR6 and T120, with and without air filters, there were boxes with an added mounting lug at the rear of the top surface. During 1961, from frame D9660 on, that of the T120 was further modified.

Meanwhile the advent of the smaller unit models had introduced another simple U bracket to act as a battery carrier and, up to 1960, a special tool pad under the seat. In 1961 this was replaced by a tool roll under the seat while on the T100SS went a narrow U bracket which carried the tools in a roll which dropped into a space under the seat between other items. At the same time a new battery carrier was introduced for the T100SS and this also went on the T90 in 1963.

1963 also saw the 650s with a new battery carrier and tooltray to suit their new frame. The carrier continued on the TR6 and T120 in 1964 and also went on all the smaller models but that for the 6T was changed to carry twin six-volt batteries. The tooltray became common to all models and was a simple open

top box with only three sides.

The next changes came for 1966 with a common battery carrier for all models and a new tooltray. The carrier was designed to take a single 12-volt battery but an alternative was offered for that year only to accommodate two six-volt ones. The tray gained a fourth side and a form that was rectangular with one corner chambered.

In 1968 the tooltray went as the toolkit was then carried in the left panel and a new battery carrier appeared. It stayed on the 500 to 1972 but the new frame for 1971 on the 650 meant changes for the larger models. The battery became supported by a tray hung from four welded on straps and the toolkit was given a folded piece of steel to drop into.

Tool pad
One of the features of the 3TA when launched was this moulded rubber tooltray. It fitted beneath the seat and had depressions formed in it to take the various items of the toolkit. For some owners this was a popular feature but others found that it prevented them from carrying their favourite tools which might not fit the spaces provided. Nor could they carry extra ones. The moulding itself was open to the weather from below and thus likely to deteriorate so for all these reasons it was only fitted up to 1960 and thus only on the 3TA, 5TA, and T100A.

Chainguards
These are parts that are usually covered in grease, damaged by chains and bent or distorted by owners struggling to fit the rear wheel. So the first job is to clean what you have which may take several sessions before you get all the grime off. Then repair and finish as any other steel item, making sure it fits as it should.

If there is any doubt you need to fit gearbox and rear wheel back into the frame assembly to check that the chain will run clear of the guard regardless of suspension movement. If it touches anywhere it will wear the finish away in no time and always rattle.

Upper chainguard
All models have one of these and the prewar one continued in 1946 on the 3T where it remained up to 1951. For the 500s a slightly modified form was used but in all cases the guard was held by two bolts and equipped with a clip near each end to carry the tyre pump. A small plate was welded on near the rear clip to keep dirt from the pump handle and to stop it falling into the spokes should it work loose.

The guard for the 500s was altered for 1948 to suit the revised mudguard stays and continued in use of all rigid frames to 1954. The TR5 alone differed with a similar form of guard but with the back, inner, part carried down to pass inboard of the lower chain run. Two guards were listed, one for rigid models and a modified version for those fitted with the sprung hub.

In 1954 the advent of the new frame brought a new guard which extended down to the rear fork leg. It was altered for 1957 with a deeper inner section and extended tail which enclosed the rear sprocket a little more. The TR models had their own version of this guard and like the road machines changed for 1957 and then continued unaltered to 1962.

The 3TA was introduced with its own guard in the same style as the pre-unit models and this went onto the other models as they came in. For the T90 and T100SS in 1963 a small supplementary part was added to bridge the gap between gearbox and chainguard and this continued to be used to 1972.

The 650s acquired a new guard for the first year of unit construction in 1963 and this changed in detail for 1964, 1965 and 1966. Meanwhile the smaller models took a new style for 1964 but kept to it to 1967. It was revised for 1968, again for 1969 when the inner part was extended down to the lower chain run but returned to the 1968 type in 1971. For the 650s there were no more changes until the new frame in 1971 which heralded a smaller and simpler guard.

Lower chainguard

This was fitted to the rigid frames from 1938–54 and to the early unit twins. Just one part served all the early models but never went on the TR5 while another fitted the 3TA, 5TA and T100A from 1957–66. The latter did not bolt to the machine at all but was welded to the rear brake torque stay.

Rear brake torque stay

This was not always fitted as for some models the back plate was anchored to a lug built into the chainstay. This was used for the first year of the sprung frame but for 1955 a stay was fitted. This same part went on all pre-unit models to 1962 and the unit 650s to 1966. Meanwhile the smaller unit models fitted a combined lower chainguard and torque stay and the more sporting T90 and T100SS had their own torque stay to 1966.

For 1967 two new stays appeared, one for the 650 and another for the smaller machines. Each had a length of wire welded to the inner side with the front end bent up and the rear down to act as chain guides. Both changed again for 1970 with the addition of a bracket hole near the front end and again for 1971 when the 500 reverted to a simple strip stay and the 650 to the same but with one extra hole in the strip.

Footrests

These are nice sturdy items that can usually be repaired. For once you have something to get hold of and the correct shape can be restored by heating the bent area and knocking it back to its right position. Clamp it in the vice to do this. If worn away it may be necessary to build the material up again and then reshape it with a file.

The methods of mounting the footrests varied over the years as the frames changed but otherwise stayed fairly constant. The pair used on the 1938 twin went onto all the road models up to 1951. For 1952 the left rest on the T100 only was modified and in 1954 both it and the T100 adopted a new right rest to suit the new frame. Meanwhile the TR5 has been fitted with its own rests for 1949–50 but then changed to those used by the 5T.

From 1955 all models used the same rests with the new 1954 Tiger right and the old 1938 left. This continued for all pre-unit machines to 1962.

The 3TA introduced a new pair of rests and these were used on all the smaller unit twins from then to 1972. In addition to these rigid rests a pair of folding ones were introduced for the T100C for 1966–69 and replaced by another pair for 1971–72.

The unit 650 had more changes. A new pair were fitted for 1963 and changed for 1964. For 1965 the left one only was altered and gained a tapped hole running along the top of the mounting boss for the brake pedal stop screw. Both rests changed for 1969 when they were Unified and again in 1971 to suit the new frame. Folding footrests were fitted to the TR6C and T120TT in 1966–67 and to the TR6C alone in 1971–72.

Footrest rubbers

It is best to replace these if possible as new ones will help to put the finishing touches to the restored machine. Just one rubber went on nearly all models from 1938 to 1972. Exceptions were the TR5 which had its own rubbers 1949–54 and the late unit 650s which had a new one for 1971–72. The 500 kept to the 1938 style for those years.

Pillion rests

These need to be cleaned up and straightened if necessary with particular attention to the pivot holes and the threaded one that enables the rest to be held in position. The pivot bolt should be tightened just enough to achieve this without making it too hard to move the rest.

For the rigid frame the rests were assembled to frame lugs but on the sprung frame bolted to the subframe silencer bracket. The same rests went on all pre-unit models and were fitted with the same rubbers. These rubbers were also used on all smaller unit twins and the unit 650 to 1970.

The 3TA had its pillion footrests held by a stud and nut and this style continued on all models until 1969 when it was Unified. It continued on the 500 to 1972 but the 650s had new rests to suit their new frame in 1971.

Brake pedal

Another part that is often damaged but is not too hard to repair. The pivot may need to be machined true and bushed if badly worn. Heat to straighten and build up worn surfaces so they can be filed to shape.

The original pedal in 1938 came fitted with a rubber pad and this continued to be listed up to 1954 although the pedal pad was altered for 1952. At that time it was reduced in width to tuck in more and given a non-slip pinnacle finish. Thus all rigid frame models effectively have the same pedal.

A new one of similar form with pedal arm, pivot bush and rod arm all forged in one was introduced for the Tiger models in 1954. It was modified during the year from engine 51200 and went on all models in 1955. It was changed to suit the duplex frame in 1960 and again for the 650s in 1963 when the frame was again altered. For 1965 the rod arm became separate with a square hole to locate to the pedal. This was now formed with a spindle so worked in a bush in the frame. For 1971 and the new frame the design reverted to a fixed spindle and a new pedal was used with the rod arm outboard of the pedal one and carrying the height adjustment bolt.

The smaller unit twins went their own way with a new pedal in the pre-unit style from 1957. This had a joggle in the rod arm and this went from 1967 when a straight arm version was introduced.

Drive side of T100S in 1968 shown with side cover removed

Rear brake rod

All the rigid models had a rod with a proper fork end at the front to connect to the pedal. With the introduction of the new frame in 1954 standards dropped and the rod was simply bent at the end and secured with a split pin.

Rods need to be straight, the thread at the end in good condition and the fork hole not worn or the rod not worn where it bears in the pedal. Damage needs to be rectified.

One type of rod was used on all rigid models but came in different lengths to suit the application. The first as introduced in 1938 went onto the 5T, T100 and 6T in turn with an alternative for use with the sprung hub and the same pair were also fitted to the TR5.

For the swinging fork models one rod was used by all from 1954–66. It and its adjuster nut changed for all in 1967 and this continued on the 500s to 1972 and the 650s until revised for the new frame in 1971.

Rear carrier

This was only fitted to models with a rigid frame and was offered as an extra for prewar models and from 1947–54. If used it will require to be refurbished so it fits correctly without straining other parts.

The prewar design was listed for 1947 but changed for the new form of rear mudguard fitted to the 5T and T100 in 1948. It was not listed for the 3T from then on but continued for the road 500s and the 6T until the new frame arrived.

12 Wheels and brakes

This is an area where a good few operations have to follow one another in a definite sequence. Due to this an early start is advised to avoid a hold-up later on when it may not be convenient. Once the machine is without wheels it becomes very hard to move about unless reduced to parts. It could be worth considering slave wheels if this could be a problem to you.

Restoration begins by removing the wheels, taking the tyres off and separating the brake backplate from the wheel assembly. Each can then be dealt with in turn.

Spoking pattern and rim offset

The wheel assembly comprises the hub assembly, the spokes, their nipples and the rim. Before doing anything else get your notepad out and measure the rim offset and draw the spoke pattern. This first is a vital piece of data and the second will give you real problems if you have to work it out from scratch. This can be done but it is not easy.

The rim offset is taken by placing a straight edge across the mouth of the brake drum and measuring from it to the edge of the rim. Just to make sure, also measure from a firm point at the other end of the hub and take the rim width. Take several measurements to see if there is any variation.

If the rim is buckled or has been taken apart, it is back to basics. You will have to work out where the rim should be in relation to the frame and you have two points of reference to help. First is that the wheels are normally central to the frame and forks. Second is the sprocket offset which you can measure on the gearbox and wheel.

Or find another machine and measure that.

You may have to do this if you start with the bare hub and don't know the spoking pattern but with a complete machine you can make notes. You consider each side and start by checking the rim to see which way round it is. No problem with a full width hub but when it is offset the spoke lengths and angles differ from side to side.

Now note where the valve hole is and check that the spokes either side run away from it to give the best access. If they don't the wheel has been built incorrectly at some time and you can expect to find most of the spokes bent near the thread. Note how the spoke to one side of the valve hole runs, whether its head points out from the wheel or into its centre and any feature of the hub which will enable you to locate that spoke into the same hole.

Relating the rim, spoke lay and hub for that first spoke will give the key to the wheel build. From it the others will fall into a pattern. Working round the rim the spokes will alternate from one side of the hub to the other. Every third spoke will be laid the opposite way to the first and its head will face the reverse way unless straight spokes are fitted. Every fifth spoke will echo the first in angle and lay.

To finish the notes for side one you need to work out the spoke cross pattern. On one side a spoke may cross one running the other way two, three or four times with two being usual. Note the position of the first spoke and the one that crosses it nearest to the hub. Trace it to the rim and note its position there from the outer end of the first spoke.

Now note how side two relates to side one. Don't forget you reverse things if you turn the wheel over. One spoke on side two will give you the start to the pattern but check it out anyway as a double-check on your side one notes.

Wheel dismantling

If you want to repaint the hub you will have to take the wheel apart and later rebuild it. Hence the notes above. The rim is removed by undoing all the spoke nipples which may be easy or could call for penetrating oil and a little heat. Note that there can be four types of spoke in each wheel with differences in length and head angle so these points need checking. Keep the spokes in batches and note which goes where on your spoke diagram or you will have to sort that out as well. Note that for some wheels certain spokes cannot come away until others have been removed. This sequence must be known, as the rebuild has to be done in the reverse order.

You now have a rim, 40 nipples and batches of 10,

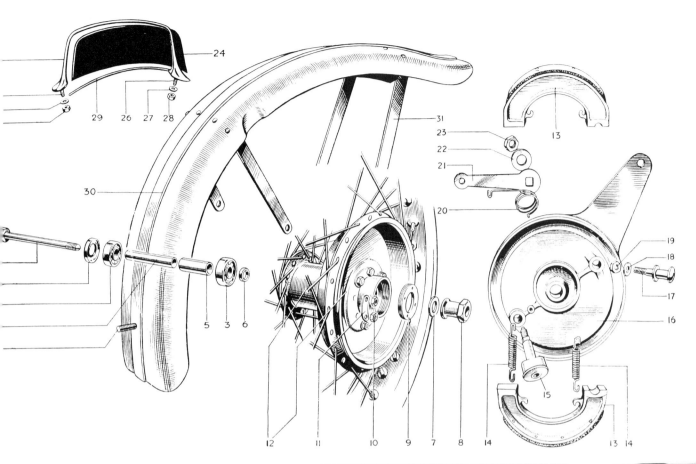

ABOVE *Front wheel and mudguard as shown in the 1946 parts list. Note typical Triumph front number plate surround*

RIGHT *8 in. front brake with air scoop and mesh as fitted to the Tiger models for 1954*

20 or 40 spokes. Plus the hub assembly with attendant brake drum and rear sprocket in one case.

Hub, drum and rear sprocket

Various forms of assembly were used by Triumph for these items and the bearings and spindle they turned on. The bearing retaining rings need to be removed, some having left-hand threads, and all the parts dismantled, cleaned and inspected. Before removing the spindle check the hub and brake drum for any run-out which will need correcting. This should not be attempted until the hub is on its new bearings to ensure accuracy.

Many Triumphs used a built-up assembly as hub

and drum and if all is well there is no need to disturb. If there is any doubt the parts should come down and all be individually inspected. This construction does allow replacement of brake drums if scored and rear sprockets if hooked but for many models the two were combined so changing one meant doing this for both. Make sure the new parts run true when on their new bearings.

If renewal is not feasible it is possible to skim the brake drum and this measure will also deal with oval or belled drums. The sprocket teeth can be built up and recut by a specialist.

The hub itself should be closely inspected for any signs of damage. Repair can be awkward depending on the construction and not attempted unless you are confident that the result will withstand the loads placed upon it.

The various parts will need careful masking before finishing and threads must be left clean or the locating rings may bind. Check this before assembly.

Front hub types

The prewar design was made to suit girder forks and turned on taper roller races. The brake drum was bolted to the hub by a ring of fixings. Postwar the same form of construction continued but mounted on ball bearing races and designed to fit the telescopic forks.

This continued to 1956 with a small modification to the hub in 1950 and a change to a more rigid cast iron brake drum in 1951. This continued on the 5T, 6T and TR5 in 1954 when the Tiger models changed to an 8 in. brake and drum to suit and this was revised for 1955 when it lost its spoke flange scallops.

In 1957 it was all change with a full width hub for the 5T, 6T and TR5 and a new drum and hub in the same 8 in. offset style as before for the T100, T110 and TR6, this last having shared the 7 in. brake of the TR5 in 1956. 1958 brought an 8 in. full width hub for these three models while the others continued with their smaller 1957 type. The 8 in. hub went onto the T120 in 1959 and the 6T in 1961 so all pre-unit models finished with the same part.

The full width hubs were of composite construction with the centre tube brazed to two conical pressings which were riveted to the cast iron hub shell and brake drum. The end of the hub without the brake was closed off by a chrome-plated cover peened into place. For 1958 only on the 650 cc models this was louvred but for all other years was plain.

The smaller unit twins used the 1957 full width hub from that year to 1968. In that year a new 8 in. hub was introduced for the T100T and T100R models only and this had straight spokes for the plain side and a flange and angled ones for the drum one. This stiffened the drum and while the end cover remained

Front hub and front mudguard stay fixing on the 3TA for 1965

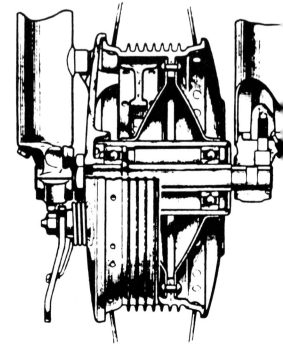

The 1957 composit full width hub built up with steel tube, steel pressings and cast iron drum

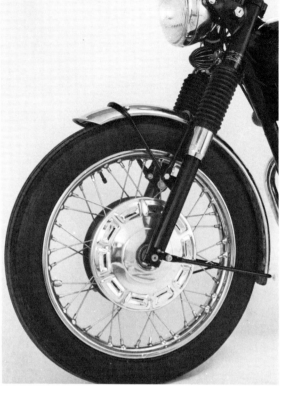

plain that year, for 1969 it gained circumferential ribs in its surface. This arrangement continued on these models to 1972.

For the T100C, T100S and the last few T90s made in 1969 there was a similar design of hub of 7 in. diameter with the same style of ribbed end cover. This also continued to 1972.

The unit 650s had more changes but began with the existing 8 in. full width hub. For 1966 there was a change for all models to the hub that was to go into the T100T in 1968 with its added flange round the brake drum. This hub was modified for 1968 to allow the use of a bigger brake backplate and at the same time the cover plate was given a ring of rectangular shaped depressions each with a slot in it to allow air in and out. This was held in place by three screws but it went for 1969 when the ribbed cover appeared and this meant a change to the hub to delete the tapped holes. For 1970 the 650s went back to their 1966 hub but fitted with the 1969 cover while for 1971–72 they used the conical hub.

Rear hub types
These were built up as at the front with hub, brake drum and sprocket bolted together to form one unit from 1938–51. After that the drum and sprocket become one part until 1966 when they became two items once more. All used as standard in rigid frames turned on taper roller bearings and these must be

ABOVE *Front end for the TR6 and T120 in 1968 showing the pierced nave plate held by three small screws*

LEFT ABOVE *1966 front end for the 650s with spoke flange round brake drum and also showing the mudguard stays of the period*

carefully adjusted to just leave a trace of play at the wheel rim. Too little and the race will wear rapidly but if correct they will run for a long time.

The sprung hub had caged angular contact ball bearings in the Mark I version and these need careful shimming to get right. The aim is free rotation with no lateral movement which is not easy but very necessary. The Mark II hubs turn on ball races so are easier to set up.

With the introduction of the swinging fork frame in 1954 the standard rear wheel bearings were changed to ball races and these remained common to all models from then on. At the same time a quickly detachable rear wheel was listed and this had a single ball race in the brake drum but taper rollers in the hub itself. This continued until 1964 but from 1965 to 1970, the last

ABOVE *The quickly detachable hub for the swinging fork frame introduced for 1954. An option for many years*

TOP *Rear wheel and rear end of a restored 1953 Thunderbird taken at Brands Hatch in 1984*

year it was offered, the qd wheel ran on three ball races.

Except where the sprung hub was fitted all Triumph twins had a 7 in. diameter rear brake. With the sprung hub this increased to 8 in.

Postwar the hub was changed from the 1938 type but carried the same drum and 46 tooth sprocket. In 1949 the speedometer drive was from the gearbox, not the rear hub, so the latter changed except for the TR5 although this model adopted the standard hub from 1951. It continued to the end of the rigid frame but from 1952 the drum and sprocket were in one in cast iron.

A new hub appeared in 1954 for the swinging fork frame but combined with the existing one piece drum and sprocket. It was modified for 1957 when the spokes changed to the butted type and thus went up a size at the hub end. The drum and sprocket changed for 1960 when the gearing was adjusted by reducing the teeth to 43 and in these forms the parts ran to the end of the pre-unit models.

The early sprung hub had few modifications from its introduction in 1947 until the second version took over in 1950 and continued to 1954.

The 3TA commenced with the combined drum and sprocket with 43 teeth as later used on the pre-unit models with its own hub in the existing style. Both changed in 1963 for the T90 and T100SS and 1964 for the 3TA and 5TA with a return to 46 teeth and the use of the 1952 combined drum and sprocket with a revised hub. For 1966 the hub continued but the sprocket became separate and once more bolted to the hub while keeping its 46 teeth. In 1970 came the final changes with Unified bolts holding modified drum and hub while using the existing sprocket.

The unit 650s began with the hub that went onto the smaller twins in 1963/64 with the same combined drum and sprocket. For 1966 they copied the smaller models with the same parts but for 1970 only altered the hub in the same way while leaving the drum alone. For 1971–72 there was the conical one-piece hub with separate 47 tooth sprocket.

The quick detachable wheel was offered from 1954 to 1970 but only from 1960 for the smaller unit models. During this period it received quite a number of alterations although the basic form remained the same. Due to this care is needed to ensure you finish up with compatible parts.

Wheel bearings

Taper rollers prewar and in the rigid rear wheel to 1954. For the rest all wheels turned on the same pair of ball races. The exception was the qd one which had taper rollers in the hub to 1964 and ball races from then on but always accompanied by the same ball race in the drum.

Ball races need to be a good fit in the hub and on the spindle. The second is easy to replace if damaged but

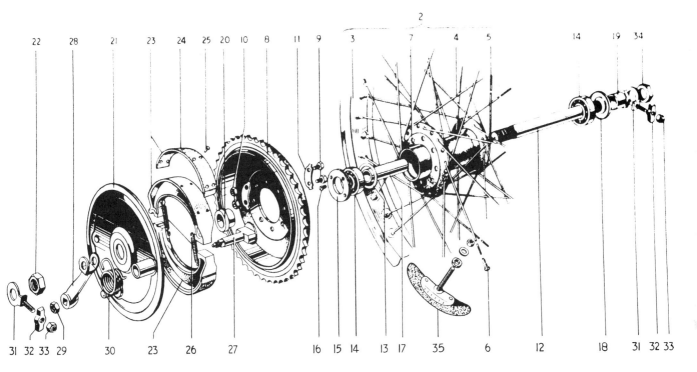

2

22 28 21 23 24 25 20 10 8 11 9 3 7 4 5 14 19 34

31 32 33 29 30 23 26 27 16 15 14 13 17 35 6 12 18 31 32 33

*Parts list drawing of the standard rear wheel fitted to the
650s in 1960*

for the first it may be necessary to use Loctite to ensure
the race does not move. Races must be fitted square
and the drift or press used must bear directly on the
race being inserted and not load the balls and their
tracks.

Sometimes it will be found that once assembled the
wheel spindle is tight. What can happen is that as you
push the outer home the inner is held back by the
spindle so finishes out of line from its nominal
position. To correct you use a hammer as a precision
tool and just lightly tap in the required direction.

Brakes

Most are single leading shoe but regardless of type
they require the same attentions. Strip, clean and
examine for wear, damage, distortion or cracks.
Repair as required. Check the fit of the backplate to
the wheel spindle, the condition of the cams, the cam
levers and the return springs. If the last are tired,
replace them.

You are likely to fit new brake shoes or to reline the
ones you have. With the former first check that the
brake drum is the standard diameter and has not been
skimmed at some time. If it has not still beware of
pattern shoes as some have minimal lining material
and will seem to be worn out even when new.

If you reline yourself you will need clamps to hold
the liners in place, drill and counter-bore to form the
holes and riveting tools. Work out from the centre and
chamfer when finished.

Should you go to an expert he will, or should, want
the wheel and backplate. He will check and skim the
drum first if this is needed and then reline the brakes
with oversize liners which can be turned down to fit.

Front brake types

The prewar backplate carried a speedometer drive
gearbox which went to the rear wheel for the 1946
models which did retain their prewar brake shoes. In
1954 an 8 in. brake with air scoop went onto the Tiger
models and for 1955–56 a blanking plate was offered
for those riders who wished to close the air scoop off.

In 1957 a new backplate carried the old shoes in the
full width drum on the 5T, 6T, TR5 and 3TA. The TR6
which had shared their brake on its introduction in
1956 moved over to join the Tigers with the 8 in. type
which had the backplate modified to suit the revised
front wheel spindle brought in for the split fork ends
of that year.

For 1958 the Tigers and TR6 changed to the full
width hub and with it a backplate that located onto a
lug on the fork leg which replaced the earlier bolted
anchorage. With the new plate came a new pair of
shoes. 1959 brought the 5TA and 1960 the T100A both
of which shared the 7 in. full width hub and brake
system.

The 8 in. hub and brake went onto the T120 in 1959
and the 6T in 1961 and for that year the shoes were
changed to fully floating with pads on the pivot pin

159

ABOVE *The T100S in 1969 showing the bellcrank lever two leading shoe front brake*

LEFT *Front wheel and brake as fitted in 1964*

ends to reduce wear. The same design but in 7 in. diameter went onto all the smaller unit twins the same year and continued on them to 1968. On the 650s the 8 in. brake ran on with a change for 1966 to wider shoes and more brake drum area.

For 1968 the T100T and T100R were fitted with the 8 in. brake used by the 650s since 1966 while the other smaller twins continued with their 7 in. type. On the 650s there was a new twin leading shoe 8 in. brake with a new backplate with air scoop. The brake cam levers were joined by an adjustable rod and the brake cable swept in from the rear to a stop cast into the backplate and on to the extended front lever. The two brake shoes were the same item fitted to suit the cams.

The design was changed for 1969 with the front lever moved round so the cable could run down the fork leg to its stop and the lever connection. As the link between the levers had to remain as it was the front lever became a bell crank. A new backplate was used with the same shoes. The same parts went onto the T100T and T100R while the other smaller twins were fitted with a 7 in. version of the same design.

This arrangement continued to 1972 for the 500s but only to 1970 for the 650s. For them 1971 brought the conical hub and a new backplate and shoes operated by very short cam levers connected directly to the inner and outer of the cable.

Rear brake types

There were fewer of these and all were of 7 in. diameter except for the sprung hub which due to its size had to be 8 in. The 1938 design continued on all rigid models with a minor modification in 1947 when a thrower was added. For the 1954 Tigers the backplate continued to be located to the frame by a lug and slot but from 1955 a torque stay was used. Thus the plate was changed for both years but then remained in use on all models to 1969.

The original brake shoes, identical with the front ones for many years, were used on all models to 1960. For 1961 the floating shoes were fitted, again common with the front ones and these stayed on the smaller models to 1972 and the 650s to 1970. The backplates changed to a Unified thread in 1970 and again for the

ABOVE *The full width hub with spoke flange round the drum as fitted to the TR6 for 1966*

LEFT *The first twin leading shoe brake used by the TR6 and T120 in 1968. Note cable run and brake shoe details*

650s only in 1971. For them there was a conical hub, new backplate and new shoes but still of 7 in. diameter with single leading shoe operation.

Spokes and nipples

These need to be straight and with good threads. It is false economy to just replace some if more than one or two are past redemption; better to re-spoke completely. Check carefully the length, gauge and head angle you require before shopping and inspect what you buy to make sure you do get what you want.

The dimensions of most Triumph spokes are listed in an appendix and if being replaced a new set of nipples are worth getting as well. Remember that their diameter is to suit the spoke gauge and that the rim holes must suit.

It is possible to buy stainless steel spokes although opinions vary as to how this material can cope with the bending of the head angle and the stress pattern spokes are subject to. If made to really close tolerances they should be no trouble but avoid anything cheap or poorly finished.

Wheel rims

All Triumph twins have steel rims of the WM section form. Diameters used were 17, 18 and 19 in. and width numbers 1, 2 and 3. All had 40 spoke holes and security bolts were fitted from 1949 on most models.

If the rim is damaged or rusty it will have to be replaced as you are unlikely to find anyone who can repair the first or willing to strip and replate to correct the second. Thus you will need a new rim and the first point to consider is the tyre size you will finally fit. In many cases it will be worth going to a WM3 section rather than keeping to the listed WM2 if you wish to fit a fatter tyre.

Next is the dimpling and the holes. For a really strong wheel the spokes must lay at the correct angle in both directions and to achieve this the rim must be pierced to suit. You also need holes for the tyre valve and any security bolts. Inspect the join in the rim as unless smooth you will never get the wheel to run really true.

The rims used for the various models are set out in an appendix along with their listed tyre size and number of security bolts. Only two of the latter were listed, one each for the WM2 and WM3 rims.

The rim finish is either chrome plating or the same with a painted, lined centre. Unless you are very sure that you can produce this really well, send it to an expert. It is an area where any flaw will be only too obvious so the cost will be worth it.

Wheel rebuilding

This is an area that many people fight shy of but with care and patience good results can be obtained. Your notes will make the job much easier and should be consulted as to the order of assembly and the precise location of each item. The rim must be the right way round.

Simply fit the first spoke and start its nipple so it cannot shift and scratch the rim. Then continue this process until you have all 40 in place. It should be obvious if you have made a mistake as either spokes won't connect at all or will be at the wrong angle. As long as spoke one is correct, the rest will fall into place.

You now have to true the wheel and could consider sending the assembly to an expert for this final important stage. Or you can do it yourself. Set the wheel vertical with the spindle held so you can spin the rim. Place a marker clear of the rim and try it for truth. Adjust spokes to suit but work to get the radial

LEFT *Adjusting the conical front brake fitted to the 650s from 1971. Note the four studs holding the fork cap in place*

BELOW *The conical front hub with its very short cam levers and simple cable connection. A 1972 T120 but the TR6 was the same*

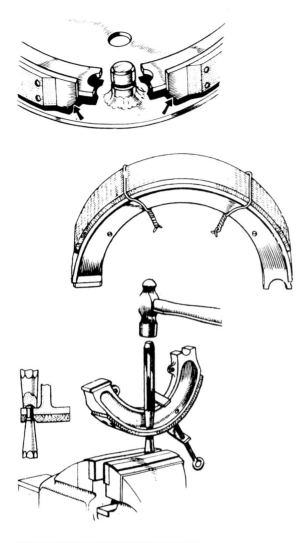

position correct first and then go on to deal with the sideways error. If you start with a good rim and work carefully you should not have much trouble. Make sure every spoke is nicely tensioned without being overstrained.

Tyres, tubes and rim tapes

Your first problem could be finding something to fit. Much easier with some models than others. You now have the choice of 'old fashioned' sizes, or some of them, more up-to-date low profile tyres or the latest metric offerings which are low profiles with their inches translated into millimetres.

Regardless of which you decide on, do fit a rim tape in good condition after you have checked the spoke nipples for protruding spoke ends. A new inner tube really is mandatory, don't even think of patches. The tyre itself must suit the rim section and the front and rear must be compatible. The faster the machine, the more important are the tyres and their type but they must never be ignored.

If you fit modern tyres you must make certain that there is ample clearance for the fatter section in all positions of the rear suspension. Fit them with care and use your slim, smooth, polished tyre levers. Don't forget the security bolts. Do forget the tyre pressure table in the old manuals which has no relevance to modern tyres. Establish the wheel loading and check the tyre data for the correct pressure. Check the rolling diameter or revolutions per mile for the old tyre and the modern replacement in case it affects the speedometer reading to any real extent.

LEFT TOP *Checking the fit of a brake shoe to its pivot at top and two stages in re-lining the shoe. Small clamps can also be used to hold the liner and the centre is rivetted first*

LEFT BELOW *The floating brake shoe design adopted for 1961*

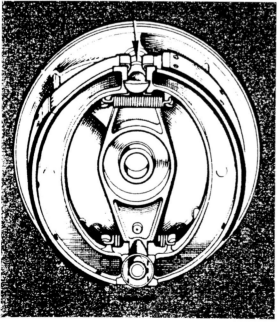

13 Cables, controls and instruments

There are few things that look worse on a restored motorcycle than cables drooping in loops and obviously far too long or ones with the adjuster screwed right out and hanging on the last thread. There are few more dangerous than cables that are tight and which could be pulled by the forks as they move.

The control cables should be the proper length, run on the right route, be neatly clipped out of harm's way and in correct adjustment. They should also be of the correct gauge for the job or the throttle will feel heavy and the front brake full of sponge.

Every cable is an assembly of inner, outer, outer ends and wire nipples at a minimum and normally all have at least one adjuster in their length. To these parts can be added end stops and fittings to attach the cable to its lever and the machine. In just about all cases the outer length determines the sweep of the final job while the inner must be chosen to suit the wear on the parts and the length of adjustment available.

Each end fitting needs to be checked over and repaired or replaced where needed. This operation should include any plating required. Nipples may be re-used but must be fully cleaned first and it is best to remove all the old solder using heat so you can properly assess the condition of the part. If past recall, they should be replaced and if exactly the right size is not available, it may be machined from another, larger, nipple. Do make sure it is a good fit on the cable, free to slide into place but no more.

Soldering

This is the technique used to attach nipple to wire and the secret of success is clean parts. Solder will not adhere to surfaces that are dirty, tarnished or greasy but is no problem on a clean surface.

The tools you need are soldering iron, solder and flux. The first may be electric, heated over a gas flame or heated by butane. The slim type used for electrical work will not have enough heat for cables and something of 60–70 watts is necessary. If you use a gas flame first clean up the iron tip with a file and let the flame play on the iron an inch back from the tip to keep it clean. When hot it can be dipped in flux to remove any oxidation and given a thin coat of solder.

The solder you use comes in a stick. Do not use flux cored electrician's solder as it is not up to the job being designed for electric wires, not steel cables. The flux can be a paste in a tin or a liquid. My own preference is for the first as it is convenient to be able to open it and dip the iron or cable in. A match is handy for putting flux onto areas where it is needed.

To cut an inner to length you use sharp, heavy duty cutters or a cold chisel and block or a hack saw. Before cutting you must tin the cable to stop it unwinding and the process is the same as any soldering. First clean the wire really well, next tin the iron and third use the iron to tin the wire, adding solder if needed. Keep it to a minimum and try to avoid blobs.

You can now cut the wire and solder a nipple on the end. To do this successfully you have to splay the wire ends out to sit in the countersink in the nipple and this operation can be done as follows. Clamp the wire vertically in the vice with the nipple sitting on top of the vice jaw. Before holding the wire firmly, slide it down to about level with the top surface of the nipple. Clamp but don't crush and then tap the wire top with the ball end of a light hammer to splay the strands. This can be started using a tack if needed.

Now hold the wire lightly in the vice with a clothes peg between the nipple and the vice jaws. Leave the vice slack enough for you to pull down on the wire. Tin the iron and apply solder to the nipple to build up as required. While it cools keep a light pull on the wire and watch. The surface appearance will change as soon as it hardens. Leave for a short while and give it a good tug. Better it flies off in the workshop than on the road. File to shape and make sure it fits its lever and can turn if necessary.

Cable making

There are two ends to a cable so there are two soldering jobs to do. As there are at least three and sometimes four or five cables to do it takes some time to make a full set from scratch.

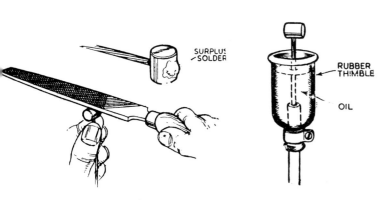

TINNED   CUT

SURPLUS
SOLDER

RUBBER
THIMBLE

OIL

Stages in soldering showing tinning the wire, cutting to length, splaying the end, filing to shape and one way of oiling the result

Start with the outer and determine its run and thus its length. Fit its ferrules having checked that they in turn will fit their housings at both ends. Solder on one nipple to the inner and assemble to the outer complete with all fittings. Some owners like to lubricate the cable at this point but this practice means that the end has to be cleaned again. My own preference is to assemble, clean, solder and then oil.

In either case the important aspect is to get the inner wire length correct. To do this connect the already soldered end and offer up the other. No need to clip anything to the frame or even have the parts on the machine at this stage as long as the operation at the ends is correct. Set the adjusters to suit the controls. Thus screw the front brake one right in if the brakes have been relined as movement will be all in one direction. The clutch is better in mid-travel as this will allow for wear and swelling plates if you have the latter problem. The throttle, air and magneto should be to allow the controls to work to their inbuilt stops without the adjusters hanging out of their housings.

Now solder the second nipple in place and clean it up. The cable can now be lubricated and the only way to be sure the oil has gone all the way through is to pour it in one end until it comes out of the other. Funnels formed round the end are a common suggestion but my own method is to use a pressure device which goes round the end and is pumped up

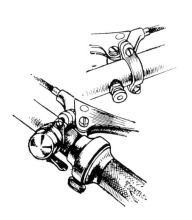

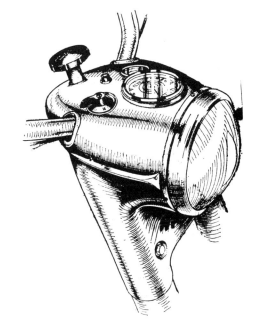

LEFT *1960 advert and price for the lubricator I use which is effective if messy. There are others as good*

RIGHT *1949 features of built in horn button, dipswitch mounting and twistgrip friction knob, nacelle and new control layout*

BELOW *The four bar tank grid and control layout of a 1966 TR6, typical of the period*

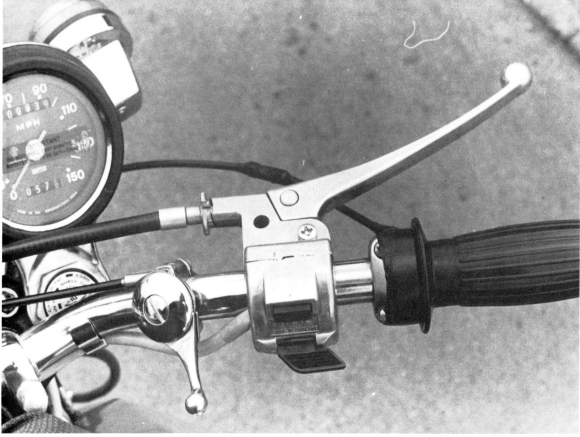

with a bicycle pump. Rather messy but very effective and there are others available.

Controls

The twins began with 1 in. diameter handlebars but while the rest of the industry settled to this size or $\frac{7}{8}$ in. Triumph chose to split the difference and use $\frac{15}{16}$ in. for many years. As many models had reduced end diameters and other packing at the fork yoke clamp, it is important that the restorer works to the parts list if he seeks originality.

The same rules apply to the controls and the use of Triumph or Amal twistgrips on some models and the optional ball end levers on others. Watch out for those models with the horn button screwed into the bars and those where the air or magneto lever is mounted on the front brake or clutch lever clamp.

Each control needs to be stripped, cleaned, inspected, renovated as required and assembled. Care will be rewarded by smooth operation and pleasant feel. Twistgrip and left bar grips should be replaced if required and the right part will enhance the final result.

The handlebars themselves may well have been changed or bent. If the former, the criterion is whether they are comfortable for you the new owner or whether you want to change them to be original. On the latter, much the same applies but beware of straightened bars as they have been known to snap due to the metal being stretched.

Instruments

The ammeter has been mentioned which leaves speedometer, rev-counter and oil pressure gauge. The

LEFT TOP *Controls of a T120 in 1969 with combined horn button and dipswitch. Ignition switch in fork shroud*

LEFT *Right bar of a 1972 T120 showing the switches built into the Lucas front brake lever and taped up throttle cable*

RIGHT TOP *The tank top instrument panel of the 1939 Tiger 100 with ammeter, oil gauge, light switch and panel light*

RIGHT *Rev-counter mounted in the nacelle of a 1952 Tiger 100 fitted with the full race kit and seen in 1984*

ABOVE *Clocks, switches and lamps for the 1967 twins*

TOP *Instrument panel of a restored 1953 Thunderbird with cut-out button in centre, aft of speedometer*

ABOVE *The 1967 layout of ammeter, warning lights and rotary light switch*

TOP *Speedometer by itself on a TR6 in 1964*

RIGHT *1968 T100S instruments and bars. The steering lock lug on the headstock is also visible*

FAR RIGHT TOP *Headlamp shell and instruments of Tiger 100 in 1968. Note slots in shrouds for horizontal beam adjustment*

last was only fitted up to 1948 and was a typical design with coiled pressure tube linked to the pointer. Repair entails instrument mechanic skills and tools for the parts are smaller and lighter than the general run of motorcycle items. A magnifier and tweezers to hold things are well worth having. Treat the scale face with care but repaint the needle if necessary.

Two types of mechanism were used in the speedometers and rev-counters fitted by Triumph with the chronometric type being superceded by the magnetic in the early 1960s. The first was generally held to be the more reliable in the long term but is a complex mechanical device that just became too expensive for a mass produced product. It has a camshaft, balance wheel, gears, levers and springs. To get at these you first have to unscrew the bezel ring without marking it which will then allow the works to be removed.

If you are an instrument fitter you should be able to strip, repair and rebuild a chronometric speedometer. If you are an instrument mechanic it could be as well to stop at the mileage recorder which Is easier to work with although it still needs delicate care.

The later magnetic type is easier to work on but only once you get inside it for the bezel is rolled on. This means care and maybe a special tool to unroll it off plus another to replace it. Once inside, it is much less complex but just as delicate as any other.

From the point of repair the rev-counter is simply a speedometer mechanism minus the distance recorder. The case is basically the same and just the dial differs with its own calibration. For Triumphs alone there was also the combined scale instrument which was a speedometer with four extra concentric scales. These used the standard needle to register the rpm in each gear and while not to road racing accuracy, it was a nice feature that gave the marque a distinctive air.

Along with the instrument head must be considered its mounting and its drive. The first must be in good order and the second comprises the cable and the drive box. The cable needs to be inspected and replaced if either inner or outer are damaged while the drive box must operate smoothly. For many years the speedometer was driven from the gearbox but late models used the rear wheel and the rev-counter various drive schemes.

LEFT TOP *1969 T120 with toggle light switch behind ammeter, itself between two warning lights*

LEFT *The rev-counter drive from the left end of the exhaust camshaft. Note the fractured exhaust pipe bracket, a victim of vibration on this 1972 T120*

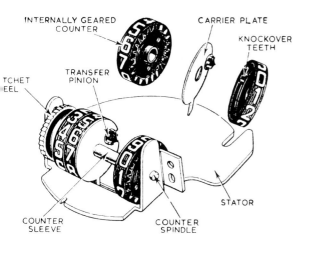

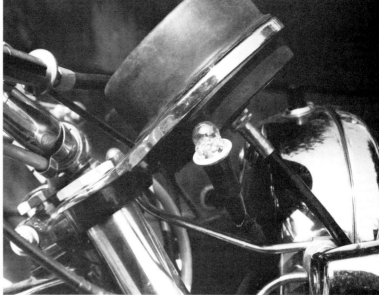

Details of the mileage recorder mechanism as used around 1960

Instrument mounting for the T120 in 1970 with push-in bulb holder. Turn switch on headlamp shell supported on bent wire brackets

Speedometer types

The first point on any speedometer is the direction of rotation of the needle which must match the cable. Next is the maximum scale reading, then whether in miles or kilometres and most important, the revolutions per mile figure.

This is normally written on the scale just under the part number and for many models a figure around 1600–1700 can be expected if it is calibrated in miles, this reducing to circa 1000 for the metric measurement. This is also the cable speed in rpm at 60 mph by definition as at that speed one mile takes one minute to travel so if the cable turns, say, 1620 times in the distance, it has done the same in the time.

The final points in speedometer selection are the presence of total and may be rip distance recorders, the method of returning the trip one to zero and the mounting of the instrument.

Up to 1948 the speedometer was mounted as a separate item but for 1949 went into the nacelle where it was retained by a clamp bar. The TR models and later sports machines retained the original style of mount.

When hunting for a replacement speedometer, most of the requirements are easy to determine and to check except for the important revs-per-mile needed to match the machine. For rear wheel driven machines, and the prewar front wheel drive ones, the factors are the tyres' revs-per-mile and the ratio between wheel and cable. The latter is controlled by the speedometer gearbox and the ratio is usually around 2:1. Where the drive is from the machine's gearbox the tyre, final drive gearing, sleeve gear ratio and layshaft skew gear pair all play their part and have to be allowed for. If any change so does the speed of the instrument cable so adjustment is needed to allow for a change of tyre size or the fitting of a wide ratio sleeve gear pair.

The optimum cable speed can be found by calculation using the data available for the model in question and applies provided it is to standard specification in respect of the features which affect it. If all is well, this is the figure to seek on the replacement speedometer, or something close to it.

On occasion the sum has to be used in reverse, in effect. If a good speedometer is to hand but with the wrong cable speed, it may be possible to achieve the correct readings by using an alternative wheel gearbox. Calculators make it easy to do the sums once the data has been collected.

Rev-counter types

Both chronometric and magnetic types were used driven from the engine in a variety of ways. Heads are made to be driven at half or quarter engine speed and the drive gearbox and the point from which it is driven must both be taken into account when selecting parts.

Direct from the camshaft or via a 1:1 box calls for a 2:1 head but if a 2:1 box is fitted you need a 4:1 head. Fit a 2:1 and you can really impress onlookers with your fast running engine.

14 Petrol tank

This has already been mentioned in chapter 8 and the tank truly is the crowning glory of any motorcycle, so its finish is important if you want the machine to look nice, but not to the extent that it does not match the rest of the machine. If the general paintwork is reasonable but a touch shabby, a super tank job will stand out and show up against it. Maybe better to leave the tank to blend in with the rest or you may find yourself renovating all the paint you meant to leave alone for a season or two.

Any tank must be checked out for damage which could be dangerous. This means looking for splits and cracks, checking brackets, examining tap bosses and badge screw threads, and looking closely at the tank bolt holes in the base. If bolts of too great a length have been used or washers left out at any time, the base of the threaded hole may have been lifted so a small crack exists. All these faults need to be corrected.

The fit of the tank cap should also be checked early on in case attention is needed in this area. Where there is no real damage but the tank interior is rusty this needs to be removed as far as possible. If left either the rust will block the carburettor or the rust area will develop a leak or both. To remove the worst of the rust, drop a handful of small nuts and bolts or sharp stones into the tank and give it a good shake. Then wash out well. After this a swill with a rust inhibitor fluid is well worth the trouble and, when the finish is complete, the inside should be treated with Petseal. This two-part liquid forms a coat on the inside of the tank and seals any small pinholes or doubtful areas so is well worth using in any tank which has a query over it. However, do look on it as an extra insurance and don't expect it to hold a cobweb of steel together with petrol in it.

The tank appearance is dependant on its external shape and if dented this will require attention. This is specialist work as has already been mentioned and usually entails cutting the tank open for access and re-welding it afterwards. Before deciding what work is needed, first remove all the loose items from the tank such as taps, cap, badges, luggage grid and panels. Then examine it to establish if it has any filled patches.

If it has and you want a good job, they must be cleared away.

Work on the tank, even if minor, usually means a welding torch and many are the horror stores on the subject. The problem is removing all the petrol and the fumes before the torch is lit up. Methods used are to wash it out with water or to allow a car exhaust to flow into it or both of these. After this many experienced workers will stand well back, light the torch and point it into the tank. The theory, and it works, is that if there is any vapour left you burn it then and there while expecting a bang.

You may not be disappointed in which case you will remember to wash the tank out better next time. What you avoid with this method is a bang when welding close up to the tank.

Tank finish

This can be simply paint with the style coming from the badges and trim, or paint plus lining, or two colours of paint plus separating line, or, worst of all to cope with, chrome plate plus painted panels plus lining.

This last was used prewar and postwar to 1949 in general and 1954 for the TR5 and is very specialized. The sequence of jobs is plate, paint and line and a good job will be expensive. It will also be worth the money.

As with any finish, preparation is all and for other than plated tanks follows the same lines as any other sheet steel item. The exception is the avoidance of polyurethene lacquer which would react with spilt petrol to lift the paint. Otherwise the final result will simply reflect the care with which the metal surface has been prepared and the skill with which the paint is applied, rubbed down and polished up. As with mudguards and the bathtub a brush finish can be fine as long as you can keep the dust off it. Care will be repaid by a smooth, glossy surface. An internal coat of Petseal may be a good idea depending on what you discovered during your early examination. Protect the tank finish while applying as a dent at this stage could annoy.

RIGHT *The 1949 petrol tank with luggage grid in place of the instrument panel. The grid soon became a standard fitting*

BELOW *The 1960 6T showing the tank fixing and its early duplex frame which quickly gained a second top tube*

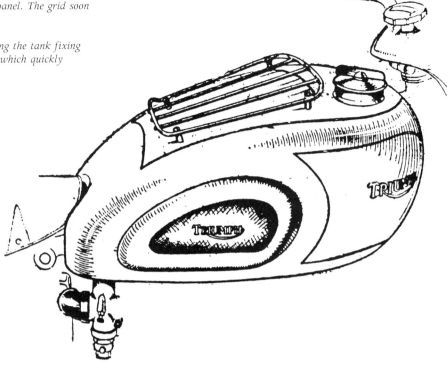

Tank types

All the early tanks were chrome plated with lined panels and fitted with a tank top instrument panel. The original 5T had a $3\frac{1}{4}$ gallon tank but the T100 one was 4 gallons and went onto both models from 1946–48. During that time the 3T had a 3-gallon tank that had been used by the T70 and T80 in prewar days.

A new series of tanks was introduced in 1949 and although still finished in the old style they no longer had an instrument panel but did carry an optional parcel grid that soon became a standard fitting and a well-known Triumph feature. The new tanks continued with 4 gallon capacity for the 5T and T100 and 3 for the 3T. They were joined by a slimmer $2\frac{1}{2}$ gallon tank for the TR5 and this was without kneegrips but could have the parcel grid fitted.

The tank style was changed in 1950 but the tanks themselves were the same parts just with a different all paint finish and new styling bands. The 6T adopted the same styling but the TR5 was unchanged. The styling continued as it was for 1951 but on revised tanks with bayonet caps in place of the hinged ones. The capacities remained as they were except for the 3T which increased to $3\frac{1}{2}$ gallons for what was to be its last year.

Except for the TR5 which was unaltered, there was a new method of tank construction for 1952 which introduced a central welded seam running from front to back of the tank top. This tank, of 4-gallon capacity continued in use on the 5T, 6T and T100 plus the T110

from 1954, all to 1956. The TR5 continued with its 1951 tank until it took the same style as the others and went to a 3-gallon capacity for 1955. This same tank was also offered as an option for the Tiger models in 1954–55. For 1956 the TR5 and new TR6 changed their construction to have the tank top seam and again this tank was an option for the Tigers. That year all models gained a chromed band which fitted over the top seam.

It was all change in 1957 with a new tank badge style which modified the tank detail but not the capacities which remained at 4 gallons for tourers and Tigers, and 3 gallons for TRs and options. The same tank went onto the T120 in 1959 with the same option but 1960 brought a change in the tank fixing. Up to then the tanks had been held by four shouldered bolts which screwed into tapped bosses on the underside of the tank. Various rubber washers insulated the tank from the frame but the bolts had to be wire locked in pairs to prevent them falling out.

For 1960 this changed with the tank sitting on rubbers and held in place by a strap. Capacities remained at 4 gallons except for the TR6 which was 3 but for 1961 the T120 adopted the 3-gallon tank as standard. For 1962 it was offered with either and the usual fitting was 4-gallon for the UK and 3 for the USA.

The first unit construction 650s all had 4-gallon tanks with a 3-gallon option available for the TR6 and T120. Fixing was by two bolts into the base at the front and a single one through a flange at the rear.

LEFT *The tank on a 1960 TR6 showing how the badge and the bands act as a split line between the two colours*

ABOVE *1963 TR6 or T120 showing the style of the grill badge first seen in 1957 on the 3TA*

ABOVE *Eyebrow style tank badge used from 1966 to 1968 and here seen on a 1967 T120*

TOP *Grill badge used 1957 to 1965 and seen here on a Thunderbird from that year*

ABOVE *Final badge adopted from 1969 with a plainer style. Here on a T100S from 1970*

TOP *Triumph kneegrip as adopted in 1968 and shown on a TR6 of that year*

RIGHT *The spring loaded taper cock petrol tap adopted from 1962 by the 650s and later by some of the 500s*

For 1966 new tanks with new badges appeared but still with the same fixings and the band over the top seam. Three capacities were used with the standard 6T, T120 and TR6 having the largest 4-gallon one. The US 6T, TR6R and Western TR6C had one of 3 gallons while the Eastern TR6C, T120R and T120TT all had 2.2-gallon tanks. In 1967 the 6T was not in the lists and the TR6C was seen as a single model with the smallest tank but otherwise there were no changes.

For 1968 just the 4-gallon tank was listed for the TR6 and T120 and in 1969 its badges changed and it was offered under two part numbers to suit the two models. Aside from colour, the distinction was the transfer applied. The same applied in 1970 but for 1971 a new 3-gallon tank was common to all models. This had a centre fixing in the middle of the top panel and sat on rubber pads. It continued for 1972 and was joined by an optional 4-gallon version.

The first small unit twin tank was in the style of the other 1957 models but held by cross bolts at front and rear. It was of 3½ gallon capacity and carried kneegrips, the parcel grid and the top seam band and in turn went onto the 3TA, 5TA, T100A and T100SS. For the latter and the T90 in 1963 and the 3TA and 5TA in 1964 a similar 3-gallon tank was adopted but changed again to 3½ gallons for 1965. This last was without the front and rear fixing lugs and reverted to four tapped holes and shouldered bolts with insulating rubbers to hold the tank to stays clamped to the frame.

For 1966 the tanks were modified to accept new badges and a 2-gallon tank was produced for the T100R and T100C. This used a different mounting bracket and had welded on kneegrip supports. It was all change again in 1967 with the three bolt fixing as on the 650s and two sizes with 3 gallons for the T90, T100S and T100T while the T100R and T100C remained at 2 gallons. The badges changed for 1969 but not the capacities and for 1970 just a 3-gallon tank

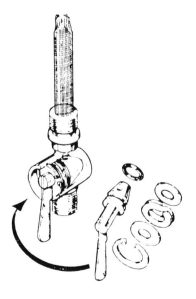

was listed for the T100S and T100T with transfers to suit. For 1971 the UK retained this size but the USA was listed with 1.8 gallon tanks with transfers and colours to distinguish the models.

Filler cap

From 1938 to 1950 hinged caps were used with a split pin acting as the fulcrum. Check the mechanism and the seal. 1951 brought in a bayonet cap which remained the same to 1972. During this time a cap with jack chain was fitted to some machines beginning with the TR5 in 1955. It was used on other off-road machines as a precaution against dropping the cap in mud or water.

Tank badges

Handle with care. Check that they are not damaged and fit as they should. Make sure the fixing screws do fit and don't bottom in their holes. Early nameplates are picked out in the machine colour which may need refurbishing.

From 1938 to 1956 all tanks carried the marque name in its special style on each side of the tank. Up to 1949 it sat there on a panel alone and this continued on the TR5 to 1954. For the rest of the range from 1950 the name was backed by a four bar chrome pressing which ran from the tank front to the kneegrip. That of the 3T differed from those used by the other models. The design of the bands was altered for 1952 when the tank construction changed and in 1955 the TR5 adopted the same style with its own bands shared with the export option Tiger tank.

In 1957 new badges of grill form were fitted with a styling band that ran fore and aft from the badge to give a split line for two-tone tank colours. The badge was common but the bands were varied to suit the tank size. Both badges and bands changed in 1960 except for the TR6 which continued with the 1957 style to the end of pre-unit models.

The same badges went onto the unit 650s fitted with 4-gallon tanks while the smaller tanks used the 1957 parts which were also fitted to the smaller unit twins. From 1961–65 the styling bands were optional on the 3TA and 5TA when a single tank colour was used. In 1966 a new pair of badges were introduced for all models in an eyebrow style with the Triumph logo on a backing with a bar above and a rib form ahead of it. In 1969 they changed again with the logo on more of a panel with picture frame surround and a slim bar shape above and running forward. This style continued to 1972.

Kneegrips

These were a feature of machines from the twenties and gradually became more common as speeds rose and the need for something to clamp onto became more pressing. As tanks fattened in the thirties they served also to protect the finish.

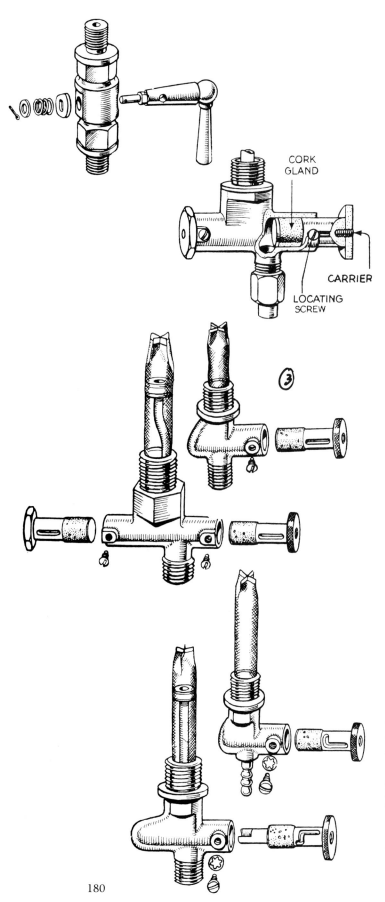

CORK
GLAND

CARRIER

LOCATING
SCREW

The early Triumph twin type fitted to plates bolted to the tank but later versions were either held by a pair of screws or simply stuck in place. The style used by the prewar 5T went onto the 3T postwar while the 1939 T100 type was used by that model and the 5T in 1946. They took a new form for 1947 and this later went on the 6T, T110 and T120.

The TR5 went without kneegrips until 1955 when it was fitted with the 1938 pattern which was used for the export Tiger tank from 1954 and went onto the TR6 in 1956. This continued on the 650 3-gallon tanks 1963–65 and was also used by the T100R and T100C in 1966.

The smaller unit twins used the 1947 pattern up to 1965 but the unit 650s changed to a stick-on type for 1963–67. This same pattern went onto the smaller models from 1966 but all changed to a new style for 1968. This remained in use on the 500s to 1972 but was not listed for the 650s for 1971–72. It did, however, appear on the 4-gallon tank offered for the 1972 UK models.

Taps

These either have a cork seal or a taper cock fitting. In either case they may need to come apart and the sealing arrangements checked over and repaired as required. Then check that the filter is undamaged and that the taps work freely. Make sure the taps don't leak and do pass a full flow of petrol before they are used on the machine. Leaks at that stage are a bind and can produce a fire.

The original 1938 tap was to stay in use for many years and was a double plunger type with one knob for the main supply and a second for reserve. Prewar the T100 had its own pair of taps but postwar it adopted two of the 1938 type while the 5T adopted a similar single tap. The 3T used a single 1938 tap. In 1949 the advent of the TR5 heralded the appearance of a taper cock tap of which two were fitted.

The 6T used the 5T tap for 1950 but in 1951 changed to a pair of taper cock taps of which the right one had a level pipe to leave a reserve turned on by the left tap. The 3T, 5T and TR5 continued as they were but the T100 joined the 6T with the same pair of taps. There were more changes for 1952 with the 5T reverting to the 1938 tap and the 6T to a single taper cock one without level pipe. The T100 and TR5 were unchanged but in 1953 the latter was altered to the T100 pair. In 1954 the 6T adopted the 1938 tap while the T110 was fitted with the taper cock pair which went onto the TR6 in 1956.

The T120 had a pair of the taper cock taps without reserve and for 1961 the 6T was fitted with the TR6 pair. For 1962 the 650s were fitted with a new pair of

A selection of petrol taps used over the years, some with reserve and some with a filter

Tap and pipe on a 1967 T100T and installed so that one side is unable to work. And on a road test machine too although the tester made no comment

taps, one with a reserve, with lever operation and these continued on the unit models to 1970. They were revised for 1971–72.

The smaller unit models were fitted with the 1938 tap from 1957 to 1970 after which they used the same taps as the 650. For the T100C and T100R from 1966–69 the tanks were fitted with the 1962 650 taps.

Parcel grid

This popular fitting first appeared in 1949 as an extra but was quickly fitted as standard. For owners who preferred to dispense with it there were four plugs to fill the tapped holes in the tank top and so stop water accumulating and rust forming.

Just one grid was listed for all from 1949–55 and this had five longitudinal bars. With one on the tank centre line the introduction of the centre seam made for an odd appearance so a new four bar grid was introduced in 1956, the year the tank centre styling band was first fitted.

The grid was on all standard models up to 1968 but was normally omitted from the off-road models. The smallest tanks lacked the tapped holes for fixing it but others retained them so the option was still available if required.

15   Seating

The seating on Triumph twins began as a saddle and pillion pad which was fitted up to 1954 and the end of the rigid frame. In 1950 the dualseat, or twinseat as Triumph preferred to call it, was first listed as an option for the 5T, 6T and T100 and in 1951 was fitted as standard to the T100 while remaining an option for the other two.

In 1954 a new dualseat was listed for the T100 and T110 while the old one continued as an option for the 5T and 6T. The new seat went onto them in 1955 when another was added for the TR5 which up to then had always been fitted with saddle and pad.

From then on only a dualseat was fitted and for this a safety strap became an option from 1957–68. In addition, some machines had a handrail during the period 1968–69.

Saddle

A saddle is an assembly and should be treated as such. On top is the cover which is sewn to shape and then fitted with clips riveted around the edge. Under that went a felt underlay and this tends to wear and fray on the springs beneath. With felt and cover removed what is left is the main frame and a series of suspension springs which run fore and aft.

At the rear of the assembly the two main springs were attached and a pivot bolt went at the front. This was supposed to pivot in a greased hole in the frame but is an area often neglected and the holes may well need repair. A good fit will allow the saddle to rise and fall on its springs as it should without side sway which can be disconcerting.

The parts need to be refurbished as with any others and then re-assembled. Once complete a new cover with underfelt can be fitted and retained with its clips. Fit the back first and work the material forward to the nose.

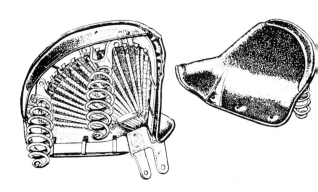

Saddle types

Just one part number covered the saddles used by 5T, 6T and T100 from 1938–54 but this included more than one make. For 1938 and 1939 Terry was the listed make for the twins but in the early postwar days when

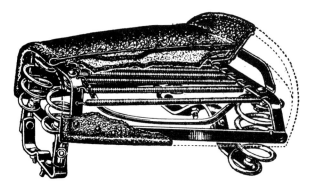

supplies were so hard to come by a seat was just a seat.

By 1950 matters had improved for both Terry and Lycett to be listed and this continued to 1954 for the 5T and 6T. From 1950 barrel-shaped saddle springs were fitted.

The 3T had a different saddle to the larger twins and like them was fitted with barrel-shaped springs in 1950. For that year both Terry and Lycett seats were listed for it but for 1951 only the Terry.

The TR5 had its own seat which in 1949 was a Lycette Aero Elastic which used rubber cords rather than tension springs under the cover. It continued in this form to 1954.

Pillion pad

When separate from a saddle passenger seats could be either sprung and built up like the saddle or simply a rubber pad with a cover. Triumph opted for the latter which was listed from 1938–54. For the TR5 only a backplate was added to spread the load on the rear mudguard but normally the pad was simply bolted in place.

If water has got into the interior it is unlikely that it can be used anymore so replacement will be necessary. Again, if the cover is damaged, a new one will be needed. Make sure you have sorted out the fixing to the mudguard before that item is finished.

When saddles and pillion seats were standard wear, it was common practice to fit a proprietary seat for the passenger and if this has been done it may require repair. If, of the spring type, this is done in the same manner as for a saddle and again the fixing to the machine needs to be finalized before finishing and not after.

Dualseat

These can be more of a problem as there were a good few variations used by Triumph over the years and they can be awkward to mend. They consist of a steel

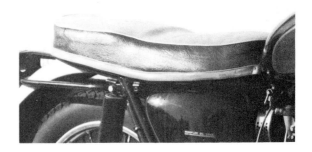

LEFT TOP *The pre-war saddle on a 1938 Speed Twin fitted with a tank in Tiger 100 colours. Wrong silencer for T100 and six stud barrel indicates year*

LEFT CENTRE *The Lycett Aero Elastic saddle fitted to the TR5 with rubber cords in place of springs*

LEFT *A 1950 Camden pillion seat constructed on the same lines as a saddle and an alternative to the pad as fitted by Triumph*

ABOVE *Dualseat on a 1966 Thunderbird*

TOP *The dualseat matched to the bathtub on a 1958 3TA and fitted with a safety strap*

CENTRE *T120 dualseat for 1964*

The dualseat as on the T100S in 1970 with ribs and suggestion of a hump at the tail, also a handrail

pan which can rust, a moulded interior which can rot and a cover which may tear or split.

The interior moulding is the greatest problem as replacement may be the only answer and unless you can locate a suitable one you will not get the desired final seat shape. The pan can be refurbished as for any other steel part and the cover replaced by another which may be stitched from basic material.

Restoration is thus a specialist job and one you can expect to farm out in most cases as not being practical for most owners. There are always exceptions of course, depending on the size of the problem and the skills and resources of the person dealing with it.

Dualseat types

The first dualseat was designed to fit to the rigid frame and thus bolted to the saddle nose lug, the saddle spring lugs and the tops of the mudguard stays using brackets attached to the seat pan. This seat remained in use to 1954 when it was joined by a new one to suit the swinging fork frame.

This was a two level design and bolted to the frame at its nose and to the area at the top of the rear units. It continued in use on the 5T, 6T, T100 and T110 to 1959 while a thinner and lighter version with flat top was introduced for the TR5 in 1955. This went onto the TR6 in 1956 and the T120 in 1959 on the later models. The first series of 1959 T120 models were fitted with the two level seat.

New seats were brought in for the pre-unit models for 1960 with the 6T and T110 being shaped to suit the bathtub enclosure also adopted that year. The two level style was continued for these which hinged on the left while the TR6 and T120 were in the same style but bolted in place as before.

The first unit 650s had a new common seat for all models based on the hinged type. The two level style continued and the hinge remained on the left as before. It was not altered until 1966 but from then on changed every year. For 1966 there was little alteration but 1967 brought a ribbed top and a raised tail with a small hump in seat level between rider and passenger. 1968 brought a thicker cushion and a change to the hinges. Up till then these had been forged into the form of a J with the seat bolted to the top and a pivot formed into the tail. They became pressings which hinged on pins welded to the frame.

The form was the same for 1969 but the base was modified to allow a grab handle to be attached. Otherwise, it interchanged with the earlier type but was changed again for 1970 for one with a new pan which lowered the seat. 1971 and a new frame meant a new seat to suit and this was altered for 1972 as part of the exercise to reduce the excessive seat height.

The smaller unit twins were fitted with the hinged seat that was to go on the 6T and T110 in 1960. This went with the bathtub and was used in turn by the 3TA, 5TA, T100A, T100SS and T90. It continued into 1966 when it was joined by a version with a black top in place of the usual grey for the Eastern T100C but both changed for 1967. The bulk of the range used the same ribbed top seat as the 650s but the T100C and T100R kept to the black top version of the same thing.

Two more versions were brought out in 1968 with thicker seat and new hinges but not as on the 650. By 1969 the smaller twins were back with the larger and used a common seat as they did again for 1970. Till 1972 they continued with this one.

Handrail

This is a tubular, chrome-plated part which bolts to the underside of the dualseat. It was listed for the T100R and T100C late in 1968 and for 1969 and as an option for the 650s in 1969. Only the one part was shown.

Safety strap

This was offered as an option and was fitted to the seat to lay across its middle. It was listed in two types for the pre-unit models from 1958–62 with one for the 5T, 6T, T100 and T110. The other went on the TR5, TR6 and T120. The latter also went on the smaller unit twins from 1957–68 and the unit 650s from 1963–66. For 1967–68 a modified form was offered.

TOP *Ribbed, two tone seat on a 1967 Daytona T100T*

ABOVE *The 1967 T100T seat hinged up showing its underside and what it covered*

16   Assembly

This is often the most satisfying part of a restoration or rebuild, culminating in that heady moment when you swing on the kickstarter and the engine bursts into life.

It is also a time for making haste slowly as rushing matters can easily damage something you have spent time, money and effort on. Slow and sure is best with plenty of reference to your notes so you work in the right sequence. In the build-up to final assembly you should have checked the fit of bolts to holes as you went along and all this work will now pay off in a straightforward fitment of the parts without snags.

The greatest problem is protecting the finish you have lavished so much care on, so cover, pad and mask where necessary and work slowly to avoid damage. Have a think about the order in which you intend to assemble the parts and arrange the items of each stage so they are together. It is good practice to do this as it is a further check that you have everything and that each item has been reworked as required. It will also ensure that you are not caught off balance with something partly together and you, short of a vital bolt and with no free hand to locate it. If this does happen, go back and dismantle rather than chance damage occurring while your back is turned.

Start the assembly with the frame and fit the rear fork, the head race cups and the main stand whether this is centre or rear. You can now put the skeleton on your machine bench and prop the front end up. If you have any doubt at all on stability, clamp the stand down. Now fit the fork crowns and the forks themselves. Add the front wheel. If you fit the mudguard at this stage, it will need protection for sure, so is best omitted for the time being.

The rear guard may well have to be fitted early on and it may be necessary to add the wiring harness at this stage or at least fit the rear section if this is threaded through frame and mudguard tubes and guides. If the machine is balanced on its centre stand, either fit the rear wheel or anchor the rear fork end to your bench.

Once you have a stable frame that is not going to rock about, fit the engine and gearbox while you have the most room to move in. Don't forget to check that you have not left anything out that must be fitted first. Sort out all engine fixings, plates and spacers in advance and place to hand. Spare rods to locate on may well be needed.

You are more likely to damage something while fitting the engine than at any other time, so first protect everything you can. Don't try to lift the weight into place unless you have at least two helpers to take the load while you slide the fixings in. With only two people, something is sure to be scratched.

Blocks underneath are one way to take the strain but better is a means of lifting it from above. In view of the cost of a rebuild, it is well worth the price of a car engine hoist which will be able to carry the load easily. Arrange the lifting sling so it is secure and holds the engine in the correct plane for its fixings to line up. If you have to tilt the engine to achieve this, you are more likely to have an accident and crushed fingers. Better to adjust the sling so the engine just drops into place.

Then fit all fixings and tighten. As with any assembly work it is best to complete a sequence fully and not leave the final tightening for later in case you forget. Not always possible, in which case leave the nut undone and give it a marker to remind you.

Continue the assembly as you wish and as the design dictates but leave the tank and seat as late as possible. Check wheel alignment once both are in place for good and adjust the chain tension correctly.

Don't try to start the engine until all is ready and keep the battery on the shelf until near the end. Before connecting it use your meter to check that the wiring is not shorting to earth somewhere and make sure you connect it the right way round. It should be fine but better be sure than chance a spark at this stage. Then disconnect the battery again while you fill the oil tank and check the gearbox and primary chain levels.

If the machine is still up on the bench, you will need help to get it down safely. Take care that you don't drop it at this stage and give yourself plenty of room to work in. Once down, you can prepare to start up by opening the workshop doors to let the exhaust fumes out.

The petrol tank will best have been left off while you get the machine down to ground level so now fit it, connect it up and pour a small amount of fuel in. Half a gallon or two litres is fine to start with. Turn on and check for leaks. Connect battery and start the engine. Keep the engine speed low and check that oil is returning to the oil tank. Hold your finger on the return to force some into the rocker box as soon as possible. Check that the generator is charging.

Next put the machine on its stand and run it up through the gears to make sure all is well in that area. Have a good look round the pipe connections to make sure there are no leaks and do your ignition timing strobe check if this is called for.

Try the machine gently to check the operation of the clutch and brakes. If you have done your paperwork and are taxed and insured, you can now get your helmet and go for a ride. If not, you will have to put it away for the moment.

For most owners in the UK that first ride of the restored machine is the prosaic one to the local dealer for its official test. Rather irksome after all your work but look on it as a top mechanic may regard scrutineering at a race meeting – a check that nothing has been overlooked. It may help to go to a dealer who knows something of older machines and who will believe that, for instance, taper roller bearing wheels should have some side play and that a 7 in. sls drum brake may lack the bite of a double disc with hydraulic operation.

A chat when booking the appointment is well worth the effort and can smooth the way to your pass.

With the machine legal, enjoy a ride. After a few miles check the oil level and give the machine a look over to see if anything has worked loose. Get some more petrol before you run short and roll off some more miles.

Then take the machine back to the workshop. Check items such as chains, brakes and cables which may have settled down a touch. Go and do your carburation check.

Enjoy your Triumph twin.

17 Paperwork

In this modern age, ownership and use of any road vehicle involves pieces of paper and some of these are documents issued by the authorities. This chapter concerns these in general and those specific to the United Kingdom in particular. Details for other countries will vary and must be checked as necessary.

The first piece of paper was mentioned in the opening chapter and is the receipt for the machine or the bundle of receipts for parts if that was the way you obtained your model. It is very desirable that they contain the engine and frame numbers so you have proof of ownership of what you actually do have. Make sure they agree with what is stamped on the machine and beware of anything that looks altered.

The other documents you will need in the UK are registration form, test certificate and insurance certificate. The first is currently known as a V5, the second as VT20 and the last is obtained privately. With them you can then tax the machine for road use.

You should consider insurance long before you get to the road as the parts and the machine as a whole need to be covered against fire or theft as soon as you get them. Try to obtain an agreed value for the machine and make sure you adjust this in line with the market. The insurance will need to be extended to cover road risks before you ride in public and it is worth shopping round for a company who specializes in older machines and caters for them. Otherwise your relatively sedate Thunderbird will be lumped in with modern 900 cc models of far higher performance and spares prices.

The V5 and VT20 are to an extent linked and also involve the number plate of your machine. Where a machine has been in use on a fairly continuous basis its original buff or green log book will have been replaced by a V5 which will record the correct engine and frame numbers along with the original registration number as displayed on the number plate.

As nothing is perfect there are even discrepancies when the documentation is all in order. For example a Triumph twin is bought for police use. It suffers an engine problem and the complete unit is changed. This is not recorded at the time, the machine is eventually withdrawn from use and finally sold off. The new owner rebuilds it and on coming to register it compares paper numbers with actual markings to find they don't tally. As they have not done for many years.

More difficult is a machine that has not been used for a period and has no V5. For the authorities to issue a form either with the existing registration number if known or one appropriate to the machine's year, they need further proof and the onus is on the owner to provide it.

It is necessary to link the number to the machine and for this old MoT certificates or old license discs are acceptable. Where not available or to back them up a letter from a recognized authority to confirm the date of the quoted engine and frame numbers and stating whether or not they were likely to have begun life together should be obtained. Acceptable sources are the owners club, Vintage MCC, service page writers of the specialist magazines (I am one of these) or the holders of the original records of the firm.

It is not normally possible to trace the original registration number from scratch and much of the official record no longer exists. The procedure needed would be to look at the firm's records to match engine and frame numbers. If this is in order the records will then give the name of the dealer to whom the machine was sent. He in turn would then need to be sought out and his records would give the registration number.

In practice few dealers from those days are still in business and fewer have kept such records for the 20 or 30 years likely to be involved.

So you have to call on your Local Vehicle Licensing Office and take all your documents with you. There you fill up a form, as you would expect to do at any government office. This will trigger off a series of events which will culminate with the issue of a V5 if all goes well.

The first thing likely to happen is a visit from the authorities or their agents to inspect your machine. This is done to check that the numbers all agree with those quoted on the form and that the machine is what you say it is and does exist.

This visit is not always carried out but for it the machine is best assembled to some degree. It is often desirable to register the machine long before the restoration is complete or there is any need to tax it for the road. At the very least it allows you to get the number plate finished.

After the visit and if all is in order, the vehicle documents can be issued. If the evidence is good the original registration number, or mark as they call it, will be retained and entered on the main computer at Swansea. If this cannot be done but there is evidence as to the age of the machine, the authorities will try to issue it an appropriate number for its period. Should there be no way of linking the machine to any period which may happen with a hybrid, a number with a letter Q suffix will be issued.

Following this the machine will have to go for its official test as mentioned in the previous chapter. Book the test, make sure you have insured the machine for road use, pass the test as after all this I would be most disappointed if you did otherwise, and you can then tax the machine for the road.

Keep all the paperwork firstly in case there are any queries at any time and secondly to go with the machine should you ever come to sell it.

Now you have to decide what to restore next year.

APPENDICES

1 Engine and frame numbers

1938–49

The year and model were used as a prefix to the engine number. For 1938–39 the final 8 or 9 was used but postwar practice was to use the last two digits, thus 46, 47, 48 or 49. The model numbers were T or 5T for the Speed Twin, T100 for Tiger 100, 3T for 350 twin and TR5 for Trophy.

Postwar engine numbers commenced at:
1946 – 72000, 1947 – 79046, 1948 – 88782 and 1949 – 100762.

The prewar frames used the prefix TH for the 5T and TF for the T100. Postwar the prefixes were TC for the 3T, TF for the rigid 5T, T100, 6T and TR5, S for all pre-unit swinging fork frames and H for the small unit machines from 1957–69. The 650 unit frames usually duplicated the engine number even if not the prefix.

1950–69

Engine numbers had a prefix indicating the model type plus a number from the list next.

1969 and onwards

During 1969 a new coding system was introduced using a two letter prefix for the month and model season year, plus model type code and a number which began at 00100 for each model year and ran on irrespective of the model it was stamped on. Model season was taken to start in August.

First letter was month and code is: A – January, B – February, C – March, D – April, E – May, G – June, H – July, J – August, K – September, N – October, P – November and X – December.

Second letter was year and code is:
C – August 1968 to July 1969, D – August 1969 to July 1970, E – August 1970 to July 1971, G – August 1971 to July 1972 and H – August 1972 to July 1973.

Year	Unit 350 and 500 cc	Pre-unit 500 and 650 cc
1950		From 100 N
1951		101NA – 15808NA
1952		15809NA – 25000NA
		then 25000 – 32302
1953		32303 – 44134
1954		44135 – 56699
1955		56700 – 70929
1956		70930 – 82799
		then 0100 – 0944
1957	H101 – H760	0945 – 011115
1958	H761 – H5484	011116 – 020075
1959	H5485 – H11511	020076 – 029363
1960	H11512 – H18611	029364 – 030424
		then D101 – D7726
1961	H18612 – H25251	D7727 – D15788
1962	H25252 – H29732	D15789 on
		Unit 650 cc
1963	H29733 – H32464	DU101 – DU5824
1964	H32465 – H35986	DU5825 – DU13374
1965	H35987 – H40527	DU13375 – DU24874
1966	H40528 – H49832	DU24875 – DU44393
1967	H49833 – H57082	DU44394 – DU66245
1968	H57083 – H65572	DU66246 – DU85903
1969	H65573 – H67331	DU85904 – DU90282

2 Model chart

Pre-unit

Model	1938	1939	1946	1947	1948	1949	1950	1951	1952	1953	1954	1955	1956	1957	1958	1959	1960	1961	1962
3T			─	─	─	─	─	─											
5T	─	─	─	─	─	─	─	─	─	─	─	─	─	─	─				
6T							─	─	─	─	─	─	─	─	─	─	─	─	─
T100		─	─	─	─	─	─	─	─	─	─	─	─	─	─	─			
T110											─	─	─	─	─	─	─	─	
T120																─	─	─	─
TR5						─	─	─	─	─	─	─	─	─	─				
TR6													─	─	─	─	─	─	─
T100c										─	─								
	1938	1939	1946	1947	1948	1949	1950	1951	1952	1953	1954	1955	1956	1957	1958	1959	1960	1961	1962

Unit

Model	1957	1958	1959	1960	1961	1962	1963	1964	1965	1966	1967	1968	1969	1970	1971	1972
3TA	─	─	─	─	─	─	─	─	─							
T90							─	─	─	─	─	─	─	─	─	
5TA			─	─	─	─	─	─	─	─						
T100A				─	─											
T100SS					─	─	─	─	─	─						
T100										─	─					
T100C										─	─	─	─	─		─
T100R										─	─	─	─	─		─
T100S											─	─	─	─		
T100T											─	─	─	─		
6T							─	─	─	─						
TR6							─	─	─	─	─	─	─	─		
TR6C										─	─	─				─
TR6R										─	─	─				─
T120							─	─	─	─	─	─	─	─		
T120R										─	─	─				─
T120TT										─	─	─				
V models																─
	1957	1958	1959	1960	1961	1962	1963	1964	1965	1966	1967	1968	1969	1970	1971	1972

3   Model alterations

These notes have been compiled from the main text and are to provide a quick guide for checking a machine for its year. The starting point should always be the engine and frame numbers and the following is mainly concerned with external details that can be inspected when purchasing.

The notes run on and are generally applicable to later models of the same series. If in doubt, refer to the main text.

The first section deals with general changes which apply to all models then in production and the feature normally continues until the end of the model or when changed as noted. The start and finish of each model run is included in this section.

General

1938	5T start, 3 piece crankshaft, pressure rocker feed, external drain pipes, flat headlamp glass.
1939	T100 start, front number plate surround, rear chain oiler with needle valve in primary chaincase.
1946	3T start, teles, separate dynamo, speedo drive from rear wheel, return line rocker feed, timed engine breather, internal oil drain.
1947	Optional sprung hub with gearbox speedo drive, domed headlamp glass.
1949	TR5 start, parcel grid with 5 bars, oil tell tale, air filter, nacelle (not TR5), no instrument panel in tank.
1950	6T start, new gearbox with speedo drive, 4 band tank styling (not TR5), E3L dynamo, MCR2 regulator, Mk.II sprung hub, built in prop stand lug, dualseat option, external drain pipes (not 3T).
1951	Bayonet tank cap. 3T end.
1952	Lug in seat tube for air hose, tapered rear lamp body, one piece brake drum and sprocket, prefocus headlamp with underslung pilot lamp (not TR5), centre tank seam (not TR5).
1953	Rectangular rear lamp.
1954	T110 start, RB107 regulator, quickly detachable rear wheel option for sprung frame.
1955	Monobloc carburettors (not 6T), rear brake torque stay, rectangular rear lamp with reflector, 4-band tank styling for TR5.
1956	TR6 start, horn grill on nacelle, prefocus headlamp with in-built pilot, centre tank seam

	for TR models, chrome seam band, parcel grid with four bars.
1957	3TA start, grill tank badge, split clamp fork leg ends, seat safety strap option.
1958	Slickshaft, revised gearbox outer shell, steering head lock. 5T end, TR5 end.
1959	5TA start, T120 start, one piece forged crankshaft with 3-bolt flywheel. T100 end.
1960	T100A start, bathtub flange reversed.
1961	T100SS start, floating brake shoes. T110 end, T100A end.
1962	End of Slickshift.
1963	T90 start.
1964	Front fork redesign.
1965	T100SS end.
1966	T100, T100C, T100R, TR6C, TR6R, T120R, T120TT start, all models 12-volt system, eyebrow tank badge, separate rear brake drum and sprocket, oil tank oil feed to rear chain, rear wheel speedo drive on 650s. 3TA, 5TA, T100, 6T end.
1967	T100S, T100T start. TR6C, TR6R, T120R, T120TT end.
1968	Concentric carburettors, finned diode heat sink, access cover in chaincase for ignition timing.
1969	Picture frame and bar tank badge, oil pressure switch, exhaust balance pipe. T90, T100C, T100R end.
1970	Engine breather design changed. T100S, T100T, TR6, T120 end.
1971	T100C, T100R, TR6C, TR6R, T120R start.

3T

1946	Integral rocker box, special crankshaft design, through studs for head and barrel, saddle, instrument panel.
1948	From engine 89333 short block studs and separate head bolts.

3TA

1957	Unit construction, distributor, bathtub, nacelle, toolpad under seat.
1961	Primary chain tensioner, no toolpad, tank band option.

1962   Siamesed exhaust pipes.
1963   Twin exhaust pipes.
1964   Points in timing cover, rear skirt in place of bathtub.
1965   Frame top strut, revised front mudguard.
1966   Welded strut, side panel, no skirt.

T90
1963   Points in timing cover, siamesed exhaust pipes, rear skirt.
1964   Twin exhaust pipes, side panel, no skirt.
1965   Frame top strut.
1966   Welded strut.

5T
1938   6 stud barrel, mag-dyno, girders, saddle, instrument panel.
1939   8 stud barrel.
1953   Alternator, access plate in outer chaincase, coil ignition.
1955   Big timing main, chaincase without access plate, sprung frame, dualseat.
1957   Full width front brake.

5TA
1959   Unit construction, distributor, bathtub, toolpad under seat.
1960   Primary chain tensioner.
1961   No toolpad, tank band option.
1962   Siamesed exhaust pipes.
1963   Twin exhaust pipes.
1964   Points in timing cover, rear skirt in place of bathtub.
1965   Frame top strut, revised front mudguard.
1966   Welded strut, side panel, no skirt.

TR5
1949   Square fin alloy head and barrel, parallel exhaust ports, siamesed exhaust pipes, special frame, saddle, separate headlamp shell.
1951   Die cast, close pitch fin, alloy head and barrel, splayed exhaust ports.
1954   Big timing main.
1955   Exhaust pipe adaptors added, sprung frame, dualseat.
1957   Full width front brake.

T100
1939   8 stud barrel, mag-dyno, girders, saddle, instrument panel, megaphone style silencers, iron barrel, optional bronze cylinder head.
1946   Tubular silencers.
1951   Die cast, close pitch fin, alloy head and barrel, dualseat, toolbox above upper chain stay.
1954   Big timing main, sprung frame, 8 in. front brake.
1958   Full width 8 in. front brake.

T100A
1960   Nacelle, bathtub, toolpad under seat.
1961   No toolpad.

T100SS
1961   Unit construction, rear skirt, separate headlamp shell.
1962   Siamezed exhaust pipes.
1963   Points in timing cover.
1964   Twin exhaust pipes, side panel, no skirt.
1965   Frame top strut.

T100C
1966   Siamezed exhaust pipes to single waist level silencer on left, trail format, no parcel grid.
1967   Twin exhaust pipes to twin waist level silencers on left.
1969   Heat shield on exhaust pipes, seat grab rail, bellcrank tls front brake.

T100R
1966   Street scrambler for US.
1967   Twin carburettors.
1968   8 in. front brake.
1969   Bellcrank tls front brake.

T100S
1967   Road model.
1969   Bellcrank tls front brake.

T100T
1967   Sports model, twin carburettors.
1968   Eight inch front brake.
1969   Bellcrank tls front brake.

T100C
1971   Street scrambler, twin exhaust pipes to twin waist level silencers on left, 7 in. tls front brake.

T100R
1971   Based on T100T, sports model, twin carburettors, 8 in. tls front brake.

6T
1950   Iron head, saddle.
1952   SU carburettor fitted.
1954   Big timing main, alternator, access plate in outer chaincase, coil ignition.
1955   Sprung frame, dualseat, chaincase without access plate.
1957   Full width front brake.
1959   Amal carburettor fitted.
1960   Duplex frame, bathtub.
1961   Alloy head with vertical runner, internal oil drain, 8 in. full width front brake.
1962   Siamesed exhaust pipes.
1963   9 stud head, points in timing cover, twin exhaust pipes, loop frame, rear skirt in place of bathtub.
1964   12 volt electric system.
1965   tdc slot in crankshaft.
1966   Side panel, no skirt.

T110
1954   Iron head engine, big timing main, dynamo, sprung frame, dualseat, 8 in. front brake.

1956	Alloy head, internal oil drain.
1958	Eight inch full width front brake.
1960	Alternator, duplex frame, bathtub.
1961	Vertical runner on head.

TR6

1956	Trail bike as TR5, big timing main, alloy head, internal oil drain, dynamo, siamezed exhaust pipe, separate headlamp shell, 7 in. front brake.
1957	Eight inch front brake.
1958	Eight inch full width front brake.
1960	Alternator, duplex frame.
1961	Revised into sporting road model with twin exhaust pipes and silencers mounted low down, vertical runner on head.
1962	Siamezed exhaust pipes.
1963	Nine stud head, points in timing cover, coil ignition, loop frame.
1964	Twin exhaust pipes.
1965	tdc slot in crankshaft.
1968	tls front brake.
1969	Bellcrank tls front brake.

TR6C

1966	Eastern US model in street scrambler form with twin waist level silencers, small headlamp. Western US model in scrambles form with twin open pipes at waist level on left, no lights.
1967	One model, twin exhaust pipes and silencers on left at waist level.
1971	New model, oil in frame, new forks, conical hubs, tls front, exhaust systems on left, centre tank fixing.
1972	Lower frame and seat, push in exhaust pipes, 5 speed gearbox option, rocker box covers in place of caps.

TR6R

1966	US street model, high rise bars.
1971	New model as TR6C except twin low level exhaust systems.
1972	As TR6C.

T120

1959	Twin carburettor version of T110, dynamo, nacelle, splayed inlet ports.
1960	Alternator, separate headlamp, duplex frame.
1961	Vertical runner on head.
1963	Nine stud head, points in timing cover, coil ignition, loop frame.
1964	Inlet balance pipe.
1965	tdc slot in crankshaft.
1968	tls front brake.
1969	Bellcrank tls front brake.

T120TT

1966	US track racer, low open pipes, no lights.

T120R

1966	US street model, high rise bars.
1971	Twin carburettor version of TR6R.
1972	As TR6C.

4 Colours

3T

1946 All painted parts in black with petrol tank chrome plated with black panels lined in ivory and mudguards with ivory stripes. Chrome plated exhaust system, headlamp rim and minor parts. Black wheel rims.

1947 As 1946, chrome variations possible due to supply problems.

1948–49 As 1946 except wheel rims chrome plated with ivory lined black centres.

1950–51 Petrol tank painted all over with styling strip on each side with four bars and Triumph logo.

3TA

1957–62 Launch model in metallic silver grey for all painted parts. For production in shell blue for forks, petrol tank, front mudguard and rear enclosure. Frame, stands, engine plates, inner rear mudguard, chainguards and oil tank in black. Chrome plated wheel rims. Metallic silver sheen for cylinder block.

1963 As 1957 plus option of shell blue parts in silver bronze.

1964 Silver bronze petrol tank, forks, mudguards and rear skirts. Black frame, stands, engine plates, chainguards and oil tank. Chrome-plated wheel rims.

1965 As 1964, colour now called silver beige.

1966 Pacific blue tank top, forks, front mudguard stays and mudguard strips. Alaskan white tank lower and mudguards. Black frame, oil tank, left side cover, chainguard and engine plates. New tank badges.

T90

1963 Alaskan white petrol tank, mudguards and rear skirts with $\frac{1}{8}$ in. black lines either side of $\frac{3}{4}$ in. gold centre stripe mudguards. Black frame, forks, oil tank, stands, mudguard stays and chainguard. Chrome-plated wheel rims and headlamp shell.

1964 As 1963 except petrol tank top in gold with $\frac{1}{8}$ in. black line between colours and running from rear of kneegrip to back of tank. No rear skirt, black left side cover.

1965 Pacific blue tank top and mudguard stripes with silver tank lower and mudguards.

Mudguard stripe and tank lining in gold. Black frame, forks, oil tank, left side cover, stands, mudguard stays and chainguard. Chrome-plated wheel rims and headlamp shell.

1966 As 1965 except blue parts in grenadier red and silver ones in Alaskan white. New tank badges.

1967 As 1965 except blue parts in hi-fi scarlet and silver ones in Alaskan white.

1968 As 1965 except blue parts in Riviera blue and silver ones remaining silver.

5T

1938–39 All painted parts in amaranth red with petrol tank chrome plated with red panels lined in gold and mudguards gold lined. Wheel rims chrome plated with red, gold lined, centres. Chrome-plated exhaust system, headlamp shell and minor parts.

1946–49 As 1938 except headlamp shell painted and wheels plated or painted depending on chrome supplies.

1950–56 Petrol tank painted all over with styling strip on each side with four bars and Triumph logo.

1957–58 New petrol tank badge. Amaranth red petrol tank and mudguards. Black frame, forks, oil tank and battery box. Chrome-plated wheel rims.

5TA

1959 Amaranth red for all painted parts with wheel rims chrome plated.

1960–62 Ruby red in place of amaranth but otherwise as 1959.

1963 As 1960 with colour known as cherry red.

1964–65 Silver petrol tank lower, mudguards and rear skirt. Black petrol tank top, frame, forks, oil tank, chainguard and engine plates. Gold $\frac{1}{8}$ in. line at tank colour join to rear of kneegrip.

1966 As 1964 except no rear skirt. Black left-side cover.

TR5

1949–54 Black frame, forks, oil tank, toolbox, headlamp shell and minor painted parts. Mudguards silver with black centre stripe, with navy blue line either side. Petrol tank chrome plated with silver panels lined blue. Wheel rims chrome plated with silver centres lined blue.

1955   Shell blue petrol tank with four bar styling strips on each side. Shell blue mudguards with black centre line lined white. Black frame, forks, oil tank, battery box, stands, mudguard stays, chainguard and headlamp shell. Chrome-plated wheel rims.

1956   As 1955 except headlamp shell chrome plated.

1957–58   New petrol tank badge. Finish in silver grey and black in 1955 style.

T100

1939   Silver mudguards with centre black stripe lined out in blue and chrome-plated petrol tank with silver sheen panels lined in blue. Other painted parts in black including frame, forks, oil tank and toolbox. Wheel rims chrome plated with silver centres lined blue. Chrome-plated exhaust systems, headlamp shell and minor parts.

1946–49   As 1939 except headlamp shell painted black, wheels painted or plated as 1939 depending on chrome supplies and navy blue lining to mudguard black stripes.

1950–53   Petrol tank painted all over in silver sheen with styling strip on each side with four bars and Triumph logo. Otherwise as 1946 with silver sheen mudguards and other painted parts in black. Wheel rims chrome plated with blue-lined silver centres.

1954–55   Shell blue petrol tank and mudguards which have central black stripe lined white. Wheel rims chrome plated with shell blue centres lined black. Other painted parts in black including frame, forks, oil tank, mudguard stays, battery box and chainguard.

1956   As 1954 except wheel rims just chrome plated.

1957   New petrol tank badge. Standard finish to 1956 style in silver grey and black. Option with ivory tank top, blue tank lower and ivory mudguards with light blue centre stripe, gold lined. Gold line at tank colour join to rear of kneegrip.

1958   Standard finish as 1957. Option with black tank top, ivory tank lower and ivory mudguards with gold lining as 1957.

1959   Standard finish as 1957. Option with ivory tank top, black tank lower and ivory mudguards.

T100A

1960   All painted parts black except tank lower in ivory. Gold lined. Chrome-plated wheel rims.

1961   Silver tank lower, front mudguard and rear enclosure, other painted parts black.

T100SS

1961–62   Kingfisher blue tank top, mudguard stripes and rear skirts. Silver tank lower and mudguards. Gold lined. Black frame, forks, oil tank and other details. Chrome-plated wheel rims and headlamp shell.

1963   To 1961 style in regal purple, silver and black.

1964   No rear skirt. To 1961 style in scarlet, silver and black. Black left side cover.

1965   To 1961 style in burnished gold for tank top and mudguard stripes, Alaskan white tank lower and mudguards with black for other parts. Black lining in place of gold.

T100

1966   New tank badge. Sherbourne green tank top and mudguard stripe, gold lined. Alaskan white tank lower and mudguard. Black frame, forks, oil tank, left side cover and other parts. Chrome-plated wheel rims and headlamp shell except shell for T100C models black.

1967   To 1966 style in Pacific blue, Alaskan white and black. All headlamp shells chrome plated.

1968   To 1966 style in aquamarine green, silver and black.

1969   To 1966 style in lincoln green, silver and black.

1970   To 1966 style in jacaranda purple, silver and black. T100S with all silver tank.

1971   Olympic flame tank and mudguards. Black frame, forks, oil tank, left side cover and other parts. Chrome-plated wheel rims and headlamp shell. T100R model has wide black bands on tank sides, lined white.

1972   To 1971 style in cherry with black details or in two tone for tank only in cherry and white.

6T

1950   All painted parts in blue grey with tank styling strips on each side with four bars and Triumph logo. Wheel rims chrome plated with blue grey centres. Gold-lined mudguards and wheel rim centres.

1951–55   To 1950 style in lighter polychromatic blue.

1956   To 1950 style in crystal grey.

1957–58   New tank badge. Bronze gold petrol tank and mudguards with white-lined black centres. Black frame, forks, oil tank, battery box and other parts. Chrome-plated wheel rims.

1959   Charcoal grey for petrol tank, mudguards and forks with black for other painted parts. Gold lining on mudguards only.

1960   Charcoal grey for 1959 items plus rear enclosure. Black frame, inner rear mudguard and other parts.

1961–62   Silver tank lower, front mudguard and rear enclosure. Black tank top, frame, fork upper legs and nacelle, oil tank, inner rear mudguard and other parts. Gold tank lining at join to rear of kneegrip. Gold lined. Silver fork legs.

1963–65   Silver tank lower, mudguards and rear skirts. Black tank top, frame, fork upper legs and nacelle, oil tank and other parts. Gold tank lining at join to rear of kneegrip. Gold lined. Silver fork legs.

1966   New tank badge, no rear skirt. Silver tank lower and mudguards. Black tank top, frame, forks, oil tank, left side cover and other parts. Gold tank lining at join to rear of kneegrip. Gold lined. For US models grenadier red tank top and mudguard stripes with Alaskan white tank lower and mudguards. Gold lined.

T110

1954–59	As T100 model for each year, including options.
1960	As 1960 T100A.
1961	Kingfisher blue tank top, fork upper legs and nacelle. Silver tank lower, front mudguard and rear enclosure. Black frame, forks, inner rear mudguard, oil tank and other details. Gold tank lining at join to rear of kneegrip. Gold lined. Silver fork legs.

TR6

1956–58	As TR5 model for each year first in shell blue and then silver grey each with black. White stripe lining. Chrome-plated headlamp shell.
1959	Standard as 1957 TR5. Export option in ivory and Aztec red lower tank, gold lined.
1960	Ivory tank top and mudguards. Aztec red tank lower and mudguard stripes. Black frame, forks, oil tank, battery box and other parts. Gold lined. Chrome-plated wheel rims and headlamp shell.
1961	Ruby red tank top and mudguard stripes. Silver tank lower and mudguards. Black frame, forks, oil tank, battery box and other parts. Gold lined. Chrome-plated wheel rims and headlamp shell.
1962	To 1961 style with polychromatic burgundy in place of ruby red.
1963	To 1961 style with regal purple in place of ruby red.
1964	To 1961 style with hi-fi scarlet in place of ruby red.
1965	To 1961 style with burnished gold in place of ruby red and Alaskan white in place of silver. Black mudguard and tank lining.
1966	To 1961 style with Pacific blue in place of ruby red and Alaskan white in place of silver for TR6 and TR6R. TR6C models have Pacific blue tank. Western TR6C only has aluminium mudguards.
1967	To 1961 style with mist green in place of ruby red and Alaskan white in place of silver. TR6C mudguards in stainless steel.
1968	To 1961 style with Riviera blue in place of ruby red.
1969	To 1961 style with trophy red in place of ruby red. White mudguard and tank lining.
1970	Spring gold tank and mudguards. Black items as 1961. Chrome-plated headlamp shell.
1971	Pacific blue and white petrol tank and blue mudguards with white stripes. Gold tank lining. Black frame, air filter boxes and side panels. Chrome-plated headlamp shell.
1972	Polychromatic blue tank top and mudguards. White tank lower and mudguard stripes. Black and chrome plating as 1971. TR6C only with chrome-plated mudguards.

T120

1959	Pearl grey tank top and mudguards. Tangerine tank lower and mudguard stripes. Gold lined. Black frame, forks, oil tank and battery box. During year changed to royal blue tank lower and mudguard stripes plus pearl grey oil tank and battery box, remainder unchanged.
1960	As 1959 except chrome-plated headlamp shell.
1961	Sky blue tank top and mudguard stripes. Silver tank lower, mudguards, oil tank and battery box. Black frame and forks. Chrome-plated headlamp shell.
1962	As 1961 except oil tank and battery box in black. Export option with flame in place of blue.
1963	Alaskan white tank and mudguards. Black mudguard stripes. Black and chrome as 1962.
1964	Gold tank top and mudguard stripes. Alaskan white tank lower and mudguards. Black lined. Black frame, forks, oil tank and left side cover. Chrome-plated headlamp shell.
1965	To 1964 style with Pacific blue in place of gold and silver in place of white. Gold lined.
1966	To 1964 style with grenadier red in place of gold. Gold lined. Aluminium mudguards for T120TT and stainless steel ones for T120R.
1967	To 1964 style with aubergine (purple) in place of gold for T120 standard. T120R and T120TT in aubergine for tank top and mudguard stripes and gold for tank lower. White lined. Both have stainless steel mudguards.
1968	To 1964 style with hi-fi scarlet in place of gold and silver in place of white. White lined.
1969	To 1964 style with Olympic flame in place of gold and silver in place of white. White lined.
1970	Tank astral red with silver side panels, mudguards astral red with silver stripes. White lined. Black and chrome as 1964.
1971	Tiger gold and black petrol tank and gold mudguards with black stripes. White lined. Black frame, air filter boxes and side panels. Chrome-plated headlamp shell.
1972	Tiger gold tank top and mudguards. White tank lower and mudguard stripes. Black lined. Black and chrome as 1971.

5   Pistons

350 pre-unit, 55 mm

E1748	6.3	3T 1946–51 std.
E1841	7.0	3T 1947–50 opt.

500 pre-unit, 63 mm

E3052	5.0	TR5 1951–59 opt.
E1969	6.0	TR5 1949–54 std.
E1563	7.0	5T 1938–58 std.
E1716	7.8	T100 1939 std.
E1908	7.8	T100 1946–54 std.
E3098	8.0	T100 1955–59, TR5 1955–58 std.
E2460	8.25	T100 1947–50
E2489	8.5	option 1949–59
E3615	9.0	option 1956–59
E2884	9.5	option 1956–59
E2671	12.0	option 1956–59

350 unit, 58.25 mm

E3689	7.5	3TA 1957–66 std.
E6908	7.5	option 1967–69
E4670	9.0	T90 1963–66 std.
E6899	9.5	T90 1967–69 std.

500 unit, 69 mm

E4004	7.0	5TA 1959–66 std.
E6906	7.0	option 1967–72
E7603	7.5	T100P 1968
E4021	9.0	T100 1960–66 std.
E6897	9.0	T100 1967 std.
E6884	9.75	T100 1967–72 std.

650 pre-unit and unit, 71 mm

E3611	6.3	option 1956–60
E2891	7.0	6T 1950–60 std.
E3415	7.5	option 1954–55
E3612	7.5	6T 1961–63 std., option 1956–60
E4899	7.5	6T 1964–66 std.
E6387	7.5	option 1967
E6895	7.5	option 1968–72
E3670	8.0	T110 and TR6 1957–60 std.
E3000	8.5	T110, 1954–55 std, option 1951–53
E3610	8.5	T110, TR6 1956 and 1961–63, T120 1959–63
E5329	8.5	TR6 and T120 1964–66
E6341	9.0	T120 and T120R 1966
E6868	9.0	T120 and TR6 1967–69
E9488	9.0	T120 and TR6 1970–72
E5317	11.0	option 1964
E5819	11.0	T120TT 1966
E6867	11.0	T120TT 1967
E3613	12.0	option 1956–60

6 Camshafts

Model	Year	Inlet	Exhaust	Tappets
3T	1946–49	E2266	E1754	E1478
	1950	E2266	E2266	E1478
	1951	E2266	E2266	E3059
3TA	1957–63	E3838	E3839	E3753
	1964–66	E3838	E5341	E3753
T90	1963–68	E4678	E4786	E3753
	1969	E10043	E10046	E3753
5T	1938–39	E1485	E1485	E1478
	1946–49	E2302	E1485	E1478
	1950	E2302	E2302	E1478
	1951–52	E2302	E2302	E3059
	1953–58	E3275	E3275	E3059
5TA	1959–63	E3838	E3839	E3753
	1964–65	E3838	E5341	E3753
	1966	E4678	E4786	E3753
TR5	1949–50	E2302	E2302	E1478
	1951–52	E2302	E2302	E3059
	1953–54	E3275	E3275	E3059
	1955–58	E3325	E3325	E3059
T100	1939	E1485	E1485	E1478
	1946–49	E2302	E1485	E1478
	1950	E2302	E2302	E1478
	1951–52	E2302	E2302	E3059
	1953–59	E3275	E3275	E3059
T100 race kit	1951–53	E2477N	E2478N	E3059
	1952–53	E3134	E3134	E3059R
T100c	1953	E3134	E3134	E3059
T100A	1960	E4022	E4023	E3753
	1961	E4038	E4039	E3753
T100SS	1961–62	E4038	E4023	E3753
	1963–65	E4678	E4786	E3753
T100 (all)	1966	E4678	E4786	E3753
T100C, T100S	1967–68	E4678	E4786	E3753
	1969	E10043	E10046	E3753
T100S	1970	E11064	E9983	E3753
T100R, T100T	1967–68	E4678	E6965	E4040
	1969	E10043	E10047	E4040
T100T	1970	E11064	E9984	E4040
T100C	1971–72	E11064	E9983	E3753
T100R	1971–72	E11064	E9984	E4040
6T	1950	E2302	E2302	E1478
	1951–52	E2302	E2302	E3059
	1953–60	E3275	E3275	E3059
	1961	E3325	E3325	E3059
	1961–62	E4220	E4220	E3059
	1963–65	E4818	E4848	E3059
	1966	E4818	E4848	E3059/ E6329
T110	1954–61	E3325	E3325	E3059
TR6	1956–61	E3325	E3325	E3059
	1962	E3134	E3325	E3059
T120	1959–62	E3134	E3325	E3059
TR6, T120	1963–65	E4819	E4855	E3059
TR6	1966	E4819	E4855	E3059/ E6329
T120	1966	E4819	E4855	E3059R E6490
TR6, T120	1967	E4819	E5047	E3059R E6490
	1968	E4819	E5047	E3059R E8801
	1969	E10040	E10041	E3059R E8801
	1970	E11063	E9989	E3059R E8801
TR6C, TR6R, T120R	1971–72	E11063	E9989	E3059R E8801

7 Valve spring lengths

Model	Year	Inner	Outer
3T	1946–51	1·5	1·312
3TA	1957–65	1·844	1·625
	1966	1·594	1·5
T90	1963–65	1·656	1·5
	1966–69	1·594	1·5
5T	1938–58	1·625	2·031
5TA	1959–65	1·656	1·5
	1966	1·594	1·5
TR5	1949–58	1·625	2·031
T100	1939–59	1·625	2·031
	1960–65	1·656	1·5
	1966–72	1·594	1·5
6T (to D11192)	1950–61	1·625	2·031
(from D11193)	1961–66	1·531	1·625
T110	1954–61	1·625	2·031
TR6	1956–65	1·625	2·031
	1966–67	1·531	1·625
	1968–72	1·531	1·5
T120	1959–65	1·625	2·031
	1966–67	1·531	1·625
	1968–72	1·531	1·5

All lengths are in inches.

8 Magnetos

Model									Years									
	1938	39	46	47	48	49	50	51	52	53	54	55	56	57	58	59	60	61	62
3T			A	A	A	A	A	A											
5T	M	M	A	A	A	A	A	A	A										
6T							A	A	A	A									
T100	M	M	A	A	A	A	A	M	M	M	M	M	M	M	M	M			
T110											M	M	M	M	M	M	A	A	
T120																M	A	A	A
TR5							M	M	M	M	M	M	M	M	M				
TR6													M	M	M	M	M	M	A

A = auto advance, M = manual advance.

Types available

1946–53	BTH with auto advance
1949–53	BTH with manual advance
1938–39	Lucas mag-dyno
1946–53, 1960–62	Lucas with auto advance
1952–61	Lucas with manual advance
1954–61	Lucas Wader
1955–59	Lucas racing

9 Spark plugs

Model	Year	KLG	Lodge	Champion
3T	1946		H14S	
	1947–50			L10S
	1951	F70	H14	L10S
5T	1938–39	831		
	1946		H14S	
	1947–50		H14	
	1951–53	F80	H14	L11S
	1954–55			L10S
	1956–58	F80	H14	L10S
T100	1939	831		
	1946		H14S	
	1947–50	F80		
	1951–53	FE80	HLN	NA10
	1954–55			NA10
	1956–58	FE100	HLN	NA10
	1959	FE100	HLN	N3
TR5	1949–53	FE80	HLN	NA10
	1954–55			NA10
	1956–58	FE100	HLN	NA10
T100c	1953	FE80	HLN	NA10
6T	1950–53	F80	H14	L11S
	1954–55			L10S
	1956–58	F80	H14	L10S
	1959–60	F80	H14	L7
	1961–62	FE100	HLN	N3
	1963–66	FE100	HLN	N4
T110	1954–55			L11S
	1956–58	FE100	HLN	NA10
	1959–61	FE100	HLN	N3
T110 (max.)	1954–55			LA11
TR6	1956–58	FE100	HLN	NA10
	1959–62	FE100	HLN	N3
	1963	FE100	HLN	N4
	1964–69			N4
	1970–72			N3
T120	1959–62	FE100	HLN	N3
	1963	FE100	HLN	N4
	1964–69			N4
	1970–72			N3

Model	Year	KLG	Lodge	Champion
T120TT	1966–67			N58R
3TA	1957–58	FE100	HLN	NA10
	1959–60	FE75	HLN	N3
	1961–63	FE75	HLN	N4
	1964–66			N4
T90	1963–69			N4
5TA	1959–60	FE75	HLN	N3
	1961–63	FE75	HLN	N4
	1964–66			N4
T100A	1960	FE75	HLN	N3
	1961	FE75	HLN	N4
T100SS	1961–63	FE75	HLN	N4
	1964–65			N4
T100	1966–69			N4
	1970			N3
	1971–72			N4

Plug equivalents

Make	Original Type	NGK	Modern Champion
KLG	F70	B5HS	L86
	F80	B7HS	L82
	FE75	B6ES	N4
	FE80	B7ES	N3
	FE100	B8ES	N2
Lodge	H14	B7HS	L85
	H14S	B7HS	L85
	HLN	B6ES	N4
		B7ES	
Champion	L7	B7HCS	L85
		B7HS	
	L10S	B6HS	L85
	L11S	B7HS	L5
	LA11	B9HN	L57R
	NA10	B8ES	N3
	N3	B8ES	N3
	N4	B7ES	N4
	N58R	B9EN	N57R

10   Carburettor settings

Model	Year	Type	Size	Main	Pilot	Slide	Needle pos.	jet
3T	1946–48	275 AD	$\frac{7}{8}$	120		5/4	3	·107
3T	1949–50	275 AQ	$\frac{7}{8}$	120		5/4	3	·107
3T	1951	275 BK	$\frac{7}{8}$	120		5/4	3	·107
3T (no air filter)	1951	275 BK	$\frac{7}{8}$	120		5/4	2	·107
3T (for AA)	1953		$\frac{21}{32}$	75		4/4	1	
5T (right side 7° float)	1938	76/112	$\frac{15}{16}$	140		6/3	3	
5T (right side 7° float)	1939	76/132	$\frac{15}{16}$	140		6/3	3	
5T	1946–48	276 AX	$\frac{15}{16}$	140		6/3$\frac{1}{2}$	3	·107
5T	1949–50	276 DK	$\frac{15}{16}$	140		6/3$\frac{1}{2}$	3	·107
5T	1951–54	276 FE	$\frac{15}{16}$	140		6/3$\frac{1}{2}$	3	·107
5T (no air filter)	1951	276 FE	$\frac{15}{16}$	140		6/3$\frac{1}{2}$	2	·107
5T	1955–58	376/25	$\frac{15}{16}$	200	30	3$\frac{1}{2}$	4	·106
T100	1939	76/117	1	160		6/3	3	
T100	1946–48	276 BN	1	160		6/3$\frac{1}{2}$	3	·107
T100	1949–50	276 DL	1	150		6/3$\frac{1}{2}$	2	·107
T100	1951–53	276 FH	1	150		6/3$\frac{1}{2}$	2	·107
T100	1954	276 GE	1	150		6/3$\frac{1}{2}$	2	·107
T100	1955–59	376/35	$\frac{15}{16}$	220	25	3$\frac{1}{2}$	4	·106
T100 (no air filter)	1949–51	276	1	160		6/3$\frac{1}{2}$	2	·107
T100c	1953	76 AS 76 AR	1	150		6/3$\frac{1}{2}$	2	·107
T100 race	1949–50	76 AJ 76 AH	1	130		6/4	3	·109
T100 race kit basic	1951–53	76 AO 76AN	1	180		6/4	3	·109
low octane				200		6/4		·109
50/50				220		6/4		·109
alcohol				660		6/4		·113
T100, TR5 (twin carb)	1956–59	76 AO 76 AN	1	180		6/4		·109
T100, TR5 (splayed head)	1957–59	376/77	1	200	25	3$\frac{1}{2}$	3	·106
T100, TR5 (not splayed)	1958–59	376/75 376/74	or use	376/35				
TR5	1949	276 DK	$\frac{15}{16}$	150		6/3$\frac{1}{2}$	3	·107
TR5	1950	276 EK	$\frac{15}{16}$	140		6/3$\frac{1}{2}$	3	·107
TR5	1951–53	276 FF	1	150		6/3$\frac{1}{2}$	2	·107
TR5	1954	276 GH	1	150		6/3$\frac{1}{2}$	2	·107
TR5 (no air filter)	1951	276 FF	1	150		6/3$\frac{1}{2}$	1	·107
TR5	1955–58	376/35	$\frac{15}{16}$	220	25	3$\frac{1}{2}$	4	·106
3TA	1957–58	375/23	$\frac{13}{16}$	110	25	3$\frac{1}{2}$	3	·105
3TA (1958 from H2330)	1958–61	375/32	$\frac{25}{32}$	100	25	3$\frac{1}{2}$	3	·105
3TA	1962–66	375/62	$\frac{25}{32}$	100	25	3$\frac{1}{2}$	3	·106
3TA (no air filter)	1957–58	375/23	$\frac{13}{16}$	120	25	3$\frac{1}{2}$	3	·105
5TA	1959–66	375/35	$\frac{7}{8}$	160	25	3	3	·105
T90	1963–67	376/300	$\frac{15}{16}$	180	20	3	3	·106
T90	1968	R624/2	24	140	20	3$\frac{1}{2}$	2	·106

Model	Year	Type	Size	Main	Pilot	Slide	Needle pos.	jet
T90	1969	R624/2	24	140		4	2	·106
T100A	1960	375/35	$\frac{7}{8}$	160	25	3	3	·105
T100A	1961	376/273	1	190	25	$3\frac{1}{2}$	3	·106
T100SS	1961–65	376/273	1	190	25	$3\frac{1}{2}$	3	·106
T100, T100R, T100C	1966	376/273	1	190	25	$3\frac{1}{2}$	3	·106
T100S, T100C	1967	376/273	1	190	25	$3\frac{1}{2}$	3	·106
T100T, T100R	1967	376/324 376/325	$1\frac{1}{16}$	200	25	$3\frac{1}{2}$	3	·106
T100S, T100C	1968	R626/8	26	190	25	$3\frac{1}{2}$	2	·106
T100S, T100C	1969	R626/8	26	180		4	2	·106
T100S	1970	R626/25	26	190		4	2	·106
T100C	1971–72	R626/32	26	170		4	2	·106
T100R, T100T	1968	L626/9 R626/10	26	200	25	$3\frac{1}{2}$	2	·106
T100R, T100T	1969	L626/9 R626/10	26	160		3	2	·106
T100T	1970	L626/27 R626/26	26	180		3	1	·106
T100R	1971	L626/34 R626/33	26	150		3	1	·106
T100R (UK)	1971	L626/38 R626/37	26	170		$3\frac{1}{2}$	1	·106
T100R	1972	L626/54 R626/53	26	150		3	1	·106
6T	1950	276 AE	1	170		$6/3\frac{1}{2}$	2	·107
6T	1951–53	276 FG	$1\frac{1}{16}$	140		$6/3\frac{1}{2}$	2	·107
6T (no air filter)	1950	276 AE	1	190		$6/3\frac{1}{2}$	2	·107
6T (no air filter)	1951	276 FG	$1\frac{1}{16}$	160		$6/3\frac{1}{2}$	2	·107
6T (SU carb.)	1952–58	MC2		·090			M9 needle	
6T (US export)	1955–58	376/42	$1\frac{1}{16}$	270	25	$3\frac{1}{2}$	4	·106
6T	1959	376/210	$1\frac{1}{16}$	270	25	$3\frac{1}{2}$	4	·1065
6T	1960	376/256	$1\frac{1}{16}$	270	25	$3\frac{1}{2}$	4	·1065
6T	1961	376/255	$1\frac{1}{16}$	250	25	$3\frac{1}{2}$	4	·106
6T (1961 from D11193)	1961–62	376/285	$1\frac{1}{16}$	220	25	4	4	·106
6T	1963–66	376/303	$1\frac{1}{16}$	230	25	4	4	·106
6T (US model)	1966	376/309	$1\frac{1}{16}$	270	25	4	4	·106
T110	1954	289X	$1\frac{1}{8}$	200		29/4	3	·107
T110	1955–59	376/40	$1\frac{1}{16}$	250	25	$3\frac{1}{2}$	3	·106
T110	1960–61	376/255	$1\frac{1}{16}$	250	25	$3\frac{1}{2}$	4	·1065
T110, TR6 (splayed head)	1958–59	376/40	$1\frac{1}{16}$	250	25	$3\frac{1}{2}$	3	·106
T110, TR6 (splayed head)	1958–59	15 GP	1	250		6	2	·107
TR6	1956–63	376/40	$1\frac{1}{16}$	250	25	$3\frac{1}{2}$	3	·106
TR6	1964–66	389/97	$1\frac{1}{8}$	310	25	$3\frac{1}{2}$	1	·106
TR6R, TR6C	1966	389/97	$1\frac{1}{8}$	310	25	$3\frac{1}{2}$	1	·106
TR6, TR6R, TR6C	1967	389/239	$1\frac{3}{16}$	330	25	4	2	·106
TR6	1968	R930/23	30	230	25	4	2	·107
TR6	1969–70	R930/23	30	230		$3\frac{1}{2}$	2	·106
TR6R, TR6C	1971–72	R930/60	30	230		$3\frac{1}{2}$	2	·106
Met. Police Mk III	1964–66	389/213	$1\frac{3}{16}$	320	25	$3\frac{1}{2}$	2	·106
T120 (sep. float chamber)	1959	376/204	$1\frac{1}{16}$	240	25	$3\frac{1}{2}$	2	·1065
T120 (sep. float chamber)	1960–61	376/233	$1\frac{1}{16}$	240	25	$3\frac{1}{2}$	2	·1065
T120 (1961 from D11193)	1961–63	376/257	$1\frac{1}{16}$	240	25	$3\frac{1}{2}$	2	·106
T120	1964–67	389/203	$1\frac{1}{8}$	260	25	3	3	·106
T120R	1966	389/203	$1\frac{1}{8}$	260	25	3	3	·106
T120R	1967	389/95	$1\frac{3}{16}$	330	25	4	2	·106
T120TT	1966–67	389/95	$1\frac{3}{16}$	330	25	4	2	·106
T120	1968	L930/10 R930/9	30	220	20	3	2	·107
T120	1969–70	L930/10 R930/9	30	190		3	2	·106
T120R	1971–72	L930/67 R930/66	30	190		3	1	·106

11 Oil tank capacity

Even Triumph data gives conflicting figures so the following should be taken more as a guide than a strict rule. For long periods only one figure was quoted for all models.

1938   5T took 6 pints.
1939   5T 6 pints, T100 8 pints.
1946   5T 8 pints at first, then 6 pints. T100 8 pints, 3T 6 pints.
1947–48   5T and 3T 6 pints, T100 8 pints.
1949–55   all road models 6 pints, T100c 8 pints.
1956–69   all models 5 pints.
1970   all models 5.5 pints.
1971–72   500 cc models 5.5 pints, 650 cc models 4 pints.

12 Transmission

Gearbox internal ratios

Gearbox	Used	Mainshaft 4	3	2	1	Layshaft 4	3	2	1	3rd	2nd	1st
1 Pre-unit standard	1938–49	25	23	19	15	19	21	25	29	1·201	1·731	2·544
2 Pre-unit wide	1938–49	27	23	18	15	17	21	26	29	1·452	2·294	3·071
3 Pre-unit close	1947–49	24	23	20	18	20	21	24	26	1·096	1·440	1·733
4 Pre-unit standard	1950–62	26	24	20	16	20	22	26	30	1·192	1·690	2·437
5 Pre-unit wide	1950–62	28	24	19	16	18	22	27	30	1·426	2·211	2·917
6 Pre-unit close	1950–62	24	23	21	18	22	23	25	28	1.091	1.299	1.697
7 Small unit standard	1957–63	26		23		23			32	1·18	1·75	2·45
8 Small unit standard	1963–72	22	24	21	16	15	20	23	27	1·222	1·606	2·475
9 Small unit wide	1967–72	23	24	20	15	14	20	24	29	1·369	1·971	3·176
10 Small unit close	1967–72	20	22	20	16	17	21	23	27	1·123	1·353	1·985
11 TR5T	1973–74	22	24	20	15	15	20	24	29	1·222	1·760	2·835
12 Unit 650 standard	1963–69	26	24	20	16	20	22	26	30	1·192	1·690	2·437
13 Unit 650 wide	1966–72	28	24	19	16	18	22	27	30	1·426	2·210	2·917
14 Unit 650 close	1966–72	24	23	21	18	22	23	25	28	1·091	1·299	1·697
15 Unit 650 standard	1970–72	26	23	20	16	20	22	26	30	1·243	1·690	2·437

16 5 speed gearbox for 1972 – 1, 1·19, 1·40, 1·837, 2·585.

Sprockets, boxes and overall gear ratios

Model	Year	Sprockets E	C	G	R	Overall ratio	Box type to 1949	from 1950
Pre-unit								
3T	1946–51	19	43	18	46	5·784	1	4
5T	1938–58	22	43	18	46	4·995	1	4
5T s/c	1938	20	43	18	46	5·494	1	
	1939–58	19	43	18	46	5·784	1	4
T100	1939–59	22	43	18	46	4·995	1	4
T100 s/c	1939–58	19	43	18	46	5·784	1	4
T100c	1953	22	43	18	46	4·995		4 or 6
T100c s/c	1953	19	43	18	46	5.784		4 or 6
TR5	1949–54	21	43	18	46	5·233	2	5
	1955–58	21	43	18	46	5·233		4
6T	1950–59	24	43	18	46	4·579		4
	1960	23	43	18	43	4·466		4
	1961–62	22	43	18	43	4·669		4
6T s/c	1950–58	21	43	18	46	5·233		4
	1959	22	43	18	46	4·995		4
	1960	20	43	18	43	5·136		4
T110	1954–59	24	43	18	46	4·579		4
	1960	23	43	18	43	4·466		4
	1961	22	43	18	43	4·669		4

Model	Year			Sprockets		Overall	Box type
T110 s/c	1954–58	21	43	18	46	5·233	4
	1960	20	43	18	43	5·136	4
TR6	1956–59	24	43	18	46	4·579	4
	1960	22	43	18	43	4·669	4
	1961–62	21	43	18	43	4·891	4
TR6 s/c	1956–58	21	43	18	46	5·233	4
T120	1959	24	43	18	46	4·579	4
	1960	22	43	18	43	4·669	4
	1961–62	21	43	18	43	4·891	4

Option engine sprockets 17 to 24T to 1949, 17 to 25T from 1950 in two types, 1950 to 1952 and 1953 to 1962.

Model Unit	Year	Sprocket E	C	G	R	Overall ratio	Gearbox
3TA	1957–63	26	58	18	43	5·329	7
	1964	26	58	19	46	5·401	8
	1965	26	58	18	46	5·701	8
	1966	26	58	17	46	6·036	8
T90	1963–69	26	58	17	46	6·036	8
5TA	1959–60	26	58	20	43	4·796	7
	1961–63	26	58	19	43	5·048	7
	1964–65	26	58	20	46	5·131	8
	1966	26	58	19	46	5·401	8
T100A	1960	26	58	20	43	4·796	7
	1961	26	58	19	43	5·048	7
T100SS	1961–62	26	58	18	43	5·329	7
	1963–65	26	58	18	46	5·701	8
T100	1966	26	58	18	46	5·701	8
T100C	1966–72	26	58	18	46	5·701	8
T100R	1966–67	26	58	19	46	5·401	8
	1968–72	26	58	18	46	5·701	8
T100S	1967–70	26	58	18	46	5·701	8
T100T	1967–70	26	58	18	46	5·701	8

Option gearbox sprockets 17 to 20 teeth.

Model Unit 650	Year	Sprocket E	C	G	R	Overall ratio	Box type to 1969	from 1970
6T	1963–66	29	58	20	46	4·600	12	
6T s/c	1963–66	29	58	18	46	5·111	12	
6T (USA)	1966	29	58	18	46	5·111	12	
TR6	1963–70	29	58	19	46	4·842	12	15
TR6 s/c	1963–65	29	58	17	46	5·412	12	
	1969–70	29	58	17	46	5·412	12	15
TR6C (east)	1966	29	58	18	46	5·111	12	
TR6C (west)	1966	29	58	17	46	5·412	12	
TR6R	1966–67	29	58	19	46	4·842	12	
	1971–72	29	58	19	47	4·947		15
TR6C	1967	29	58	18	46	5·111	12	
	1971–72	29	58	18	47	5·222		15
TR6RV	1972	29	58	19	47	4·947		16
TR6CV	1972	29	58	19	47	4·947		16
T120	1963–70	29	58	19	46	4·842	12	15
T120 s/c	1963–65	29	58	17	46	5·412	12	
	1969–70	29	58	17	46	5·412	12	15
T120R	1966–67	29	58	19	46	4·842	12	
	1971–72	29	58	19	47	4·947		15
T120TT	1966–67	29	58	17	46	5·412	12	
T120RV	1972	29	58	19	47	4·947		16

Option gearbox sprockets 15 to 20 teeth.

Chains

Primary
Pre-unit 0.5 pitch × 0.335 roller diameter × 0.305 in.
between inner plates.

No. of pitches

3T	1946–51	74
5T	1938–54	78
T100	1939–53	78
	1954	70
TR5	1949–54	76
6T	1950–54	80
T110	1954	70
5Ts/c	1938–54	77
T100s/c	1939–53	77
6Ts/c	1950–54	78
ALL	1955–62	70

(5T, 6T, TR5, TR6, T100, T110, T120)

Unit 0.375 × 0.250 × 0.225 in duplex. 350 and 500–78
links, 650–84 links.

Final drive 0.625 × 0.400 × 0.380 in.

No. of pitches

3T	1946–51	90	T100A	1960–61	101
5T	1938	92	T100SS	1961–63	101
	1939–51	93		1964–65	102
	1952–54	92	T100	1966	102
	1955–58	100	T100C	1966–72	102
T100	1939–51	93	T100R	1966	102
	1952–53	92		1967	103
	1954–59	100		1968–72	102
TR5	1949–54	90	T100S	1967–70	102
	1955–58	100	T100T	1967–70	102
6T	1950–51	93	6T	1963–65	103
	1952–54	92		1966	102
	1955–59	101	TR6	1963–65	103
	1960–61	99		1968–70	104
	1962	98	TR6C	1966	102
T110	1954–59	101		1967	104
	1960–61	99		1971–72	106
TR6	1956–59	101	TR6R	1966	103
	1960–61	99		1967	104
	1962	98		1971–72	106
T120	1959	101	T120	1963–65	103
	1960–61	99		1968–70	104
	1962	98	T120R	1966	103
3TA	1957–63	100		1967	104
	1964	103		1971–72	106
	1965–66	102	T120TT	1966	102
T90	1963–69	102		1967	103
5TA	1959–63	101			
	1964	103			
	1965	104			
	1966	103			

13　Rear suspension springs

Colour codes as used from 1958

Rate – lb/in.	Colour	Used
90	yellow/white	1955–62
100	green/green	1958–67
100	plain	1957–59
100	chromed	1969, 1971–72
110	purple/blue	1955–62
110	red/red	1960–68
110	chromed	1971–72
130	red/yellow	1954–62
130	red/orange	1960–68
145	blue/yellow	1960–68
145	chromed	1969–70
150	blue/red	1955–62

Fitments

Pre-unit models

1954–56	130 standard, 150 sidecar, 90 road racing, 110 option.
1957	110 standard, 150 sidecar, 90 road racing, 130 option.
1958–62	100 standard, 150 sidecar, 90 road racing, 110 and 130 option.

Unit models

1957–59	100 standard.
1960–68	350 and 500 – 130 standard, 110 and 145 option.
1963–66	6T and T120 – 145; TR6 – 100.
1966	US T120 – 100.
1967	TR6 and T120 – 145; TR6C, TR6R, T120R, T120TT – 100.
1968	TR6 and T120 – 145.
1969	145 chromed for unit 650s and T90, T100S, T100T; 100 chromed for T100C and T100R.
1970	All models – 145.
1971–72	500 – 100, 650 – 110.

14 Wheels, brakes, tyres

Rim part numbers and use

Model	Year	Front	Rear	Sprung hub	QD rear
3T	1946–51	W351	W79A	W653	
3TA	1957–60	W1274	W1272		W1272
	1961–65	W1274	W1435		W1435
	1966	W1373	W1471		W1471
T90	1963–65	W1373	W1471		W1007
	1966–69	W1373	W1471		W1471
5T	1938–39	WM2-20	WM2-19		
	1946–56	W351	W79A	W643	W79A
	1957–58	W1230	W79A		W79A
5TA	1959–60	W1274	W1272		W1272
	1961–65	W1274	W1435		W1435
	1966	W1373	W1471		W1471
TR5	1949	W870	W270A	W643	W643
	1950–54	W870	W270A	W894	
	1955–56	W870	W1007		W1007
	1957–58	W1230	W1007		W1007
T100	1939	WM2-20	WM2-19		
	1946–57	W351	W79A	W643	W79A
	1958–59	W1230	W79A		W79A
T100A	1960	W1274	W1272		W1272
	1961	W1274	W1435		W1435
T100SS	1961–62	W1230	W1007		W1007
	1963–65	W1373	W1471		W1007
T100	1966	W1373	W1471		W1471
T100C	1966–69	W1230	W1007		W1007
T100R	1966–69	W1230	W1007		W1007
T100S	1967–70	W1373	W1471		W1471
T100T	1967	W1373	W1471		W1471
	1968	W1374	W1471		W1471
	1969–70	W1230	W1471		W1471
T100C	1971–72	W1230	W1007		
T100R	1971–72	W1230	W1007		
6T	1950–56	W351	W79A	W643	W79A
	1957–59	W1230	W79A		W79A
	1960	W1373	W1378		W1378
	1961–62	W1374	W1378		W1378
	1963–65	W1374	W1471		W1007
	1966	W1374	W1471		W1471
T110	1954–57	W351	W79A		W79A
	1958–59	W1230	W79A		W79A
	1960–61	W1374	W1378		W1378
TR6	1956	W870	W1007		W1007
	1957	W351	W1007		W1007
	1958–66	W1230	W1007		W1007
	1967–70	W1230	W1471		W1471
	1971–72	W3818	W3784		
T120	1959–60	W1230	W79A		W79A
	1961–62	W1230	W1007		W1007
	1963–65	W1374	W1471		W1007
	1966	W1374	W1471		W1471
	1967–70	W1230	W1471		W1471
T120TT	1966–67	W1230	W1007		W1007
T120R	1966–67	W1230	W1007		W1007
	1971–72	W3818	W3784		

Rims

Part number	Size	Year used
W79A	WM2-19	1946–60
W270A	WM3-19	1949–54
W351	WM2-19	1946–57
W643	WM2-19	1947–54
W870	WM1-20	1949–56
W894	WM3-19	1950–54
W1007	WM3-18	1955–72
W1230	WM2-19	1957–72
W1272	WM2-17	1957–60
W1274	WM2-17	1957–65
W1373	WM2-18	1960, 1963–70
W1374	WM2-18	1960–66, 1968
W1378	WM2-18	1960–62
W1435	WM2-17	1961–65
W1471	WM2-18	1963–70
W3784	WM3-18	1971–72
W3818	WM2-19	1971–72

Spokes

These are listed by length from shortest to longest and detailed from Triumph parts lists. The length is normally given as a fractional measurement but is decimal for ease of reading. The gauge is a British Standard and both single diameter and butted spokes were used by Triumph over the years. The angle is that between the spoke and its head so that spokes with their heads pointing at the wheel centre usually have an angle quoted as less than 90 degrees. The final number is the Triumph part number. Some models had straight spokes and this is indicated by 'st'.

Length	Gauge	Angle	Part no.
4·312	8/10	78	W1730
4·312	8/10	100	W1731
4·781	8/10	78	W1708
4·875	8/10	100	W1709
5·062	8/10	st	W1275
5·625	8/10	st	W1328
6·0	10	80	W1060
6·0	8/10	80	W1166
6·0	8/10	95	W1167
6·0	8/10	st	W1236
6·375	10	83	W933
6·375	10	94	W934
6·406	10	83	W662
6·406	10	94	W663
7·562	9	90	W1126
7·562	8/10	90	W1107
7·562	8/10	110	W3402
7·875	9	100	W1127
7·875	8/10	90	W1108
7·937	10	81	W942
7·937	10	96	W943
8·0	10	70	WX10
8·0	10	99	WX10X
8·0	8/10	90	W1104
8·312	9	79	W1008
8·312	9	98	W1009
8·344	10	88	W660
8·344	10	90	W661
8·375	8/10	90	W1106
8·437	9	79	W1010
8·437	9	98	W1011
8·75	9	100	NW125X
8·75	9	76	NW125
8·875	9	80	W107
8·875	9	97	W107X
9·375	10	70	W354
9·375	10	99	W354X

Brake diameters

Only two sizes were used by Triumph, these being 7 in. and 8 in. as follows.

First with 7 in. brakes front and rear:

3T	1946–51	3TA	1957–66
5T	1938–58	5TA	1959–66
TR5	1949–58	T100A	1960–61
T90	1963–69	T100SS	1961–65
T100	1966	T100C	1966–69
T100S	1967–70	T100C	1971–72

Second with 8 in. front and 7 in. rear:

T110	1954–61	T100R	1971–72
T120	1959–72		

Thirdly, those that changed were:

Model	Both 7 in.	8 in. front, 7 in. rear
T100	1939–53	1954–59
6T	1950–60	1961–66
TR6	1956	1957–72
T100R	1966–67	1968–69
T100T	1967	1968–70

Fourth, the sprung hub. This had an 8 in. brake and was fitted to the 3T, 5T, 6T and TR5 as an option for 1947–54 and to the T100 for 1947–53.

Tyre sizes

These are the one item not listed in the parts books. All rear tyres are of studded or universal pattern but some front were ribbed and are marked R in the tables.

Model	Year	Front	Rear
3T	1946–51	3·25 × 19	3·25 × 19
3TA	1957–65	3·25 × 17 R	3·25 × 17
	1966	3·25 × 18 R	3·50 × 18
T90	1963–69	3·25 × 18 R	3·50 × 18
5T	1938–39	26 × 3·0 R	26 × 3·5
	1946–58	3·25 × 19	3·50 × 19
5TA	1959–65	3·25 × 17 R	3·50 × 17
	1966	3·25 × 18 R	3·50 × 18
TR5	1949–54	3·00 × 20	4·00 × 19
	1955–56	3·00 × 20	4·00 × 18
	1957–58	3·25 × 19	4·00 × 18
T100	1939	26 × 3·0 R	26 × 3·5
	1946–47	3·25 × 19	3·50 × 19
	1948–59	3·25 × 19 R	3·50 × 19
T100A	1960–61	3·25 × 17 R	3·50 × 17
T100SS	1961–62	3·25 × 19 R	3·50 × 18
	1963–65	3·25 × 18 R	3·50 × 18
T100	1966	3·25 × 18 R	3·50 × 18
T100C	1966	3·25 × 19	4·00 × 18
	1967–69	3·50 × 19	4·00 × 18
T100R	1966	3·25 × 19	4·00 × 18
	1967–68	3·25 × 19 R	4·00 × 18
	1969	3·25 × 19	4·00 × 18
T100S	1967–70	3·25 × 18 R	3·50 × 18
T100T	1967–68	3·25 × 18 R	3·50 × 18
	1969–70	3·25 × 19 R	3·50 × 18
T100C	1971–72	3·50 × 19	4·00 × 18

Model	Year	Front	Rear
T100R	1971–72	3·25 × 19	4·00 × 18
6T	1950–56	3·25 × 19 R	3·50 × 19
	1957–59	3·25 × 19	3·50 × 19
	1960–66	3·25 × 18 R	3·50 × 18
T110	1954–59	3·25 × 19 R	3·50 × 19
	1960–61	3·25 × 18 R	3·50 × 18
TR6	1956	3·00 × 20	4·00 × 18
	1957–60	3·25 × 19	4·00 × 18
	1961–66	3·25 × 19 R	4·00 × 18
	1967–70	3·25 × 19 R	3·50 × 18
TR6C	1966	3·25 × 19	4·00 × 18
	1967	3·50 × 19	4·00 × 18
TR6R	1966–67	3·25 × 19 R	4·00 × 18
TR6C	1971–72	3·25 × 19	4·00 × 18
TR6R	1971–72	3·25 × 19	4·00 × 18
T120	1959–60	3·25 × 19 R	3·50 × 19
	1961–62	3·25 × 19 R	4·00 × 18
	1963–66	3·25 × 18 R	3·50 × 18
	1967–70	3·00 × 19 R	3·50 × 18
T120TT	1966	3·25 × 19	4·00 × 18
	1967	3·50 × 19	4·00 × 18
T120R	1966–67	3·25 × 19 R	4·00 × 18
	1971–72	3·25 × 19	4·00 × 18

Tyre equivalents

Section

Original	Low profile	Metric
3.00	3.60	90/90
3.25	3.60	90/90
3.50	4.10	100/90
4.00	4.25/85	110/90

Revolutions per mile

3.25 × 17	872	3.25 × 19	807
3.50 × 17	858	3.50 × 19	795
3.50 × 18	825	4.00 × 19	783
4.00 × 18	812	3.50 × 19 s/c	803

Data from Avon Tyres Ltd or by calculation.
Sidecar tyre included for reference from modern list.

Security bolts

Fitted from 1949–72 in two sizes as part D106 for WM2 rims and part WM3 for that section. For 1971–72 the latter became part W3468.

Model	Year	Part	Number
3T	1949–51	D106	1
3TA	1960	D106	1
	1966	D106	2
T90	1963–69	D106	2
5T	1949–58	D106	1
5TA	1960	D106	1
	1966	D106	2
TR5	1949–54	WM3	1
	1955–58	WM3	2
T100	1949–59	D106	1
T100A	1960	D106	1
T100SS	1961–62	WM3	1
	1963–65	D106	2
T100	1966	D106	2
T100C	1966–68	WM3	2
T100R	1966–69	WM3	2
T100S	1967–70	D106	2
T100T	1967–70	D106	2
T100C	1971–72	WM3	2
T100R	1971–72	WM3	2
6T	1950–63	D106	1
	1964–66	D106	2
T110	1954–61	D106	1
TR6	1956–59	WM3	2
	1960–63	WM3	1
	1964–67	WM3	2
	1968–70	D106	2
	1971–72	W3468	2
T120	1959–63	D106	1
	1964–70	D106	2
	1971–72	W3468	2

15 Headlamp, ammeter, switches

These varied and moved about a good deal over the years and while much of the data given below is also to be found in the main text a summary may help. The headlamp may have a separated shell or be fitted to a nacelle. The fitment of an ammeter was usual and the switches were for lights and ignition in the main and could be separate or built as one combined assembly.

3T	1946–48	Tank top instrument panel with oil gauge, ammeter, panel lamp and light switch.
	1949–51	Nacelle with light switch, ammeter, ignition cut-out and speedometer.
3TA	1957–63	Nacelle with combined lights and ignition switch, ammeter and speedometer.
	1964–66	Nacelle with ignition switch, light switch, ammeter and speedometer.
T90	1963	Separate shell with ammeter, left skirt fitted with ignition switch and light switch.
	1964–65	1966 as 1964 plus red ignition warning light in shell. Separate switches mounted on left side panel, otherwise as 1963.
	1967	Separate shell with ammeter, light switch, red warning light, green warning light. Ignition switch on left side panel.
	1968–69	Ignition switch on left fork shroud, toggle light switch, otherwise as 1967.
5T	1938–48	as 3T.
	1949–52	as 3T.
	1953	Nacelle with ammeter, light switch, ignition switch and speedometer.
	1954–58	Combined light and ignition switches, otherwise as 1953.
5TA	1959–63	as 3TA.
	1964–66	as 3TA.
TR5	1949–58	Separate shell with small panel carrying ammeter and light switch.
T100	1939–48	as 3T.
	1949–59	as 3T.
T100A	1960–61	Nacelle with ammeter, light switch, cut-out button and speedometer.
	1961	After engine H22430 as 3TA.

T100SS	1961–62	Separate shell with ammeter, left skirt fitted with combined lights and ignition switch.
	1963	as T90.
	1964–65	as T90.
T100	1966	as T90.
T100C	1966	Small separate shell with light switch and dip switch. Cut-out button on handlebars.
	1967	Red warning light in shell, otherwise as 1966.
	1968–69	Green warning light added, otherwise as 1967.
T100R	1966	as T90.
	1967	as T90.
	1968–69	as T90.
T100S	1967	as T90.
	1968–70	as T90.
T100T	1967	as T90.
	1968–70	as T90.
T100C	1971–72	Separate shell with toggle light switch and red, green and amber warning lights. Ignition switch on left fork shroud.
T100R	1971–72	as T100C but with larger shell.
6T	1950–53	as 3T.
	1954–62	as 5T.
	1963–66	as 1953 5T.
T110	1954–61	as T100.
TR6	1956–59	as TR5.
	1960–62	Separate shell with ammeter, light switch on small panel under seat nose on right.
	1963–65	as 1966 T90.
	1967	as T90.
	1968–70	as T90.
TR6C	1966	as T100C.
	1967	as T100C.
TR6R	1966	as T90.
	1967	as T90.
TR6C	1971–72	Separate shell with toggle light switch and red, green and amber warning lights.
TR6R	1971–72	Separate shell with light switch and red, green and amber warning lights. Ignition switch behind right side cover.

T120	1959	as T100.
	1960–62	as TR6.
	1963–65	as 1966 T90.
	1967	as T90.
	1968–70	as T90.
T120TT	1966–67	No lights, cut-out button on handlebars.
T120R	1966	as T90.
	1967	as T90.
	1971–72	as TR6R.

16 Part numbers

Pre-unit		1938	1939	1946	1947	1948	1949	1950
1 Cylinder block 3T				E1740	←	E2461[1]	←	←
2	5T	E1451	E1666	E2257	←	←	←	E2927
3	6T							E2895
4	T100		E1666	E2257	←	←	←	E2927
5	T110							
6	T120							
7	TR5						E2474TR5	←
8	TR6							
9 Cylinder head 3T				E2014	←	E2645[1]	←	←
10	5T	E1454	←	E2258	←	←	←	E2928
11	6T							E2896
12	T100		E710	E2258A	←	←	←	E2929
13	T110							
14	T120							
15	TR5						E2875	←
16	TR6							
17 Inlet valve 3T				E1751	←	←	←	←
18	5T	E1473		E1955	←	←	←	←
19	6T							E2903
20	T100		E1473	E1955	←	←	←	←
21	T110							
22	T120							
23	TR5						E2115	←
24	TR6							
25 Exhaust valve 3T				E1752	←	←	←	←
26	5T	E1474	←	E1956	←	←	←	←
27	6T							E2904
28	T100		E1474	E1956	←	←	←	←
29	T110							
30	T120							
31	TR5						E1956	←
32	TR6							
33 Valve guide 3T				E1759				
34 Inlet	5T, 6T, T100, T110, TR6	E1480	←	←	←	←	←	E2899
35	TR5						E2899	←
36	T120							
37 Exhaust	5T, 6T, T100, T110, TR6	E1604	←	←	←	←	←	E2900
38	TR5						E2900	←
39	T120							
40 Valve spring inner ⎱ 5T,6T,T100,T110,TR5,TR6		E1488	←	←	←	←	←	←
41 outer ⎰ to 1960		E1487	←	←	←	←	←	←
42 inner ⎱ T120 & T110,								
43 outer ⎰ TR6 – 1961 on								

[1] from 89333

	1951	1952	1953	1954	1955	1956	1957	1958	1959	1960	1961	1962
1	←											
2	←	←	←	←	←	E3525	←	←				
3	←	←	←	←	←	E3332	←	←	←	←	←	←
4	E2957	E2958	←	←	←	E3591	←	←	←			
5				E3332	←	←	←	←	←	←	←	
6									E3332	←	←	←
7	E2957	E2958	←	←	←	E3591	←	←				
8						E3332/TR6	←	←	←	←	←	←
9	←											
10	←	←	←	←	←	←	←	←				
11	←	←	←	←	←	←	E3873	←	←	←	E3924	←
12	E3005	←	←	←	←	E3593	←	←	←			
13				E3333	←	E3608[2]	E3644	E3924	←	←	←	
14									E4019	←	←	←
15	E3021	←	←	←	E3005	E3593	←	←				
16						E3608[2]	E3644	E3924	←	←	←	←
17	←											
18	←	←	←	←	←	←	←	←				
19	←	←	←	←	←	←	←	←	←	←	E3310	←
20	E2969	←	←	←	←	←	←	←	←			
21				E3310	←	←	←	←	←	←	←	
22									E3310	←	←	←
23	E2969	←	←	←	←	←	←	←				
24						E3310	←	←	←	←	←	←
25	←											
26	←	←	←	←	←	←	←	←				
27	←	←	←	←	←	←	←	←	←	←	E3927	←
28	←	←	←	←	←	←	←	←	←			
29				E2904	←	←	←	E3927	←	←	←	
30									E3927	←	←	←
31	←	←	←	←	←	←	←	←				
32						E2904	←	E3927	←	←	←	←
33	←											
34	←	←	←	←	←	←	←	←				
35	←	←	←	←	←	←	←	←				
36									E3827	←	←	←
37	←	←	←	←	←	←	←	←	←	←	←	←
38	←	←	←	←	←	←	←	←				
39									E3828		←	←
40	←	←	←	←	←	←	←	←	←	←		
41	←	←	←	←	←	←	←	←	←	←		
42									E3001	←	←	←
43									E3002	←	←	←

[2] from 80599 use E3644

Pre-unit		1938	1939	1946	1947	1948	1949	1950
1	Valve spring inner 6T							
2	outer 6T							
3	inner 3T			E1777	←	←	←	←
4	outer 3T			E1778	←	←	←	←
5	Crankshaft timingside 3T			E1747	←	←	←	←
6	drive side 3T			E2200	←	←	←	←
7	flywheel 3T			E1745	←	←	←	←
8	timing side 5T	E1459	←	←	←	←	←	E2915
9	6T							E2902
10	T100		E1459	←	←	←	←	E2915
11	T110							
12	TR5						E1459	E2915
13	TR6							
14	drive side 5T	E1460	←	←	←	←	←	E2914
15	6T							E2901
16	T100		E1460	←	←	←	←	E2914
17	T110							
18	TR5						E1460	E2914
19	TR6							
20	flywheel 5T	E1510	←	E1510A	←	←	←	E2916
21	6T							E2908
22	T100		E1510T	E1510A	←	←	←	E2916T
23	T110							
24	TR5						E1510A	E2916
25	TR6							
26	one piece T100							
27	650							
28	flywheel All							
29	Crankcase 3T			E2250	←	←	←	←
30	3T			E2251	←	←	E2251A	←
31	5T	E1452	E1652	E2219	←	←	←	←
32	5T	E1453	E1667	E2220	E2220A	←	←	←
33	6T							E2892
34	6T							E2893
35	T100		E1652	E2219	←	←	←	←
36	T100		E1667	E2220	E2220A	←	←	←
37	T110							
38	T110							
39	T120							
40	T120							
41	TR5						E2219	←
42	TR5						E2220A	←
43	TR6							
44	TR6							

	1951	1952	1953	1954	1955	1956	1957	1958	1959	1960	1961	1962
1											E4221[1]	←
2											E4222[1]	←
3	←											
4	←											
5	←											
6	←											
7	←											
8	←	←	←	←	E3453	←	←	←				
9	←	←	←	E3431	E3454	←	←	←				
10	E2915T	E2915	←	E3430	E3453	←	←	←				
11				E3431	E3454	←	←	←				
12	←	←	←	E3430	E3453	←	←	←				
13						E3454	←	←				
14	←	←	E3112	←	E3329	←	←	←				
15	←	←	←	E3330	←	←	←	←				
16	E2914T	E2914	E3112	E3329	←	←	←	←				
17				E3330	←	←	←	←				
18	←	←	E3112	E3329	←	←	←	←				
19						E3330	←	←				
20	E2918	←	←	←	E3306	←	←	←				
21	←	←	←	E3306	←	←	←	←				
22	E2918T	←	E1510	E3306	←	←	←	←				
23				E3306	←	←	←	←				
24	E2918	←	←	E3306	←	←	←	←				
25						E3306	←	←				
26									E3891			
27									E3894	←	←	E4493
28									E3906	←	←	E4479
29	←											
30	←											
31	←	←	E3109	←	E3425	E2892	←	←				
32	←	←	←	←	←	E3314	←	←				
33	←	←	←	←	←	←	←	←	←	←	←	←
34	←	←	←	E3314	←	←	←	←	←	←	←	←
35	←	←	←	E3281	←	←	←	←	←			
36	←	←	←	←	←	←	←	←	←			
37				E2892	←	←	←	←	←	←	←	
38				E3282	←	←	←	←	←	E3314	←	
39									E2892	←	←	←
40									E3282	E3314	←	←
41	←	←	←	E3281	←	←	←	←				
42	←	←	←	←	←	←	←	←				
43						E2892	←	←	←	←	←	←
44						E3282	←	←	←	E3314	←	←

[1] from D11193

Pre-unit	1938	1939	1946	1947	1948	1949	1950
1 Connecting rod 3T			E1749	←	←	←	←
2　　　　　5T	E1489	←	←	←	←	←	E2932
3　　　　　6T							E2921
4　　　　　T100		E1489T	E1489	E1489T	←	←	E2932T
5　　　　　T110							
6　　　　　TR5						E1489T	E2932T
7　　　　　All							
8 Drive main 3T			E1592	←	←	←	←
9 Timing main 3T			E1769	←	←	←	←
10 Drive main 500 & 650			E1591	←	←	←	←
11 Timing main 5T	E1592	←	←	←	←	E2877	←
12 Timing main TR5, T100, 650s		E1592	←	←	←	E2877	←
13 Oil pump			E2140	←	←	←	GS326
14 Release valve			GS253	←	←	E2795	←
15 Timing cover 3T			E2252	←	←	←	←
16　　　　　5T	E1455	E1651	E2218	←	←	←	←
17　　　　　6T							E2218
18　　　　　T100		E1651	E2218	←	←	←	←
19　　　　　T110							
20　　　　　T120							
21　　　　　TR5						E2218	←
22　　　　　TR6							
23 Engine sprocket	E1440	E1680	←	←	←	E2826	←
24 Exhaust pipes 3T			E2236A/7A	←	←	←	←
25　　　　　5T	E1519/20	←	←	←	←	←	←
26　　　　　6T							E1519/20
27　　　　　T100		E1728/9	E1519/20	←	←	←	←
28　　　　　T110							
29　　　　　T120							
30　　　　　TR5						E2866	←
31　　　　　TR6							
32 Silencers 3T			E2238/39	E2646/7	←	←	←
33　　　　　5T	E1567/8	←	E2276/86	E1567/8	←	←	←
34　　　　　6T							E1567/8
35　　　　　T100		E1726/7	E2276/86	E1567/8	←	←	←
36　　　　　T110							
37　　　　　T120							
38　　　　　TR5						E2827	←
39　　　　　TR6							
40 Gearbox shell	T264A	←	←	T264B	←	←	T909
41　　　　outer cover	T411	←	←	←	←	←	T935
42　　　　inner cover	T410	←	←	←	←	←	T931
43　　　　filler cap	T400	←	←	←	←	←	←

	1951	1952	1953	1954	1955	1956	1957	1958	1959	1960	1961	1962
1	←											
2	E2921	←	←	←	E3328							
3	←	←	←	E3328	←							
4	E2921T	←	←	E3328T	←							
5				E3328T	←							
6	E2921T	←	←	E3328T	←							
7						E3606	←	←	←	←	←	←
8	←											
9	←											
10	←	←	←	←	←	←	←	←	←	←	←	←
11	←	←	←	←	E1591	←	←	←				
12	←	←	←	E1591	←	←	←	←	←	←	←	←
13	←	E3072	←	←	←	←	←	←	←	←	←	←
14	←	←	←	←	←	←	←	←	←	←	E4191	←
15	←											
16	←	←	E3110	←	←	←	←	←				
17	←	←	←	E3110	←	←	←	←	←	←	←	←
18	←	←	←	←	←	←	←	←	←			
19				E2218	←	←	←	←	←	E3310	←	
20									E2218	E3310	←	←
21	←	←	←	←	←	←	←	←				
22						E2218	←	←	←	E3110	←	←
23	←	←	E3108	←	←	←	←	←	←	←	←	←
24	←											
25	←	←	E1519/E3127	E3315/6	E3350/E3426	←	←	←				
26	←	←	←	E3315/6	E3350/E3426	←	←	←	←	←	←	E4409/10
27	E2985/87	←	←	E3346/49	←	←	←	E3629/33	←			
28				E3347/50	←	←	←	E3628/32	←	E3632/E4133	←	
29									E3628/32	E3632/E4133	←	←
30	E3014/5	←	←	←	E3462/3	←	←	←				
31						E3472/3	←	←	←	E4125/30	E4177/79	E4409/10
32	←											
33	←	←	←	E3323/4	←	←	E3651/2	←				
34	←	←	←	E3323/4	←	←	E3651/2	←	←	E4118/9	←	E4413
35	←	←	←	E3323/4	←	←	E3651/2	E3816/7	E3651/2			
36				E3323/4	←	←	E3651/2	E3816/7	E3651/2	E4118/9	←	
37									E3651/2	E4118/9	E4132/76	E4174/5
38	←	←	←	E3407	E3470	←	←	←				
39						E3470	←	←	←	E4132	E4132/76	E4175
40	←	←	←	T909/T1201	T1201	←	←	←	←	←	T1505	←
41	←	←	←	←	←	←	←	T1534	←	←	←	←
42	←	←	←	T1217	←	←	←	T1531	T1562	←	←	←
43	E1564	←	←	←	←	←	←	E732	←	←	←	←

Pre-unit		1938	1939	1946	1947	1948	1949	1950
1	Frame front 3T			F2385	←	←	←	←
2	5T, 6T	F1616	←	F2400	←	←	F2938	←
3	T100		F1911	F2400	←	←	F2938	←
4	TR5						F2988	←
5	s/a							
6	Frame rear 3T			F2385A	←	←	F2963	F3100
7	5T, 6T	F1616A	←	←	←	F2751[1]	F2939	F3102
8	T100		F1616A	←	←	F2751[1]	F2939	F3102
9	s/a							
10	s/a 6T, T110							
11	TR6, T120							
12	Rear fork s/a							
13	Rear stand	F1834	←	←	←	←	←	←
14	TR5						F1834	←
15	Centre stand							
16	TR6, T120							
17	Front fork assy. 3T			H501	←	←	H709	←
18	5T	Girder	←	H502	←	←	H692	←
19	6T							H692
20	T100		Girder	H502	←	←	H692	←
21	T110							
22	T120							
23	TR5						H728	←
24	TR6							
25	Nacelle top 3T						H618	←
26	5T						H618	←
27	6T							H618
28	T100, T110						H618	←
29	T120							
30	Front hub	W348	←	W573	←	←	←	W573A
31	Front brake drum 7in.	W305	←	W576	←	←	←	←
32	8 in.							
33	Front hub & drum 7in.							
34	8 in.							
35	Rear hub – rigid	W98	←	W652	←	←	W861	←
36	TR5						W652	←
37	s/a							
38	Brake drum	W311	←	←	←	←	←	←
39	Sprocket	W56	←	←	←	←	←	←
40	Sprung hub wheel				W646	←	W879	W925[2]
41	3T				W646A	←	W877	W923[2]
42	TR5						W877	W891
43	QD rear wheel road							
44	TR							
45	T120							

[1] from TF17790   [2] from frame 7439 – Mk II

	1951	1952	1953	1954	1955	1956	1957	1958	1959	1960	1961	1962
1	←											
2	←	F3292	F3292A	←								
3	F2400	F3292	F3292A									
4	←	F3295	←	←	F3893	F3904	←	F4414				
5				F3634	F3892	F3904	←	F4414	←	F4608	F4846	←
6	←											
7	←	←	←	←								
8	F3178	←	←									
9				F3635	←	←	←	←	←			
10										F4609	←	←
11										F4684	←	←
12				F3646	F3778	←	F4131	←	←	←	←	←
13	←	←	←	←								
14	←	←	F3146	←								
15				F3730	←	←	F4304	←	←	←	←	←
16										F4763	←	←
17	←											
18	←	H791	H813	H922	H994	←	H1101	H1197				
19	H777	H797	←	H924	H996	←	H1104	H1198	←	H1310	←	←
20	←	H791	←	H923	H995	←	H1102	H1198	←			
21				H923	H995	←	H1102	H1198	←	H1310	←	
22									H1198	H1311	←	←
23	←	H788	←	←	H956	←	H1103	H1200				
24						H956	H1105	H1200	←	H1311	←	←
25	←											
26	←	H761	H812	H917	←	←	←	H1206				
27	←	H761	←	H917	←	←	←	H1208	←	H1144	←	←
28	←	H761	←	←	←	←	←	H1207	←	H1298	←	
29									H1278			
30	←	←	←	←	←	←	W1260					
31	W940	←	←	←	←	←						
32				W1056	W1165	←	←					
33							W1231	←	←	←		
34								W1325	←	←	←	←
35	←	←	←	←								
36	W861	←	←	←								
37				W1017	←	←	W1158	←	←	←	←	←
38	←	W951	←	←	←	←	←	←	←	W1276	←	←
39	←											
40	W925A	←	←	←								
41	W923A											
42	W924A	←	←	←								
43				W1027	W1119	←	W1309	←	←	W1403	←	←
44					W1124		W1310			W1404	←	←
45										W1405	W1404	←

[1] from TF17790   [2] from frame 7439 – Mk II

TRIUMPH TWIN RESTORATION

Pre-unit		1938	1939	1946	1947	1948	1949	1950
1	Front mudguard	H209/8	←	H410A	H427	H566	←	←
2	TR						H716	←
3	6T, T110							
4	TR6, T120							
5	Alt. valanced guard							
6	Rear mudguard 3T			F1722	←	←	←	←
7	tail 3T			F1723A	←	←	←	←
8	5T, 6T	F1725B/8	F1725BS/9	F1724	←	F2756	←	←
9	tail 5T, 6T	F1725A/8	F1725AS/9	F1725A	←	F2758	F3012	←
10	T100		F1733BT/9	F1724	←	F2756	←	←
11	tail T100		F1733AT/9	F1725A	←	F2758	F3012	←
12	TR5 rigid						F2998	←
13	TR5 sprung						F3064	←
14	s/a frame							
15	TR							
16	TR6, T120							
17	6T, T110							
18	Bathtub left 6T, T110							
19	right 6T, T110							
20	Outer chaincase 3T			T478A	←	←	←	←
21	5T	T480	T480A	←	←	←	←	←
22	6T							T480A
23	T100		T480A	←	←	←	←	←
24	T110							
25	T120							
26	TR5						T478A	←
27	TR6							
28	Inner chaincase 3T			T725	←	←	←	←
29	5T	T43	T483A	T483	←	←	←	T483A
30	6T							T483A
31	T100		T483A	T483	←	←	←	T483A
32	T110							
33	T120							
34	TR5						T885A	←
35	TR6							
36	Chainguard, top 3T			T148A	←	←	←	←
37	gen.	T148A	←	T148B	←	T766	←	←
38	TR						T891	←
39	s/a							
40	Chainguard, lower	F1730	←	←	←	←	←	←

	1951	1952	1953	1954	1955	1956	1957	1958	1959	1960	1961	1962
1	←	←	←	←	←	←	←	H1211	←			
2	←	←	←	←	←	←	←	H1216	←			
3										H1097	←	←
4										H1294	←	←
5				H768	←	←	←					
6	←											
7	←											
8	←	←	←	←								
9	←	←	←	←								
10	←	F3330	←									
11	←	←	←									
12	←	←	←	←		ꙏ						
13												
14				H3629	←	←	←	F4394	←			
15					F3685	←	←	←	←			
16										F4687	←	←
17										F4674	←	←
18										F4676	←	←
19										F4677	←	←
20	←											
21	←	←	T1056	←	T1232	←	←	←				
22	←	←	←	T1056	T1237	←	←	←	←	←	←	T1651
23	←	←	←	T1190	←	←	←	←	←			
24				T1190	←	←	←	←	←	T1601	←	
25									T1190	T1601	←	←
26	←	←	←	←	T1190	←	←	←				
27						T1190	←	←	←	T1601	←	←
28	←											
29	←	T1030	T1055	←	T1231	←	←	←				
30	←	T1030	←	T1055	T1231	←	←	←	←	T1603	←	←
31	←	T1030	←	T1186	←	←	←	←	←			
32				T1186	←	←	←	←	←	T1603	←	
33									T1186	T1600	←	←
34	←	T1029	←	←	T1186	←	←	←				
35						T1186	←	←	←	T1600	←	←
36	←											
37	←	←	←	←								
38	←	←	←	←	F3807	←	F4138	←	←	←	←	←
39				F3570	←	←	F4130	←	←	←	←	←
40	←	←	←	←								

Pre-unit		1938	1939	1946	1947	1948	1949	1950
1	Petrol tank 3T			F1845	←	←	F2966B	F2966PB
2	5T	F1846	F1846R	F1930R	←	←	F2964R	F2964PR
3	6T							F2964TB
4	T100		F1930	F1930	←	←	F2964S	F2964PS
5	T110							
6	T120							
7	TR5						F2995	←
8	TR6							
9	Export T100, T110, T120							
10	Parcel grid						F2933	←
11	Oil tank 3T			F1645A	←	←	←	←
12	5T	F1645	←	F1909A[1]	F1645A	←	←	←
13	6T							F1645A
14	T100		F1909	F1909A	←	←	F1645A	←
15	T110							
16	T120							
17	TR5						F2969	←
18	TR6							
19	T100c							
20	Handlebars	H225	←	←	←	←	H659	←
21	TR						H440	←
22	T120							
23	Saddle	F1729T	←	←	←	←	←	←
24	3T			F1897	←	←	←	←
25	TR5						F2992	←
26	Dual seat 5T, 6T, T100							F3153
27	s/a							
28	TR5, TR6, T120							

[1] Early only, later F1645A

	1951	1952	1953	1954	1955	1956	1957	1958	1959	1960	1961	1962
1	F3184PB											
2	F3183PR	F3280PR	←	←	←	←	F4415	←				
3	F3183TM	F3280TM	←	←	←	F3280TG	F4415	←	←	F4640	←	←
4	F3183PS	F3280PS	←	F3280BS	←	←	F4115	←	←			
5				F3280BS	←	←	F4415	←	←	F4640	←	
6									F4115	F4640	F4700	F4640/F4700
7	F3185	←	←	←	F3360	F3914	F4116	←				
8						F3914	F4116	←	←	F4700	←	←
9				F3360	←	F3914	F4116	←	←			
10	←	←	←	←	←	F3917	←	←	←	←	←	←
11	F3175											
12	F3175	F3321	←	←	F3856	←	←	←				
13	F3175	F3321	←	←	F3856	←	←	←	←	F4476A	←	←
14	*F3175*	F3321	←	F3591	F3856	←	←	←	F4513			
15				F3591	F3856	←	←	←	F4513	F4476A	←	
16									F4529	F4702	←	F5066
17	F3186	←	←	←	F3856	←	←	←				
18						F3856	←	←	F4513	F4702	←	F5067
19			F3370									
20	←	←	←	←	←	H1009	←	←	←	←	←	←
21	←	←	←	←	H932	H1003	←	←	←	←	←	←
22									H1009	H811	←	←
23	←	←	←	←								
24	←											
25	←	←	←	←								
26	←	←	←	←								
27				F3647	←	←	←	←	←	F4239	←	←
28					F3785	←	←	←	←	F4691	←	←

350/500 Unit	1957	1958	1959	1960	1961	1962
1 Crankshaft	E3875	←	E3998	←	←	←
2 Flywheel	E3712	←	←	←	←	←
3 Connecting rod 350	E3702	←	←	←	←	←
4 500			E4001	←	←	←
5 500 (late)						
6 Crankcase	E3687	←	E4005	←	←	←
7 Crankcase	E3688	←	←	←	←	←
8 Main bearing, right	E3790	←	←	E4137	←	←
9 , left	E3835	←	←	←	←	←
10 Cylinder block 350	E3698	←	←	←	←	←
11 500			E4000	←	←	←
12 Cylinder head 3TA	E3879	←	E4017	←	←	←
13 5TA, T100			E4007	←	←	←
14 T90						
15 T100C, T100S						
16 T100C						
17 T100T, T100R						
18 Inlet valve 3TA	E3738	←	←	←	←	←
19 T90						
20 500			E4012	←	←	←
21 Exhaust valve 350	E3739	←	←	←	←	←
22 5TA, T100			E4013	←	←	←
23 T100						
24 Oil pump	E3878	←	←	←	←	←
25 Release valve	E2795	←	←	←	E4191	←
26 Timing cover – distributor	E3693	←	←	←	←	←
27 with points						
28 Oil pressure switch						
29 Gearbox inner cover	T1448	←	←	←	←	←
30 Gearbox outer cover	T1450	←	←	←	←	T1637
31 Primary chaincase	E3701	←	←	←		
32 (tensioner)				E4122	←	←
33 Exhaust pipes 5TA, T100A			E3992/94	←	←	E4467/8
34 3TA	E3864/5	←	E3992/94	←	←	E4467/8
35 T90						
36 T100SS					E4467/8	←
37 T100C						
38 T100S						
39 T100R, T100T						
40 Silencers gen.	E3935/6	←	←	←	←	E4415
41 T100A, T100R				E4157/8	←	
42 T100SS, T90					E4415	←
43 T100C						
44 UK models						

	1963	1964	1965	1966	1967	1968	1969	1970	1971	1972
1	←	←	←	←	←	←	E9490	←	←	←
2	←	←	E5870	←	←	←	←	←	←	←
3	←	←	←	←	E6964	←	←			
4	←	←	←	←	←	←	←			
5						E6856	E8834	←	E9915	←
6	←	←	E5868	←	←	←	E9746	E11268	←	←
7	←	←	E4645	←	←	←	E9747	E11269	←	←
8	←	E4322	←	←	←	←	E9494	←	←	←
9	←	←	←	←	←	←	E9493	←	←	←
10	←	←	←	←	←	←	E9718			
11	←	←	←	←	←	←	E9719	←	←	←
12	←	E4779	E5956	←						
13	←	E4785	←	←						
14	E4784	←	←	←	E6699	←	E9506			
15					E6700	E6966	E9507[1]	←	E10277	E12644
16							E10277[2]			
17					E6966	←	←	E9507	←	E12643
18	←	←	←	←						
19	E4640	←	←	←	←	←	←			
20	←	←	←	←	E6853	←	←	←	←	←
21	←	←	←	←	←	←	←			
22	←	←	←	←	←					
23					E6854	←	←	←	←	←
24	←	←	←	←	E6928	←	←	←	←	←
25	←	←	E5896	←	←	←	E6595	←	E12210	←
26	←									
27	E4630	←	←	←	←	←	E9250	←	←	←
28							D2133	←	←	←
29	←	←	←	←	←	←	T3754	←	T4301	←
30	←	T1870	←	←	←	←	T3755	←	←	←
31										
32	←	←	←	←	←	E7359	E9249	←	←	←
33	E3992/94	←	←	←						
34	E3992/94	←	E5325/27	←						
35	E4467/8	E5325/27	←	←	←	E7637/8	←			
36	←	E3992/94	←							
37				E4513/4	E7020/22	←	E10017/19		←	E12646/7
38					E3992/94	E7639/40	E9662/3	←		
39					E5325/27	E7637/8	E9662/3	←	E12037/8	E12628/9
40	E3935/6	←	←	←	←	←	E4157/8	←	←	E12017/8
41				E4157/8	←	←				
42	←	E3935/6	←							
43				E3470	E6974/5	←	E9669/70		E9669/70	E12019/20
44									E11710	

[1] T100S only   [2] Other years as line above

350/500 unit	1957	1958	1959	1960	1961	1962
1 Chainguard, top	F4198	←	←	←	←	←
2 lower	F4199	←	←	←	←	←
3 Left side panel, 2 switch						
4 1 switch						
5 blank						
6 Frame front	F4157	←	←	←	F4849	←
7 Frame strut						
8 Frame rear	F4158	←	←	←	←	←
9 T100SS					F5146	←
10 Rear fork	F4190	←	←	←	←	←
11 Centre stand gen.	F4402	←	←	←	←	←
12 T100SS, T90, T100R					F5153	←
13 Prop stand 3TA, 5TA, T100A	F4388	←	←	←	←	←
14 T100SS, T90, T100					F4388	←
15 T100C, T100R						
16 Nacelle top 3TA, 5TA	H1144	←	←	←	←	←
17 T100A				H1298	←	
18 Front hub & drum	W1231	←	←	←	←	←
19 left hub plate	W1334	←	←	←	←	←
20 hub & drum T100T, T100R						
21 left hub plate T100T, T100R						
22 Rear hub	W1266	←	←	←	←	←
23 Sprocket & drum	W1276	←	←	←	←	←
24 Brake drum						
25 Sprocket						
26 QD rear wheel				W1386	W1436	←
27 T100SS					W1429	←
28 Front mudguard 3TA, 5TA, T100A	H1097	←	←	←	←	←
29 T100SS, T90, T100					H1294	←
30 T100C						
31 Bath tub left	F4144	←	←	F4768	←	←
32 right	F4145	←	←	F4769	←	←
33 mudguard	F4297	←	←	←	←	←
34 Rear mudguard					F4858	←
35 US						
36 Skirt left					F5094	←
37 right					F5096	←
38 valances						
39 Petrol tank	F4232	←	←	←	←	←
40 T100C, T100R						
41 UK T100R						
42 oil tank	F4233	←	F4476	←	F4476/F4851	←
43 Seat	F4239	←	←	←	←	←
44 T100C						

	1963	1964	1965	1966	1967	1968	1969	1970	1971	1972
1	←	F5409	←	←	←	F7707	F9753	←	F7707	←
2	←	←	←	←						
3		*F5559*	←	F6931						
4					F7361					
5				F6964	←	F8042	←	←	←	F11358
6	←	F5406	←	F6912	F7312	←	F10034	←	←	←
7			F4862							
8	←	F6223	←	F6913	F7313	F8038	←	←	←	←
9	←									
10	←	←	←	F6936	F7375	←	←	←	←	←
11	←	F5529	←	F5153	F7692	←	←	←	F7693	←
12	←	←	←	F4891	F7693	←	←			
13	←	←	←	F3617						
14	←	F3723	←	F3617	F7373	←	F7849	F11560	←	←
15				F5539	F7356	←				
16	←	H1781	←	←						
17										
18	←	←	←	←	←	←	W3325	←	←	←
19	←	←	←	←	←	←	W3443	←	←	←
20						W1722	←	←	←	←
21						W1332	W3460	←	←	←
22	←	W1472	←	←	←	←	←	W3586	←	←
23	←	W951	←							
24				W1498	←	←	←	W3585	←	←
25				W1499	←	←	←	←	←	←
26	←	W1587	W1601	W1746	←	←	←	←		
27	←	W1496	W1602	W1745	←	←	←	←		
28	←	H1689	H1901	←						
29	←	H1675	←	←	H1997	←	H1996	H3882	←	←
30				H1677/87	H1677	H1676	H3677		H3884	←
31	←									
32	←									
33	←	F5963	←							
34	←	F5984	←	←	←	F8143	←	F11617	F12995	←
35				F6965/6	F6965/7	F8126/44	←		F12876	←
36	←	F5978	←							
37	←	F5362	←							
38		F5323/4	←							
39	←	←	F6140	F7001	F7393	←	F9759	F11805/6		
40				F7002	F7192	←	F9760		F11803/4	←
41									F9759	
42	←	F5381	←	F6877	←	F7836	←	F11763	F13290	←
43	←	←	←	←	F7776	F9517	F9714	F11573	←	←
44				F4360A	F7482	F9502				

650 Unit	1963	1964	1965	1966	1967
Crankshaft	E4643	←	←	←	←
Flywheel	E4479	←	E5783	E6327	←
Connecting rod 6T	E3606	←	←	E3606T	←
TR6, T120	E3606T	←	←	←	←
Main bearing, right	E1591	←	←	←	←
, left	E1591	←	←	E2879	←
Crankcase	E4533	←	E5871	←	←
Crankcase	E4534	←	←	E6303	←
Oil pump	E3878	←	←	←	E6928
Release valve	E4191	←	E5896	←	←
Cylinder block	E4546	←	←	E6304	←
head 6T, TR6	E4552	←	←	←	E7031
T120	E4928	E5348	←	←	←
T120TT, T120R				E5727	←
Inlet valve 6T, TR6	E3310	←	←	←	E4603
T120	E3310	E4603	←	←	←
Exhaust valve 6T, TR6	E3927	←	←	←	E2904
T120	E3927	E2904	←	←	←
Timing cover	E4567	←	←	←	←
Sprocket cover plate	E4577	←	←	←	←
Primary chaincase	T1727	←	←	←	←
Gearbox inner cover	T1703	←	←	T2112	←
outer cover	T1705	T1986	←	←	←
Exhaust pipes 6T	E4716/18	←	E5957/8	←	
TR6	E4409/E4846	E4716/18	E5957/8	←	←
T120	E4716/18	←	E5957/8	←	←
TR6C (east)				E4884/86	
TR6C (west)				E6370/72	
T120TT				E5959/61	←
TR6C					E7024/26
Silencers	E4949	←	←	←	←
US 6T, TR6R, T120R				E5866	←
TR6C (east)				E4132/76	
TR6C					E6974/5
Frame front	F5448	←	F6442	F6903	F7371
Frame rear	F5449	←	F6443	F6904	F7372
Rear fork	F5302	←	←	F6933	←
Centre stand (3.50 tyre)	F5345	F5928		←	
(4.00 tyre)	F5330	F5932	←	←	←
Chainguard	F5371	F5737	F6257	F7067	←

650 Unit	1968	1969	1970	1971	1972
Crankshaft	←	←	←	←	E13097
Flywheel	E7332	E9687	←	E12425	←
Connecting rod TR6, T120	←	E9525	←	←	←
Main bearing, right	←	←	←	←	E3835
, left	←	←	←	←	←
Crankcase	←	E9748	E11266	←	←
Crankcase	E7330	E9749	E11267	E12274	E13098
Oil pump	←	←	E9421	←	←
Release valve	←	E6595	←	E12210	E6595
Cylinder block	←	←	←	←	←
head 6T, TR6	←	E9362	←	E12354	E12806
T120	←	E9418	←	E12356	E12807
Inlet valve 6T, TR6	←	←	←	←	←
T120	←	←	←	←	←
Exhaust valve 6T, TR6	←	←	←	←	←
T120	←	←	←	←	←
Timing cover	E8797	E9246	←	←	←
Oil pressure switch		D2133	←	←	←
Sprocket cover plate	E7037	←	←	←	←
Primary chaincase	T2439	E9245	←	←	←
Rotor cover	T2440	←	←	←	←
Gearbox inner cover	←	T3766	←	T4293	←
outer cover	T3628	T3760	←	←	←
Exhaust pipes TR6	←	E9363/4	←		
T120	←	E9363/4	←		
TR6C				E11900/1	E12334/E12632
T120R, TR6R				E12753/56	E126⋯7
Silencers	←	E5866	←		
TR6C				E12019/20	←
T120R, TR6R				E12382	←
Frame front	F7843	←	F11354	F12089	F14283
Frame rear	F8036	←	←		
Rear fork	F7845	F10045	←	F12513	←
Centre stand (4.00 tyre)	←	F9365	F11267	F12627	←
Chainguard	←	←	←	F12641	←

650 Unit	1963	1964	1965	1966	1967
Prop stand (3.50 tyre)	F4388	←	←	←	
(4.00 tyre)	F4712	←	←	F6940	
gen.					F7357
TR6C, T120TT					F7373
Nacelle top 6T	H1447	H1781	←	←	
Front hub	W1325	←	←	W1722	←
cover plate	W1332	←	←	←	←
Rear hub	W1472	←	←	←	←
Sprocket & drum	W951	←	←		
Sprocket				W1499	←
Brake drum				W1498	←
QD rear wheel	W1310	←	W1600	W1745/6	W1813/4
Petrol tank 4 gal. 6T, TR6, T120	F5260	←	←	F7004	←
3 gal. TR6, T120	F5416	←	←		
US 6T, TR6R				F7003	←
TR6C, T120R, T120TT				F6728	←
Parcel grid	F3917	←	←	←	←
Oil tank	F5327	F6308	←	F6877	←
Skirt left	F5319	←	←		
right	F5320	←	←		
valances	F5323/4	←	←		
Left side panel, 2 switch	F5394	←	←	F6931	
1 switch					F7359
blank				F6962	←
6T				F6930	
Seat	F5366	←	←	F5239	F7776
TR6C, T120TT					F7482
Front mudguard 6T	H1097	H1689	H1901	←	
TR6	H1294	H1675	←	←	H1677
T120	H1478	H1675	←	←	H1677
US 6T, TR6C (east), TR6R					H1677
TR6C (west), T120TT					H1687
T120R					H1997
Rear mudguard 6T	F5579	F5953	←	F5984	
TR6, T120	F5579	F5984	←	←	←
US 6T, TR6C (east)				F6965	
TR6C (west)				F5955	
T120R				F6967	←
TR6R				F6965	←
TR6C					F6967
T120TT				F5955	F7397

650 Unit	1968	1969	1970	1971	1972
Prop stand gen.	F7849	←	F11560	←	←
Front hub	W1995	W1693	W1722	W3658	←
cover plate	W1992	W3460	←		
Rear hub	←	←	W3586	W3773	←
Sprocket	←	←	←	W3747	←
Brake drum	←	←	W3585		
QD rear wheel	W1813	W2106	W3670		
Petrol tank 4 gal. 6T, TR6, T120	←	F9703/4	F11799/800		F12881
3 gal. TR6, T120				F12996	←
Parcel grid	←				
Oil tank	F7836	←	F11763		
Left side panel, blank	F8042	←	←	F12502/4	F13859/60
Seat	F8205	F9714	F11573	F13634	F14288
Front mudguard TR6	H2268	H1677	H3882		
T120					
TR6C (west), T120TT	H1997				
T120R	←				
TR6R, T120R				H4260[1]	H4271
TR6C				H4065[1]	H4270
Rear mudguard TR6, T120	F8126	←	F11617		
T120R				F13566	←
TR6R				F13566	←
TR6C				F13565	←

Later models as 1972

[1]Later models as 1972

Picture indexes

This is compiled in date order, by machine and by item to give the maximum benefit. Due to space it is not possible to have a picture of each side of every model for every year but by using this index it is often possible to find a picture that helps. This is because the cycle parts were often common for several models in any one year so any picture from that year will help.

Thus one of a T120 can help with a TR6 except around the carburettor area and a 3TA and 5TA will help one another.

So look for your model and year but also check other models of the same year. It can also be worth looking at the same model in the years before and after as the feature you are checking may not have changed.

Some of the references are for detail parts only so check the index, list the relevant pages and have a look at each to see if it helps.

Component picture index

Index